SOLICITORS ACCOUNTS

An Industry Accounting and Auditing Guide

SOLICITORS ACCOUNTS

An Industry Accounting and Auditing Guide

Gervase MacGregor, BSc(Hons), ACA

Stoy Hayward

Accountancy BOOKS

The Institute of Chartered Accountants
in England and Wales
Chartered Accountants' Hall
Moorgate Place
London EC2P 2BJ

ISBN 1 85355 402 2

British Library Cataloguing-in-Publication Data.
A catalogue record for this book is available from the British Library.

Typeset by Type Study, Scarborough
Printed in Great Britain by T. J. Press (Padstow) Ltd, Padstow, Cornwall

Contents

APPENDICES

Preface

It was a great pleasure to undertake the writing of this book. It is an area of work in which I have had an interest for over a decade, and I enjoyed putting down on paper what I had learnt in the last ten years.

My aim has been to give accountants involved with law firms sufficient background to the industry, regulation of and the problems arising from partnerships to enable them to be aware of the relevant issues should they need to report to the Law Society or to advise their client in the running of their practice.

The section on the Solicitors Accounts Rules 1991 is prescriptive, as it needs to be. The sections on the format of a solicitor's accounts and practice management are discursive. This is because I believe it is unwise to try and change the practices of any business without understanding the reasons for those practices. Therefore, although I hope to have covered all of the different methods of, for example, profit sharing used by lawyers, I do not advocate one over another, so use this book with care!

I am aware that there will be some areas within the book where practising accountants have a contrary view or have experience of an issue which I do not. There will inevitably be changes in the solicitors' industry in the future. Therefore I should be most grateful if readers would let me know of any peculiar difficulties with the Solicitors Accounts Rules which would be of general interest.

There are a large number of people to thank for their help in writing this book, first of all my fellow partners at Stoy Hayward. I would particularly like to mention Stephen Greene for his early support of the project and Jeremy Newman for reading the text (twice) and providing invaluable criticism. I would also like to thank all of those lawyers and bankers I have met with over the last year and to whom I gave an undertaking of confidentiality in my research.

Gervase MacGregor
London
July 1993

PART I

Background to the solicitors industry

This section is designed to give a general introduction to the solicitors' industry to an accountant with little or no previous experience of the sector.

The individual chapters examine how solicitors are organised in firms, the size and spread of those firms, the type of work which solicitors undertake, what the Law Society does, legal aid and future possible developments in the industry.

There is also a chapter on how solicitors are required to conduct themselves professionally.

Chapter 1 – The solicitors industry in England and Wales

1.1 Introduction

An auditor is required to have an understanding of the industry in which the business he is auditing operates; this enables him, *inter alia*, to consider some of the audit risks he faces when carrying out his assignment and, further, to undertake his assignment more efficiently. The specific requirements for the accountant reporting to the Law Society (hereafter the 'reporting accountant'), or any accountant advising a solicitors' practice, are rarely stated. It is as if, the accountant and the solicitor being 'professionals' giving advice to similar types of client, accountants will naturally have sufficient knowledge of what solicitors do.

In practice this is rarely the case, as any senior sent on a Solicitors' Accounts Rules audit for the first time is likely to attest. Additionally, many experienced partners in accountancy firms may be surprised, despite their large circle of solicitor friends, at how superficial their knowledge is. Yet solicitor clients will be among the most perilous that an accountant has, because of the handling of client money and the strict requirements of the Accountant's Report Rules.

This chapter attempts to give a background to the industry (as it stood in 1992) in which solicitors operate in England and Wales. The statistical information is based on three excellent publications by the Law Society, the first of which, the *Annual Statistical Report*, is required reading every year.

- *Annual Statistical Report 1992*, John Jenkins
- *Solicitors in England and Wales: Practice, Organisation and Perceptions – First Report: The Work of the Solicitor in Private Practice*, Gerry Chambers and Stephen Harwood- Richardson, 1991
- *Solicitors in England and Wales: Practice, Organisation and Perceptions Second Report: The Private Practice Firm*, Gerry Chambers and Stephen Harwood-Richardson, 1991

1.2 Solicitors and practices

The term solicitor denotes a person who is qualified to act as a solicitor of the Supreme Court of England and Wales; such persons are only permitted to practice if they hold a current practising certificate. Solicitors in practice can carry out such a wide variety of activities that one should look to see what a person who is not qualified to act as a solicitor cannot do. By section 20 of the Solicitors Act 1974, unqualified persons are not allowed to:

> act as a solicitor, or as such issue any writ or process, or commence, prosecute or defend any action, suit or any other proceeding, in his own name or in the name of any other person, in any court of civil or criminal jurisdiction; or act as a solicitor in any cause, civil or criminal, to be heard or determined before any justice or justices or any commissioners of Her Majesty's Revenue.

Solicitors are therefore individuals who issue certain types of documents, writs, and who act in certain types of proceeding. Sections 22 and 23 also forbid unqualified individuals from preparing instruments relating to real or personal property, and grants of probate or letters of administration. As a catch all, section 21 makes unlawful any unqualified person impersonating a solicitor.

As well as the specific activities of preparing certain documents and appearing in various tribunals, solicitors give advice, principally in the law, but also, like accountants, on a wide range of commercial and business matters.

As at 31 July 1992 there were 72,449 solicitors on the Roll, of whom 59,566 had practising certificates. Of these, 49,785 worked in private practice. The number of solicitors has been increasing in recent years by about four per cent per year. Over the thirty years since 1961, the numbers have nearly tripled; the majority of this increase is accounted for by women, who currently comprise about a quarter of all practising solicitors, compared to about ten per cent ten years ago.

The industry is 'young' with an average age of 39 years; 58 per cent of all practising solicitors are less than 40 years old and three-quarters have been practising for less than 20 years.

Of the 49,785 solicitors in private practice, just over 53 per cent are partners, eight per cent are sole practitioners and the remainder are mainly assistant solicitors. The recent trend has been for a slow down in the number of partners being created and an increase in the number of sole practitioners, both being due to the current recession. As at 31 July 1992, the solicitors in private practice were employed in 9,755 firms in 14,059 offices. The number of private practice firms has been falling recently (there were 10,243 at 31 July 1991) and is currently back at 1989 levels; the number of offices has also been falling. In addition to the solicitors employed there were about 23,000 other fee earners, and about 100,000 other staff. The total staff employed by private practice firms is therefore about 170,000 people.

As at 31 July 1991, of 8,113 private practice firms, 3,064 were sole practitioners, 3,503 were firms of between two and four partners, 1,140 between five and ten partners and 406 firms of above ten partners; these last three categories being called small, medium and large firms.

Most firms are therefore small businesses; research by the Law Society based on surveys in 1989 shows that the typical firm has 3.6 partners and 21 total staff and partners. The 21 staff comprise 6 solicitors, 3½ paralegals, ½ managerial staff and 11 administrative staff. In addition, 75 per cent of solicitors are equity partners. These ratios are quite different from accountancy practices, with their higher staff to partner and professional to non-professional staff ratios. ('Paralegals' is used to described those professional staff without a practising certificate, that is articled clerks, legal executives, licensed conveyancers and clerks.)

However, within the groupings of firms there are variances which have an impact on the profitability of firms. The largest firms have the highest ratio of solicitors (fee earners) to all staff, and the lowest ratio of clerks. They also have the highest ratio of managerial staff. The smaller firms, especially sole practitioners, have the highest ratio of clerks.

1.3 Types of work and the way it is carried out

If one glances through any of the major law firm directories, such as the *Chambers & Partners' Directory* (1992/93, Orbach and Chambers Limited) or *The Legal 500* (John Pritchard, 1992, 5th edition, Legalise Limited), one sees an extreme diversity of specialisation, including public law, charities, capital markets, insolvency, shipping, pensions and sports law. These directories describe the work of solicitors within the 'top' one thousand or five hundred legal firms, where many individuals will specialize in one type of law only in a large department similarly focused. In general, the larger the firm, the greater the range of specialist departments but, interestingly, there are areas of the law, in which even the biggest firms do not have an expertise, or where there are certain much smaller firms a client would go to for advice in a particular area. This is in marked contrast with the accountancy profession where the largest firms tend to try to cover all areas. Size is obviously a major factor here; as some of the largest law firms would not be considered large when compared with a big six accountancy practice.

As indicated above, this specialism is not restricted to the large and medium sized practices, but appears widespread across the profession. The study by the Law Society on the work of the private practice firm (Gerry Chambers and Stephen Harwood-Richardson, 1991) found that 70 per cent of solicitors surveyed described themselves as specialists, with only 30 per cent describing themselves as general practitioners, the same number describing themselves as extreme specialists.

Despite the apparent degree of specialisation, it does appear that across the profession solicitors are exposed to many different types of work. The Law Society survey grouped all of the different areas of law into 15 categories being:

- commercial property;
- business and commercial affairs;
- residential conveyancing;
- housing, landlord and tenant;
- probate, wills and trust;
- personal bankruptcy, insolvency and debt;
- personal financial management and advice;
- family, matrimonial and child custody;
- child care and wardship;
- personal injury, accident and medical negligence;
- crime;
- welfare benefits and social security rights;
- consumer problems;
- employment law; and
- other.

The survey found that half of solicitors have handled cases in at least two thirds of the above categories, and, as is to be expected, the greatest exposure to different types of work occurred in sole practitioners and more experienced solicitors.

Having said that, the survey also found that 50 per cent of solicitors only ever handled up to three types of work, and 34 per cent four to six types of work. It is clear therefore that although solicitors in practice will have a broad range of experience, specialisation is common throughout the profession. (It is also interesting to compare the types of work in the directories, where corporate work is split into as many as 50 categories, to the Law Society's split, where there is a much greater emphasis on private client work.)

In terms of the actual work which solicitors regularly handle the survey found that business affairs, residential conveyancing, commercial property and probate work were the most popular, with other areas such as welfare and child care being regularly handled by very few solicitors. This again emphasises the specialisation of certain areas of the law. The survey also estimates that over half of total solicitor time is devoted to business affairs, domestic conveyancing and commercial property work.

An area which shows a great contrast with the accountancy profession is the way in which solicitors handle their work. Again taking the results of the survey, 42 per cent of solicitors work without another solicitor on all or almost all of their cases, and 40 per cent on most of their cases. Only half of solicitors received assistance from articled clerks or paralegals.

1.4 Financial information

1.4.1 Turnover

The estimated gross fees of all solicitors for the year ended 31 July 1991 was £5.7 billion, or about £690,000 per firm. This equates, on average, to gross fees per equity partner and sole practitioner of about £200,000, £124,000 per solicitor and £80,000 per fee earner. The increases in fees in the last part of the 1980s saw a fall off from 20 per cent increases, to about 10 per cent. This reduction was most pronounced in the year ended 31 July 1989, a period which also saw annual inflation approaching 10 per cent.

The performance of London firms indicates that this decline has only recently taken place, with such firms experiencing 20 per cent growth up to the year ended 31 July 1990. However, the figures for 31 July 1991 show an increase of about 10 per cent, in line with the rest of the country, and recent anecdotal evidence indicates that this figure now may be much lower. Outside of London, the south of England has experienced a particularly sharp decline, with the majority of firms experiencing either zero or negative growth. In addition, the results by size of firm indicate that the most serious effects have been on partnerships with less than 11 partners; these firms have, on average, been witnessing a fall in the real level of fees. Therefore, in turnover terms alone, the recession has hit particularly severely and early the small and medium size partnerships in the south.

1.4.2 Sources of fee income

The sources of fee income are particularly interesting when the experiences and expectations of the legal profession in 1989 are examined. When the detailed survey for the Law Society, referred to above, was carried out. At this time, the highest proportion of fees, 29 per cent, was earned from business affairs work. However, residential conveyancing accounted for 21 per cent of fees and commercial property for 17 per cent. Outside London, residential conveyancing was the most important source of fees.

The expectations of such firms indicated that by 1994 business affairs would increase in importance, as would commercial property; the Law Society's

Report states that there was an overall confidence in commercial property work as a major source of fees. Just over half of firms expected residential conveyancing to be of less importance due, it seems, to increasing competition. In fact, the number of total property transactions was showing a marked decline, even in 1989, from the high levels of 1988. By the first quarter of 1992 there were only 258,000 transactions compared with 530,000 four years before.

After commercial property, at 7 per cent comes probate and trust work, then family, personal injury and crime at four to five per cent each as sources of total fee income. Of much less importance are housing, employment, insolvency, welfare, child care and consumer advice.

Many of these areas do not appear to show much increase although matrimonial, crime and insolvency are obvious exceptions. However, insolvency can only be carried out by specialists and criminal work depends on the legal aid system (see below). As the recession continues, particularly in the property market, many firms see little prospect for growth.

1.4.3 Profitability of firms

The static or declining levels of turnover growth obviously have a direct impact on the profitability of firms. Solicitors' practices tend to have very high levels of staff costs relative to turnover and property costs are another important overhead. The ability to reduce the cost of these is either limited or is itself expensive. The 1989 survey asked firms to grade particular types of work according to profitability. The most profitable areas of work were commercial property and then business affairs. Residential conveyancing was generally profitable and, in fact, most other types of work were profitable. However, criminal and family work often indicated low profitability or a loss and some of the other types of work not generally carried out by some solicitors such as welfare, housing, employment and consumer advice appeared to be unprofitable.

The Report's conclusions on profitability, based on 1989 experiences, are worth repeating:

> The effect of a substantial reduction in these profitable areas of work coupled with low rates of pay for legal aid work could force firms either to seek higher payment for currently unprofitable private client work in order to make such work profitable or to give up such work completely. If they did nothing, firms would risk going out of business completely.

The continuing recession, with the consequent effects of higher write-offs of debts and time, would indicate that the economic climate for many firms is very difficult indeed.

1.5 Legal aid

At the time of writing, the future of the provision of legal aid is uncertain. There are proposals by the Lord Chancellor's Department, which administers the legal aid scheme, which would appear to limit the rates of legal aid, the number of individuals entitled to receive it and the number of solicitors practices which can offer legal aid advice. The profession itself has come up with a number of proposals to counter those of the Lord Chancellor including freezing legal aid rates and restricting the number of lawyers attending court hearings. Whatever is decided, the result will inevitably be a decrease in the total amount of legal aid payments made by Government to the legal profession. Accountants with solicitor clients deriving a substantial amount of their fee income from legal aid payments should keep abreast of future developments.

Legal aid is aimed to help those 'who might otherwise be unable to obtain advice, assistance or representation on account of their means.' This means that below certain income levels, depending on the sort of case, certain people pay no money at all towards the costs of advice or representation; above certain levels, individuals have to make a contribution. It is often said that only the very rich and the very poor can afford lawyers. The current plans by the Lord Chancellor's office, which would tend to reduce these income levels, will lower the numbers of people able to claim free or subsidised advice.

Legal aid is paid, in most cases, by the Legal Aid Board although about one quarter of the expenditure on legal aid is in respect of criminal representation in the higher courts and is paid direct by the Lord Chancellor's Department. In the year to 31 March 1992 the total legal aid bill was £967 million, of which £732 million was paid to solicitors. The increases on the previous year's payments were 32 per cent and 28 per cent respectively. The payments to solicitors compares with the total fees earned by solicitors of £5,742 million to 31 July 1991. Legal aid payments therefore represent a significant part of the industry's income, and it is estimated that about 79 per cent of all solicitors' offices received legal aid payments to 31 March 1992.

The 1989 survey found that about 10 per cent of firms derived more than half of their fees from legally aided work, although 74 per cent of firms did legal aid work. However, because such work was considered to be unprofitable by a number of firms, 40 per cent of firms that did legal aid work expected it to diminish in importance in the five years to 1994.

Legal aid work has been seen to be unprofitable by solicitors both because the rates given for work are subject to a scale of charges which are generally less than the commercial rates and also because of the delays in getting paid by the Legal Aid Board.

There are variations in the importance of legally aided work, with small firms having more legal aid cases than large, and north of England firms carrying out a greater proportion than those in the south.

1.6 The future and the solicitor

At the time of writing it is clear that the legal profession is going to face a number of severe financial problems in the near future. Conveyancing, for many years the major source of revenue for the majority of firms, is now of less importance than litigation, the prospects for a recovery in the housing and commercial property markets are not good, and any new work can be expected to be the subject of fierce competition between firms.

The other main area of work, commercial, is still suffering from the recession. Even worse, from the point of view of some solicitors, is the prospect of the low-balling or predatory pricing, where firms will undercut a client's existing solicitor with the offer of very low cost work, as has been seen in the accountancy profession over the last three years. The publication of what purports to be the average profit share of partners in the largest firms, with increases as the recession has continued, may encourage clients either to use smaller firms, or to ask firms for fixed price quotations for work. In this respect, the solicitors profession will start to resemble the accountancy profession.

As has been noted above, the provision of legal aid is also under pressure and any fall in what is a significant source of income for the profession as a whole, and the main source for many specialist practices, will be very painful.

The financial problems facing the solicitors' industry will be reflected in increasing changes within practices. One can expect to see mergers, splits and various disputes over drawings, profit shares and management. Additionally, some firms will face severe cash flow and financing problems which will result in bankruptcies and voluntary arrangements. All of this is discussed in future chapters because it all has an implication for the accountant advising his solicitor clients.

1.7 The future and the accountant

The solicitors' industry in general, and certain types of firms in particular, are facing and will continue to face economic problems. This has the unfortunate but inevitable effect of making the reporting accountant's work more risky. Previous recessions have witnessed increased levels of default by solicitors of their clients' money, and the current recession is not proving to be an exception. With increasing resources devoted to policing and investigating compliance, the Law Society will uncover more fraud, fraud which the accountant should, perhaps, have detected in his work.

It is likely too that accountants' fees will come under pressure. This will unfortunately lead to increasing risk of non-detection or negligence by the accountant.

However, the accountant who has a thorough understanding of his clients' business (and the above comments are no more than wide generalisations) can provide independent and constructive advice on how to deal with the current problems. This may include advising on critical appraisals of the profitability of all types of business, the staffing mix, the quality of debtor management or improvement of financial control. Inevitably there will be changes in firms as, for example, the legally aided and non-legally aided sides of a practice split up or firms merge to cut costs, and the accountant will be expected to advise here as well. Therefore, although certain types of work will be under pressure, from fees as well as risk, there are good opportunities for the accountant to advise in new areas. In all cases, the accountant will be best-prepared to recognise a problem or to advise if he knows his client and his industry.

Chapter 2 – Role of the Law Society

2.1 Introduction

This chapter looks first of all at the general role of the Law Society, to provide an overview to accountants of the various functions of the Law Society. Secondly, it considers in more detail the two areas of the Society with which the reporting accountant will have contact, the Professional Ethics Division and the Solicitors Complaints Bureau. It is hoped that accountants will deal more with the former than the latter, and indeed contact with the former may obviate the need for the Complaints Bureau to deal with the reporting accountant at all!

Finally, the chapter looks in detail at the two arms of the Society which provide compensation where loss has arisen by the actions of a solicitor, the Solicitors Indemnity Fund and the Solicitors Compensation Fund.

2.2 General

The Law Society is to solicitors what the various accountancy bodies are to accountants; therefore one finds great similarities between what these bodies do.

The Law Society is run by a Council of 75 members headed by an elected President. The work of the Council is delegated to a number of Standing Committees. The actual administration of the Society is carried out by an Executive Office and two directorates, Legal Practice and Professional Standards and Development. The administration is headed by a Secretary-General.

One of the most important functions is to maintain professional standards. This is done primarily through practice rules and other regulations made by the Council of the Law Society, which have statutory force. Enforcement is carried out through the Solicitors Complaints Bureau and the Solicitors Disciplinary Tribunal. There is also a Financial Services Monitoring Unit dealing with the compliance of firms authorised to conduct investment business.

The Society also controls the legal education of solicitors and aspiring solicitors through the Training Committee. This covers academic training, articles and continuing professional education.

The Society provides advice concerning the interpretation and application of the Practice Rules through the Professional Ethics Division of the Professional Standards and Developments Directorate, and on matters of law and practice through the Legal Practice Directorate.

Other important aspects of the Law Society's work are the representation of the profession to the Government or its committees, publications including the Law Society's *Gazette*, sent free to members every week, and international representation. Local Law Societies are independent from the Law Society.

The Society operates from both Law Society's Hall and Law Society House in Chancery Lane, and Redditch, where the Professional Standards and Development Directorate is located, and Leamington, from where the Solicitors Complaints Bureau operates.

2.3 Areas of the Law Society with which the reporting accountant may have contact

The areas of the Law Society with which the reporting accountant will have most contact will be first of all the Professional Ethics Division, located at Redditch, and the Solicitors Complaints Bureau, which moved from Victoria to Leamington in March 1993.

The Policy Department is responsible for the *Guide to the Professional Conduct of Solicitors* and therefore the Solicitors' Accounts Rules 1991 (SAR91) and the Accountant's Report Rules 1991 (ARR91). The SAR91 and the ARR91 are actually written by the Accounts Rules sub-committee of the Law Society. The Department is continually looking at policy problems regarding the Rules, the need for changes and amendments, new rules and clarification. Changes to the Rules, or guidance thereto are notified to solicitors first of all in the Law Society's *Gazette* and then the detailed rules or guidance are issued in the regular professional up-dates, *Professional Standards Bulletin*. The *Professional Standards Bulletin* is an up-date to the *Guide to the Professional Conduct of Solicitors*. To enable the reporting accountant to keep abreast of changes which affect his work it is vital that he has access to each of these publications.

Changes to the Rules or guidance are often the result of individual solicitors expressing difficulties to the Policy Department regarding certain interpretational or practical aspects of the Rules. For example, since the issue of the SAR91, there have been new rules on the treatment of professional disbursements and bulk legal aid payments where it was thought that solicitors would have problems in implementing the 1991 provisions.

However, clarification is often required where it is felt that a particular interpretation of a rule could lead to that rule not meeting a problem it was designed to solve. Hence, guidance was issued in November 1992 concerning the rate of interest to be paid on undesignated deposits where it was felt there was the risk of abuse.

On matters where the reporting accountant may have difficulty with the SAR91 which contains policy implications, he is advised to contact the Policy Department, preferably in writing, for guidance. However, in normal circumstances, the reporting accountant's difficulty will be interpretational, because, for example, he finds it hard to see how the Rules apply to a particular set of circumstances. In this case the accountant should contact one of the executives in the guidance section of the Professional Ethics Division. The guidance section will give good, practical and consistent advice over the telephone. However, it must be remembered that for particularly involved issues the matter should be dealt with in writing.

The most common query received by the guidance section from reporting accountants concerns interest, where, of course, the reporting accountant's responsibilities are limited. After queries on interest, the next most frequent enquiry concerns client account reconciliations, often because the accounts do not reconcile and the accountant does not wish to qualify his report.

A department formed only very recently is the Accounts Rules Monitoring Unit at Redditch which is also available to answer general queries.

The advice to the reporting accountant must be that if he is in any doubt concerning the SAR91 or the ARR91 he should contact the guidance section of Professional Ethics Division.

All accountants' reports are received by the accountant's report section which is part of the Administration of the Law Society, in Redditch. This section is responsible for reminding solicitors to submit their reports, and will also deal with applications for any of the various dispensations allowing a solicitor not to file an accountant's report. It is also the part of the Law Society to be contacted if a solicitor wishes to extend the deadline for the submission of the accountant's report. Such extensions, normally for a month, are often given when the solicitor wishes to change his accounts year-end, or if his accounting system has changed.

All late accountants' reports, that is those which have not received an extension, are automatically sent by the accountants' report section to the regulation and conduct section of the Solicitors Complaints Bureau. There are generally two types of penalty that this section will take in respect of late filed reports. First, it can issue what is called a section 12 condition to the solicitor's practising certificate, which means that at the next occasion the solicitor applies for his certificate he has to give at least six weeks notice and find two other solicitors to certify that he is a fit and proper person. The second penalty is an immediate recommendation for disciplinary action to be taken. It is therefore recommended that the reporting accountant ensures his work is planned to allow his report to meet the six months deadline.

All qualified accountant's reports are sent by the section at Redditch to the investigation accountants at the Solicitors Complaints Bureau. The Bureau was set up in 1986 and also deals will all complaints from members of the public. It is overseen by an investigation committee, the majority of which comprises lay members.

The Law Society currently receives about 1300 qualified reports a year. When it is considered that there are over 8000 firms (although not all will hold client money), this may be thought to be a low incidence of qualification given the strictness of the Rules regarding when the reporting accountant must qualify his report. This aspect of reporting under the ARR91 is dealt with in Chapter 5; however, there is a belief by many involved in the industry, including accountants in practice, that the incidence of qualification is low because reporting accountants do not always qualify when they should.

The investigation accountants also receive all accountants' reports where there is no qualification but where there is a difference on one of the client account reconciliations, with no explanation; such reports are automatically treated as qualified. (The continued incidence of this is surprising given that the Law Society issued guidance on this aspect of the accountants' report in 1991.)

The investigation accountants' section employs qualified and experienced accountants. The action taken as a result of receiving a qualified report is primarily a matter for their judgement. Of the 1300 qualified reports, in 900 cases no further action is taken based solely on the information contained within the report. Of the remaining 400 a large proportion are satisfactorily explained after seeking further information.

There are four courses of action which the investigation accountants can take or recommend, depending on their view of the seriousness of the breach. These are as follows:

(a) a letter to the solicitor concerned warning him not to breach the Rules again;
(b) a request for further information from the solicitor or the reporting

accountant, on the receipt of which it may be decided to take no further action, or one of the two following courses may be taken;

(i) the matter is referred to a separate unit at Redditch, the Accounts Rules Monitors; or

(ii) the breach is so serious that it requires an inspection.

The Accounts Rules Monitors carry out investigations both on a random basis, to ensure compliance by the profession as a whole, and as a result of complaints or qualified reports referred by the Solicitors Complaints Bureau. An investigation by the Monitors requires one week's notice to be given to the solicitor. Such investigations are not as detailed as the inspections undertaken by the investigation accountants.

Of the inspections undertaken in 1992, only 13 per cent were as a result of a qualified accountant's report. Nearly half were caused by the suspicion aroused by financial difficulties and 18 per cent were on the grounds of a suspected fraud or a dishonest partner.

Inspections are normally undertaken when it is thought that there is high risk of a shortfall of client money, and the accountants who carry out this work have procedures designed to uncover fraud. Forty eight hours notice is needed for such an inspection, at which the solicitor is required to present his accounting records; failure to do so is itself a disciplinary offence.

After all inspections a report is submitted to the regulations and conduct department of the Law Society; breaches are referred to the conduct committee.

The conduct committee will take one of a number of actions:

(a) note the breach with regret;
(b) deprecate the breach;
(c) give a rebuke;
(d) give a severe rebuke;
(e) the chairman may give a verbal rebuke; or
(f) recommend that disciplinary proceedings are taken against the solicitor.

If an inspection uncovers a shortfall in client funds which is unreplaced or where the solicitor is a sole practitioner, the Bureau will institute an 'intervention'. This is where another firm of solicitors closes down the practice, and takes over dealing with the clients and the client money. The solicitor in breach loses his practising certificate and will be struck off the Roll.

Wherever an inspection uncovers a shortfall in client money the accountants look to see whether there was also a shortfall in the client account reconciliation dates to which the last accountant's report refers. If there was a shortfall then the matter is reported to the conduct and regulation department which will ask the reporting accountant for his observations. If the observations are not considered to be satisfactory then the accountant will be disqualified from undertaking any further reporting responsibilities under the ARR91 and the individual will be reported to his institute. This is likely to result in disciplinary proceedings.

This sequence of possible events indicates how vital it is that the reporting accountant undertakes his work to the highest possible professional standards. The recent highly publicised cases of dishonesty by solicitors concerning large amounts of client money strongly emphasise the importance of the reporting accountant's role. Where loss has occurred there are two possible sources of reimbursement within the Law Society which can provide compensation and these are considered next.

2.4 Solicitors Indemnity Fund Limited (SIF)

The SIF provides indemnity cover to solicitors in practice where there is a claim other than where there is dishonesty and the firm is a sole practitioner or the partners in the firm colluded in the theft or fraud. The exceptions are dealt with by the Solicitors Compensation Fund. The SIF provides cover up to a maximum of £1,000,000 except in personal injury cases where the maximum is £500,000.

Recently there has been a considerable increase in the amount paid by firms to the SIF as the SIF has had to deal with a growing number of claims; between 1987 and 1992 the number of claims on the SIF increased by 17 per cent per annum, and the average cost of settling each claim by 7.3 per cent per annum. It is estimated that in 1992/93 the costs of meeting claims will be £270 million, of which a large proportion will be met directly by the firms themselves on 'deductibles' (see below) and that the SIF will need to raise contributions to the fund from firms of nearly £180 million. (The financial information in this and succeeding paragraphs is extracted from two articles in the Law Society's *Gazette* by John Young, the Chairman of SIF: *Professional Indemnity*, 13 May 1992, and *Professional Indemnity Costs 92/93*, 24 June 1992.)

The contribution required from each firm is calculated as a percentage of the gross fees per partner, such percentage decreasing with increasing average gross fees. There are also fairly large discounts given depending on the size of the firm, with firms comprising more than 15 partners receiving the maximum discount of 32 per cent (but subject to a maximum amount, currently £225,000). There are further discounts available for firms involved in low-risk work (criminal and certain types of debt collection).

Deductibles represent the excess payable by the firm on a claim. Prior to 1992/93 the standard deductible was £500 per partner per claim, subject to a minimum of £2000 and a maximum of £5000 per firm. The deductible arising on multiple claims within the same indemnity period could not exceed five times the standard deductible. From 1 September 1992, the standard deductible is equivalent to 1 per cent of the gross fees of the practice concerned, subject to a minimum of £3000 and a maximum of £150,000 per claim. The deductible arising on multiple claims is three times the standard deductible.

The recent changes have been designed to increase the contributions payable by the sole practitioner and two-partner firms who it was felt were being subsidised by the larger firms, and to put more of the costs of meeting claims back onto the firms responsible for the claims. The maximum cover of £1,000,000 (or £500,000, as noted above) provided by the SIF is non-negotiable. Where a firm wishes to obtain cover above this amount then it needs to contact professional brokers.

The SIF can use independent accountants to investigate and substantiate claims; an important part of this will be to determine how the reporting accountant has discharged his responsibilities.

2.5 Solicitors Compensation Fund (SCF)

'The Law Society maintains a Compensation Fund... The object of the Fund is to enable the Society to make grants to those who have suffered loss by reason of the dishonesty of a solicitor . . . Grants may also be made in the event of hardship suffered as a result of a solicitor failing to account for monies due (but only where money or money's worth has been misappropriated by the solicitor) . . .' (guidance notes issued by the Law Society for persons who wish to apply for a grant from the SCF). The SCF will not therefore make grants in respect of damages or consequential loss arising from acts of the solicitor.

The SCF is funded by standard payments mainly from solicitors holding client money. For 1992/93 the amount is £1045, and for the 24,000 solicitors not holding client money the amount is £150. The total amount of money raised is £30 million (see Law Society's *Gazette*, 10 June 1992). It is anticipated that these amounts will need to be increased in future because of the rapid increase in applications to the Fund. For example, the beginning of 1992 saw increases of 60 per cent by number and 65 per cent by value. £11.7 million was paid out in 1991 (an increase of 11 per cent on the previous year) and at the end of that year unprocessed claims amounted to £33 million, nearly £20 million more than the value of the Fund (see Law Society's *Gazette*, 3 June 1992 – *Solicitors Face Bill of up to £1800 for Fund*).

The majority of grants arise from conveyancing transactions; mortgage frauds, some of which run into millions, account for 20 per cent of applications.

Because of the nature of claims against the Fund, the investigation and substantiation of claims is run from the Solicitors Complaints Bureau. An important part of their work will also be to determine whether a reporting accountant is in any way to blame for the loss. Actions for negligence in this area are rare, as most will be settled out of court. However, there is a general duty of care owed by reporting accountants to the Law Society, and this is considered in Chapter 7.

As noted in Chapter 7 the whole issue of default by solicitors is the subject of a protracted debate. It is apparent that reporting accountants are going to receive a large proportion of the blame, sometimes from a failure to understand what it is the reporting accountant is supposed to do, but also because reporting accountants sometimes fail to carry out what they are supposed to do. Possible changes to the reporting accountant's duties are considered in Chapter 7; however, as fraud claims and investigations increase, the work carried out by an increasing number of reporting accountants will come under greater scrutiny.

Chapter 3 – Professional conduct of solicitors

3.1 Introduction

Solicitors are bound to conduct themselves by certain statutes and Law Society rules. These are contained in the Guide to the Professional Conduct of Solicitors, published by the Law Society in 1990. Since publication there have been a number of changes, notably the Solicitors' Practice Rules 1990 (SPR90), the Solicitors' Publicity Code 1990 (SPC90) and the Solicitors' Introduction and Referral Code 1990 (SIRC90) as well as various changes and new rules contained in the Professional Standards Bulletins.

The various rules, codes and guidelines provide an insight into the way solicitors carry out their business and are summarised below.

3.2 Practice

Persons are not qualified to act as solicitors unless they have been admitted as a solicitor, their name is on the Roll and they have a current practising certificate. This prohibits individuals generally from calling themselves solicitors, acting as solicitors, appearing before certain tribunals, drawing up certain types of documents or administering oaths. Solicitors are not allowed to discriminate on the grounds of race or sex, and have a duty to persuade clients to modify instructions regarding any discriminatory choice of a barrister.

Solicitors are under a duty to ensure that offices where they practise from are supervised to comply with certain minimum standards. For example, on days when offices are open to the public or telephone calls they need to have a solicitor in attendance who has been admitted for three years, and need to be managed by a practising solicitor or legal executive.

Sole principals are required to have been admitted for three years before they can practise on their own or supervise their own offices. Where they are absent from the office due to illness or vacation they still have an ongoing duty to clients and arrangements must be made to facilitate this. They also have to make a will which contains provisions for the running of the practice in the event of death. If a solicitor is not appointed as executor to do this then the executors have to appoint a solicitor to do so.

For solicitors practising in partnership, there is a principle that *prima facie* each is responsible for the acts or omissions of the firm including the staff. This is particularly important where there is a breach of the Solicitors' Accounts Rules 1991 as each partner could be disciplined and knowledge will be imputed to the partners.

All partners within a firm are required to hold practising certificates and the effect of a partner not holding a practising certificate is to render the partnership illegal which means the partnership is effectively dissolved. Where there is a material alteration in a firm clients have to be notified promptly and a material change is held to be, for example, one partner leaving in a four partner firm. Additionally, where one firm takes over another or a firm splits up clients have to be notified. In the case of a split clients have to be offered a choice of firm as to which firm the client wishes to retain.

If a salaried partner's name appears on the firm's notepaper then he must hold a practising certificate and is treated as a partner by the Law Society with regard to responsibilities under the Solicitors Accounts Rules.

Solicitors are not allowed to operate, participate in or control businesses, other than the practice of solicitor which offers specific services. These services are basically the normal activities of a solicitor's practice, plus property selling and investment advice. The only exceptions to the rule are management consultancies and company secretarial services which only draft legal documents or offer legal advice as an ancillary service, and overseas practices. However, solicitors are allowed to set up service companies to carry out the administrative functions of the firm.

Law centres are generally companies limited by guarantee which are funded by grants; Citizens' Advice Bureaux (CABs) are similar organisations funded by grants and charity. At both legal advice is given and casework undertaken. In many ways they resemble solicitors practices and will employ solicitors. The Law Society treats law centres and CABs, in many respects, like practices and employed solicitors have to hold a practising certificate and comply with the Practice Rules. Law centres can also hold client money and may therefore be obliged to submit an accountant's report to the Law Society.

3.3 Clients

Rule 1 of the SPR90 prohibits a solicitor from doing anything in practice which impairs or compromises his independence or integrity, a person's freedom to instruct the solicitor of his choice, his duty to act in the best interests of his client, the reputation of the solicitor or his profession, his standard of work and his duty to the Court. Solicitors are allowed to publicise themselves, but within the provisions of the SPC90. As well as the normal rules regarding advertising, such as good taste, solicitors are not allowed to make comparisons with or criticisms of other firms. They are not allowed to make unsolicited visits or phone calls or name clients without their permission, and references to fees must be clear.

Within the principles of Rule 1 and under the SIRC90 solicitors are allowed to accept work from or refer work to third parties, but they must not accept instructions where the third party has stipulated to the potential client that the solicitor must act. Solicitors are not allowed to reward introducers of work with commissions and have to be wary of becoming reliant on a limited number of referrers. At six monthly intervals firms are required to review their compliance with the SIRC90 and confirm that the giving of advice has not been tainted by their relationship with introducers. It is recommended that no more than 20 per cent of a firm's business should come from a single source. Where a solicitor himself refers work he must have regard to the client's interest and must pass on to the client commissions in excess of £20.

A solicitor is free to decide whether to accept instructions, but must not act where he has insufficient experience or resources, where he believes the client is acting out of malice or vindictiveness, where a solicitor is already acting in the matter or where he suspects the instruction has been made under duress or undue influence.

Solicitors can only terminate the retainer with a client for good reason, for example where he cannot obtain clear instructions and upon reasonable notice. The solicitor is required to deliver to his former client all papers and property subject to any lien he has.

The solicitor must keep his client's affairs confidential, must not take advantage of his client, must keep him properly informed and comply with his reasonable requests for information. The duty of confidentiality extends to staff, and applies to all information irrespective of its source. It also includes such information as the client's address. The only exceptions to the rule regarding confidentiality are when the client (or former client) consents, or where the solicitor has a duty, for example in legal aid cases, or under a court order. There is a similar duty for the solicitor to disclose to his client information pertinent to his client, regardless of its source, and to use that information.

3.3.1 Conflicts of interest

The solicitor must also not act where there is a conflict of interest or a risk of a conflict, that is a conflict between the firm and the prospective client, or between an existing client and a former or prospective client, or a former client and a prospective client or two existing clients.

A conflict between the firm and a client can arise where a solicitor acts in a personal capacity, or where a partner or employees are interested, where the solicitor has a family interest, or where a directorship is held. A conflict may also exist where the solicitor or a related party holds an office. For example, there would be a conflict between a solicitor acting in respect of proceedings following a death where the solicitor or a partner was the coroner who investigated the death.

Conflicts with former clients will arise where the solicitor acquires relevant knowledge, which is obviously confidential, yet which he would be under a duty to disclose to the present client if material to the case; for example this could be the case in matrimonial or partnership disputes. The same rules apply where existing clients of a firm or solicitor have a conflict of interest. The solicitor may not be allowed to act for either client, unless the consent of the other client is given and the solicitor does not have relevant knowledge.

3.3.2 Way in which work is to be carried out

When acting for a client, solicitors are required to carry out the client's instructions with diligence and reasonable care and skill. Inadequate professional service includes professional and organisational incompetence. Where a solicitor is aware of an intention by a client to make a claim, or where he becomes aware of an act or omission which would justify a claim, the solicitor is required to inform his client that the client should take legal advice.

3.3.3 Communications

Solicitors are required to deal with correspondence from clients and former clients promptly. In dealing with the client generally the solicitor is required to follow the client care provisions of Rule 15 of the SPR90 which provide that the client must be made aware of:

(a) whom the client deals with in the event of a complaint;
(b) who is responsible for the work on a day to day basis, and the partner responsible for supervision;
(c) what the issues raised by the case are and how they will be dealt with;
(d) the progress of the case and the reasons for serious delays.

The solicitor should also let the client know:

(e) when and if the persons responsible for the case change, the fact and the reasons;
(f) when it is appropriate to instruct counsel;

(g) who will represent the client at any hearings;
(h) the effect of important documents;
(i) on taking instructions, as best he can the level of costs, how these are to be met and whether the client might qualify for legal aid.

3.3.4 Costs

There are a separate set of professional standards dealing with informing the client as to costs. These are that the solicitor should inform the client:

(a) on taking instructions the best information concerning the likely cost of the case or how the fee shall be calculated, how the charges will be met and whether they may be eligible for legal aid or covered by insurance;
(b) on confirming instructions, in writing any agreed fee, what it covers, whether it includes VAT and disbursements, and what payments the client may have to make and when;
(c) in advance, the reasons for substantial variations of the fee from the estimate;
(d) that he can set an upper limit for costs beyond which the solicitor may not go without referring to the client;
(e) every six months the costs to date;
(f) that it is often not possible to estimate costs in advance;
(g) in legally aided cases the obligations and effect on the client of, for example, becoming liable to pay a contribution;
(h) in contentious cases that the client remains liable for the solicitor's costs, and of the effects of orders by the courts for costs;
(i) whether the likely outcome will justify the expense or risk involved.

As well as complying with the above code, solicitors are forbidden from entering into arrangements for accepting contingency fees from cases which involve the institution of proceedings (this therefore excludes debt collections where the debts are collected without legal proceedings) or sharing fees with any person other than his employee or another solicitor. Solicitors are allowed to ask for money in advance of costs or disbursements.

On completion of work, the solicitor must render a bill of costs within a reasonable time, and the bill should contain sufficient information regarding the work being charged for. The bill must distinguish between disbursements and profit costs. Solicitors cannot generally sue on unpaid bills until one month after delivery. For non-contentious business the solicitor is required to inform the client of his right to have the bill taxed by the High Court and to require a remuneration certificate from the Law Society regarding what sum charged would be fair and reasonable for the work. Once notice has been given, the solicitor has the right to charge interest on the bill. For contentious bills the client has the right to request the solicitor to deliver a new bill containing a detailed breakdown.

Solicitors are not allowed to take unfair advantage by overcharging their clients. Where, for example, more than half of a non-contentious bill is reduced by a taxing master, he is required to inform the Law Society.

Where professional disbursements are concerned, even though the solicitor has not received payment from his client he will remain responsible for the costs incurred, unless for example he makes it clear to the other professional that the solicitor restricts his liability to the amount allowed on taxation. A barrister does not have a contractual relationship with his solicitor and therefore cannot sue for his fees; however, in non-legal aid cases where fees are unpaid or unchallenged within three months of the conclusion of the case, this can be raised as a matter of professional conduct with the Law Society; this applies regardless of whether the solicitor has been paid by his client. In legal aid cases a delay on the part of a solicitor in submitting the bill for taxation may also result in disciplinary action.

3.4 Third parties

The solicitor also has duties to four other classes of persons, being third parties, other solicitors, the bar and the court.

There is a set of duties regarding professional undertakings given by the solicitor generally either written or oral. Professional undertakings are those given to persons who will rely on them. Professional undertakings bind the solicitor personally. Undertakings that are ambiguous are interpreted in the recipient's favour. They are outside the law of contract, that is they can be given without consideration, bind the solicitor when given by his staff, and bind all of the partners in the firm. Undertakings can also be given by the solicitor on behalf of someone else, for example a client. Therefore an undertaking to pay an accountant's costs in a matter would be enforceable.

The rules regarding third parties generally, over and above the normal professional requirements, cover solicitors stopping client account cheques, preparing conveyancing contracts for a vendor where the purchaser has not taken legal advice or where he is instructed to deal with more than one purchaser, action to be taken when administering oaths, and writing letters on behalf of clients before an action. This last rule stops solicitors demanding anything other than that recoverable by law.

Solicitors are required to act with complete frankness and good faith towards other solicitors, and must not, for example, write offensive letters, or behave in an acrimonious or offensive manner. Solicitors are also not allowed, in general, to communicate with persons in a matter where those persons have retained another solicitor, without that solicitor's consent.

The duties regarding the bar require the solicitors to instruct counsel adequately and with enough notice, and to attend proceedings where counsel has been instructed, except for those in certain lower courts where the interests of the client will not be affected.

As far as the courts are concerned, solicitors are forbidden to deceive or mislead the court, offer to make contingent payments to witnesses, discuss the merits of a case with the judge without the presence of a representative for the other side, or to continue to act where a client has admitted to misleading the court or perjury unless this is fully disclosed to the court. There are also duties regarding the solicitor acting as advocate before a court, such as not acting for a client as advocate where a member of the solicitor's firm is to be called upon to give more than formal evidence, or dealing with scrupulous fairness and dispassionately when prosecuting a criminal case.

PART II

An audit under the Solicitors Accounts Rules

This section is designed to provide a comprehensive guide to carrying out an audit under the Solicitors' Accounts Rules.

The chapters include section by section analyses of the Solicitors' Accounts Rules and the Accountant's Report Rules, as well as comments on the most recent changes to these and guidance by the Law Society on their application.

The heart of this section is a chapter presenting a programme of work to carry out an audit. The recommended approach is structured and attempts to use the same discipline an auditor would adopt in carrying out a Companies Act audit. Reference is made to a substantial appendix containing model forms for the audit work.

The section also looks at difficulties which may arise in carrying out an audit, and although the author recognises that there are many other areas, these are the ones on which he is commonly asked to advise.

An important part of developing a structured approach to an audit is the assessment of risk and the determination of statistical sample sizes, and one chapter deals with these issues.

Finally, there is a chapter on possible changes to the work of an accountant in this area and his liability in the event of negligent work.

Chapter 4 – The Solicitors Accounts Rules

4.1 Introduction and Regulatory Framework

Under the Solicitors Act 1974, the Law Society has the power to regulate the custody of client and controlled trust money held by solicitors. The regulation is to cover the:

(a) opening and keeping by solicitors of accounts at banks or building societies for such money and the location of the branches where accounts are to be kept;
(b) keeping of accounts containing information as to such money received or held or paid by the solicitor on account of the client or the trust; and
(c) empowering of the Council of the Law Society regarding compliance with the regulations. (Solicitors Act 1974, section 32)

Section 33 of the Act covers interest on client money, and requires rules to be made to require solicitors to keep client money in separate deposit accounts, or make good to the client the interest which would have accrued if the client money had been kept in a separate account, to be determined by the amount and length of time of the deposit. The section does not make a solicitor liable to account for interest on client accounts held generally (except as provided by the rules) nor does it affect arrangements made in writing between the solicitor and his client.

By section 34 of the Act, all solicitors, subject to certain exemptions, have to submit a signed accountant's report once in every 12 month period ending 31 October, and six months after the end of the accounting period to which the report refers. Section 34 also empowers the Council to regulate the qualifications of reporting accountants, the format of the report and the nature and scope of the examination.

The current rules designed to achieve the above are the Solicitors' Accounts Rules 1991 (SAR91) and the Accountant's Reports Rules 1991 (ARR91). The SAR91 have two main objectives:

(a) to ensure that a solicitor meets the legal requirements as set out above; and

(b) to ensure that a solicitor accounts to his clients for interest on money so held on a fair and reasonable basis.

The SAR91 are divided into three main parts:

- *Part I* covers the maintenance of client accounts, movements of client money and the various books which a solicitor is required to keep.
- *Part II* deals with the maintenance of accounts in respect of controlled trusts, movements of controlled trust money and the records required to be kept for controlled trusts.
- *Part III* deals with accounting to clients for interest.

(There are two further Parts which deal with the exercise of compliance with the Rules by the Council of the Law Society and the application of the Rules.)

The Law Society has a number of methods of trying to ensure that these objectives are met. First, the SAR91 provide the detail of the manner in which books should be kept and when interest should be paid. Secondly, the Law Society issues clarifications to the SAR on areas of the rules which are unclear or being abused. The Law Society operates its own regulatory bodies to enforce the rules as described in Chapter 2. Finally, it is required that all solicitors holding money within a practice year have their books open to examination by an independent accountant, the reporting accountant, who reports to the Law Society on his findings.

As most firms of solicitors hold client money, this generates a great deal of work for the accountancy profession. The work which the reporting accountant is required to do, and the way he reports is set out in the ARR91. The revised SAR91 and the ARR91 came into force with effect from 1 June 1992; for details of previous solicitors' accounts and accountants' report rules, together with details of transitional arrangements for solicitors whose accounting periods span 1 June 1992, the reader is referred to *Business Briefings No 32* (1992, Accountancy Books). Since the issue of the SAR91, there have been amendments and guidance, published in Professional Standards Bulletins of the Professional Standards and Development Directorate of the Law Society. The amendments also came into force from 1 June 1992.

4.2 The SAR91 Rule by Rule

1 Date of commencement
2 Definitions (see Appendix 1)

4.2.1 Part I – General

Payments of client money in

3 Requirement to keep client money in a client account and to pay it in without delay.

4 Money which may be paid into a client account (trust money, to open or maintain account, replace withdrawals made in error, mixed money under Rule 5).

5 Mixed money, that is client or trust money plus other, for example, office money, may be split on receipt or paid into a client account.

5A Full or partial settlements of fees can be paid into a client account, but can only remain there for up to seven days.

6 No other money can be paid into a client account.

Withdrawals from a client account

7 Money which may be withdrawn from a client account. (Client money: payment to, on behalf of, client; reimbursement of solicitor, on client's authority, for solicitor's bill where it, or written intimation, is delivered to client; transfer to other client account. (N.B. note the definition of costs in Appendix 1, and implications for unpaid professional disbursements included in the solicitor's bill.) Trust money: in execution of trust, transfer to separate bank account for the trust. Other money: paid in under Rules 4, 5 and 5A, or paid in in error.)

8 Money to pay solicitor's bill or repay any other money belonging to solicitor must be transferred to a non-client account or by cheque in favour of the solicitor; no money other than as allowed by Rule 7 can be withdrawn without express permission of the Law Society.

Money not to be paid into a client account

9 No obligation to pay client money into a client account if: cash and paid to client or third party, cheque endorsed over to client or third party, paid into separate account in name of client or other person on client's instruction.

The solicitor shall not pay into a client account money which the client instructs not to so pay, money in respect of the reimbursement of solicitor or, subject to Rule 5A, money in respect of a bill of costs.

Transfers

10 No transfers from one client account to that of another unless each transfer would have been permissable under the Rules.

Books

11 Requirement to keep accounts written up to show:

- client money received, held or paid and other money dealt with through client accounts, money to be shown separately in respect of each client separately, distinct from other money received held or paid by the solicitor and current balance on each client ledger;
- above movements in a client cash account and client ledger.

- Solicitors are allowed to open one client account when they act for both borrower and an institutional lender in a conveyancing transaction.
- Solicitors are required to keep records of bills of costs, which distinguish profit costs from disbursements and written intimations.
- Requirement to carry out and preserve reconciliations of total of a client's ledger balances with cash account balance and cash account balance with bank statements every five weeks at least.
- Withdrawals from a client account, other than those from one general client account to another general client account, are only to be made by individuals where at least one is a solicitor with a practising certificate, an employee of such a solicitor being a solicitor or a Fellow of the Institute of Legal Executives who is confirmed as being of good standing and who has been a Fellow for three years, is a registered foreign lawyer or, in an office dealing solely with conveyancing, a licensed conveyancer who is an employee of a solicitor with a practising certificate.

Requirement to preserve all books, ledgers, records and bank statements for at least six years, and all cheques and authorities to withdraw money from a client account for at least two years. The requirement regarding cheques is relaxed if the bank confirm that they will retain them.

4.2.2 Part II – Controlled trusts

12 Requirement to pay controlled trust money not dealt with as client money into a controlled trust account without delay.

13 Money which may be paid into a controlled trust account (money belonging to that trust, to open or maintain account, replace withdrawals made in error).

14 Mixed money, that is controlled trust money plus other money, for example, office money, may be split on receipt or paid into a client account.

15 No other money can be paid into a controlled trust account.

16 Money which may be withdrawn from a controlled trust account (in execution of trust, transfer to a client account, paid in under Rule 13 or in error.)

17 No money other than as allowed by Rule 16 can be withdrawn without express permission of the Law Society.

18 No obligation to pay controlled trust money into a controlled trust account if: cash and paid in execution of trust without delay, cheque endorsed over in execution of trust.

19 Where controlled trust money is not paid into a client account and treated under Part II, the solicitor is required to keep accounts of his

dealings with controlled trust money separate from other money and to preserve the accounts and bank statements for at least six years. It is also required that these accounts are kept centrally or that a central register of controlled trusts is maintained.

4.2.3 Part III – Interest

20 This requires that solicitors who hold client money account to the client for interest if the money is held in a separate designated account for the money, or if undesignated under Rule 21.

21 This requires that solicitors account for interest on client money held where the following minimum sums are held for the following number of weeks:

Number of weeks	*Minimum balance*
8	£1,000
4	£2,000
2	£10,000
1	£20,000

In addition, sums of £20,000 held for less than a week should have interest paid where it is fair and reasonable to do so, and where there are amounts held, either continuously or intermittently, which vary significantly over a period of time where it is fair and reasonable to do so.

22 Where money is held for a client for part of the time in a separate designated account and for part of the time on the general account, and for the time that the money was on the general account no interest would be payable under the table in Rule 21, then the fair and reasonable basis applies and regard has to be taken of the interest which would have been payable if the money had been held in a general account for the whole period.

23 To determine the interest to be paid on general account, reference is to be made to interest payable on a separate designated account at the bank or building society where the money is held, or if the money is held at successive accounts at different banks or building societies, the highest rate of interest on the day when interest commenced to accrue.

24 Where interest is payable on money held by the solicitor as stakeholder the interest is payable to whomever the stake is paid.

25 Clients who are aggrieved at the interest received can apply to the Law Society for a certificate of the interest which should have been earned.

26 The interest rules do not affect any arrangements in writing between the solicitor and the client, do not apply to controlled trust money, or to

other trust money where the solicitor holds the money in a capacity as trustee rather than as solicitor.

4.3 Recent changes

4.3.1 Legal aid payments

By the Solicitors' Accounts (Legal Aid Temporary Provision) Rules 1992, solicitors are allowed to pay into office accounts payments from the Legal Aid Board which relate to the unpaid fees of professionals, experts, other lawyers etc. This is therefore a relaxation of the rule requiring amounts received in respect of unpaid professional disbursements to be paid into a client account. To the extent that the unpaid professional disbursements have not been paid within 14 days of the receipt of the legal aid payment, the amount relating to the unpaid professional disbursements must be paid into the appropriate client account.

4.3.2 Interest rates to be used for the purposes of Part III

In the Professional Standards Bulletin Number 8, published in November 1992, the Law Society gave guidance on the rates of interest to be used in conjunction with Part III of the SAR91. The Law Society recognised that banks and building societies offer many different interest rates, and the rates for businesses may be lower than that for the public because interest is credited quarterly rather than annually. Additionally, the Law Society is aware that businesses receive lower rates because they may choose not to be debited with certain bank charges such as for cheques and therefore it is not appropriate to look at the artificially low rates but rather at the range of rates paid to the bank's solicitor clients. Further, it may be important to consider the rates applicable to accounts which offer instant access compared to the rates paid on longer-term deposit accounts if instant access is not important, or if it is, then to the different types of instant-access account. Also, some banks will automatically deposit money in a very low interest bearing account unless there is instruction from the solicitor, despite the availability of higher rates.

The Law Society stated that it was inconceivable that a court would consider that a solicitor's obligations to clients would have been fulfilled by placing large sums in separate accounts for any length of time at very low rates and similarly, it would be inappropriate to calculate interest payable for general accounts by reference to accounts yielding low rates. However, solicitors are not liable to pay the rate that a client could have obtained personally or a higher rate than the solicitor actually received unless the rates were being kept artificially low. The Law Society summarised by stating that the rate applied should be reasonable for separate designated accounts and fair for the general account.

4.3.3 Contracting out of the deposit interest provisions

Also in the Professional Standards Bulletin Number 8, the Law Society gave guidance regarding contracting out of the deposit interest provisions, under Rule 26, as noted above.

First of all, it is acceptable for a solicitor to arrange with his client to contract out of the *de minimis* provisions of Rule 21 and, as an alternative, stipulate in the standard terms of business that interest will only be paid if it amounts to more than £20. This would be appropriate where, for example, interest rates are falling and use of the table may give rise to very low rates of interest payable.

However, the Law Society considered that it was improper for a solicitor to enter into an arrangement by, for example, the use of standard terms of contract, where the client receives no interest at all. Additionally, a solicitor may be in breach of the fiduciary duty to a client if the client did not have an opportunity to give an informed consent. The Law Society advised that each case had to be taken on its merits and although there were instances where such an arrangement could be made, the client should receive something in return. Solicitors are required to act fairly towards their clients and to provide them with sufficient information to make an informed consent. Contracting out is never appropriate where it is against the client's interests.

With regard to stakeholder money, similar considerations apply and although a solicitor can make a charge for the services of acting as stakeholder, this should be fair and reasonable and a maximum charge should be fixed. Again, solicitors are not allowed to take an unfair advantage and they should be particularly careful where the other party is not represented.

4.4 Client money

Solicitors hold client money for a variety of reasons, for example:

(a) in conveyancing transactions where deposits are held in and the principle passes through client account. This is the primary source of client money for most solicitors;
(b) where the solicitor undertakes probate work and handles money as executor;
(c) where the solicitor acts as agent and receives money by, for example, the collection of a debt;

(d) monies deposited by both sides in a dispute;
(e) monies held by way of retention under, for example, a sale and purchase agreement pending resolution of a warranty claim.

It can be seen that one of the primary purposes of the SAR91 is to control the movement of client money and to ensure that it does not become mixed with other money, such as the solicitor's own. This is the reason behind the rule that solicitors cannot treat themselves as clients, and thereby pay their own money into a client account. There are relaxations of this rule, but only in very specific circumstances. Similarly, client money must be paid into a client account on receipt, and only in specified circumstances is this rule relaxed.

With movements out of a client account there is more difficulty because, although the solicitor will only be paying out money in accordance with the matter with which he his dealing for his client, this will include the settlement of his own bills of cost. Hence the rules regarding the notice the solicitor has to give his client when he wishes to apply any money to his own costs. These movements can be summarised as shown on the next page.

Because the client bank accounts may include the money of a large number of clients, any payment on behalf of one client in excess of the money held on his behalf will result in the other clients subsidising that client, and such an application of client's money would be a clear breach of the SAR91. This is the reason for the prohibition on overdrawn client accounts. Solicitors are allowed to pay their own money into a client's account to meet a shortfall which is not expected to be immediately made up by the client; however, in these circumstances that money becomes the client's money and the debt owed by the client to the solicitor is a separate matter and any further money placed into client account cannot be withdrawn by the solicitor to meet the liability unless such a withdrawal is in accordance with the rules.

Accounts may become overdrawn if a payment out of a client account is made in respect of a cheque which does not clear. Solicitors are advised to come to an arrangement with the bank to pay dishonoured cheques out of an office account, to wait for the cheque to clear or to have them specially cleared.

As well as the above, client money is afforded protection by the requirements regarding books of account to be kept, the regular reconciliations between the client ledgers, cash book and bank statements and the submission of an Accountant's Report every 12 months.

4.5 Trusts

Section 32 of the Solicitors Act 1974 has a requirement for the Law Society to make rules regarding controlled trusts. Controlled trusts are defined as those

Description	*Receipts*	*Payments*
Client money	Must be paid into a client account without delay (SAR91-3), but subject to the provisions of the Solicitors' Accounts (Legal Aid Temporary Provision) Rules 1992	May be paid: (a) to or on behalf of the client (b) for the reimbursement of the solicitor on client's authority (c) on client authority (d) for the solicitor's fees after delivery of a bill or written intimation (e) into another client account (SAR91-7(a))
Trust money	May be paid into a client account (SAR91-4(a))	May be paid in execution of the trust or into the trust bank account (SAR91-7(b))
Solicitor's own money	May be paid in only for the purpose of opening or maintaining the account (SAR91-4(b)). Subject to SAR91-5A regarding clients' remittances	May be paid out of the account when no longer required (SAR91-7(c))
Mixed receipts (which contain a proportion of client money)	May be paid into a client account intact or split by the solicitor (SAR91-4(d) and 5(b))	The proportion which is not client or trust money may be paid out (SAR91-7(d))
Correction of mistakes	Money to replace any sum withdrawn in contravention of the rules (SAR91-7(c))	Money paid in contravention of the rules (SAR91-7(d))
Other	No other payments in are allowed (SAR91-6)	No other withdrawals are allowed without the express permission of the Council (SAR91-8(2))
Transfer between ledger accounts	Only permissible if the payment in and the withdrawal would have been permissible under the above rules (SAR91-10(i))	

trusts where all of the trustees are partners or employees in the same firm. Solicitors are allowed to treat controlled trust money like client money but where they do not, then the rules implemented by Part II apply.

As far as other trusts are concerned, money in respect of these may be treated as client money, but there is no specific requirement to do so, or to keep certain records. The presence of other trustees is considered to be sufficient protection for the funds of such trusts.

4.6 The treatment of interest earned on client money

By section 33 of the Solicitors Act 1974 a solicitor is allowed to retain interest earned on client money unless it arises on a separate designated account. The solicitor is only required to make good to the client for money held in the general account for interest which would have been earned if the money had been held in a separate account and only then subject to the amount and the length of time deposited. Interest actually earned on general account does not have to be paid across to the client as such.

There are two important implications of section 33. First of all, interest earned on the general account is not client money and as such it should be removed from the client account as it is credited. Secondly, the compensatory payment made by the solicitor need not and probably will not be based on the actual amounts of interest received.

This degree of latitude given to the solicitor is understandable. All money held by the solicitor will attract interest but it will certainly be uneconomic to account to clients for very small amounts, hence the guidance from the Law Society of a *de minimis* level of £20. At the time of writing, interest rates are the lowest they have been for some considerable time, and the amount of interest actually earned on any deposit will be substantially lower than, say, two years ago.

However, the rules are open to abuse (especially if they are looked at in isolation from the other provisions of the Guide to Professional Conduct) and they have led the Law Society to provide further guidance to solicitors on what is fair and reasonable as referred to above. As noted in Chapter 2, the subject of interest is the cause of many of the complaints received by the Solicitors Complaints Bureau.

As far as interest on trust money is concerned, where the solicitor is joint trustee with a lay person then the rules of Part III apply. Where the solicitor is trustee in a capacity other than that of solicitor, or where the trust is a controlled trust then the solicitor is subject to the general legal principle that a trustee is precluded from obtaining any benefit from the trust without express authority. Therefore, although Part III does not apply to such trust money, the solicitor has a legal duty to account to the trust for all of the interest received.

The responsibility of the accountant to ensure that the solicitor accounts for interest in a proper manner are limited, and understandably so. However, the accountant does have specific and extensive responsibilities for ensuring compliance with Parts I and II of the SAR91 and these are described in the next chapter.

Chapter 5 – The Accountants Report Rules

5.1 Introduction

Within six months of the end of his financial year and once every practice year, the solicitor must deliver to the Law Society an Accountant's Report. The qualification requirements of the accountant, scope of his work and format of his report are set out in the Accountant's Report Rules 1991 (ARR91), issued by the Law Society which came into effect on 1 June 1992. These Rules replaced the Accountant's Report Rules 1986. The ARR91 have been amended by new rules regarding the accountant's responsibilities in respect of controlled trusts, and these amendments also came into effect on 1 June 1992.

5.2 The ARR91 Rule by Rule

1 Date rules came into effect

2 Definitions (all definitions in both the Solicitors' Account Rules 1991 (SAR91) and the ARR91 are included in Appendix 1)

3 Deals with qualifications of an accountant. To make a report under the ARR91 a person must be a member of either the English, Scottish or Irish Institutes, or the Chartered Association of Certified Accountants, and must not have been found guilty of misconduct by their professional association. In addition, the Law Society may inform accountants that they are not qualified to give an Accountant's Report where it comes to their attention that a person has been negligent in the preparation of a report under the ARR91 in the past. It should be noted that, because an Accountant's Report is signed in the name of an individual rather than a firm, disqualification affects the individual accountant signing the report and not any other person or partner within his firm.

Employees or co-employees of the solicitor subject to the report are also disqualified from reporting.

4 This rule covers the work which the accountant needs to carry out in order to make the report and is the longest rule of the ARR91.

The accountant is required to ascertain particulars of all of the solicitors' accounts and make an examination of them. The prescribed examination of the accounts (other than any controlled trust accounts) is as follows:

- examine book-keeping system to ensure it complies with rule 11 of the SAR91 and designed so that there is a ledger account for each client;
- that the ledgers show separately movements of client money;
- that movements of money through the client account are separate from office money.

As noted in Chapter 4, Rule 11 covers the requirements to maintain:

- books of accounts;
- records containing client money and other money dealt with through client account;
- the balance on client ledgers;
- the format of the client cash book and the client ledger;
- records of bills of costs;
- five weekly reconciliations;
- client account cheque signing requirements; and
- the preservation of accounting records.

There is also a requirement to ensure that the records are sufficient to enable Rule 13 of the Solicitors' Investment Business Rules 1990 to be complied with. Rule 13 requires that a solicitor authorised in the conduct of discrete investment business shall ensure that:

- all bills of cost shall record the amount attributable to discrete investment business separately from the amount of costs attributable to other work;
- all bills of cost containing an item attributable to discrete investment business shall be identified separately from other bills in the bills delivered book or file of copies of bills, or recorded in a separate bills delivered book or file of copies of bills maintained solely for such bills;
- records are maintained to enable the solicitor to complete the paragraphs of the form required to be sent to the Law Society every year for their annual authorisation to conduct investment business in respect of the amounts received (see Appendix 3).

The accountant is then required to make certain tests and test checks, being:

- posting to client ledger from client cash records;
- casts of client ledger and cash records;
- comparing entries on client bank statements to client cash records;
- system of recording costs and making transfers from the client account in respect of costs.

There is then a general requirement to test documents to ensure that financial transactions evidenced by the documents are in accordance with Part I of the SAR91 and the entries in the books of accounts reflect the transactions in a manner complying with Part I of the SAR91.

The accountant is then to carry out an extraction of the list of client ledger balances, compare the total with the client cash account balance, and reconcile the cash account balance with the individual client bank balance confirmed direct to the accountant.

The accountant is also required to ensure that the five weekly reconciliations have been kept, test whether client accounts have been overdrawn, check the office accounts to determine whether client money has not been paid into client accounts, and to ascertain transactions where, with the client's consent, client money is not held in the client account.

In respect of controlled trust accounts the accountant is required to ascertain the record keeping system in respect of such accounts, make test checks of postings to the accounts from the cash book, check the casts of the accounts, undertake the general examination of documents to ensure compliance with Part II of the SAR91, ascertain and test the cost recording system and transfers in respect of costs, and carry out a comparison of the balance on each of the accounts with the bank balance confirmed direct to the accountant on the last day of the year.

Rule 4 then limits the scope of the above examinations and tests by stating that the accountant is not required to extend enquiries beyond the information contained in the relevant documents or supplemented by information and explanations from the solicitor relating to any client matter; or to enquire into stocks, share, securities or other documents of title held on behalf of clients; or to consider whether the books have been properly written up at any time other than when the examination takes place.

Rule 4 then deals with the restriction of the work to be carried out in checking the extraction of ledger balances carried out by a computer, by allowing the accountant not to check the extraction of all of the balance if the accountant is satisfied that there is a satisfactory system of control in place, and that the books balance.

The accountant is required to make further examinations if it appears that Rules I and II have not been complied with, however, except for client money deposited in a separate designated account, the accountant is not required to check compliance with Part III, that is the deposit interest rules.

5 The solicitor is given the right to decline to produce any document to the accountant on the grounds of privilege; if this happens, the accountant is required to qualify his Report.

6 The Accountant's Report is to be in the format set out in the Schedule (this is included in Appendix 2).

7 This covers the exceptions to the requirement to deliver an Accountant's Report during a practice year, that is where no client or controlled trust money was held at any time in the previous practice year; or the solicitor ceased to hold such money during the previous practice year and delivered an Accountant's Report confirming this; or the solicitor is exempt from complying with the SAR91.

The section also states that partners of solicitors who hold or receive client or controlled trust money are also deemed to have held or received such money.

8 This section deals with those solicitors who deliver their first Accountant's Report or who become under an obligation to deliver having previously been exempt under section 7, and states that the accounting period begins on the day client or controlled trust money is held or received, and that the accounting period may therefore cover less than 12 months. Accounting periods can also be less than 12 months where a solicitor ceases to hold client or controlled trust money.

9 Section 9 also allows an accounting period to be less than 12 months for solicitors who become, or cease to be, members of a firm of solicitors. For solicitors with more than one place of business, separate Accountant's Reports may be delivered.

10 Deals with giving notice to solicitors under the rules.

11 Deals with giving notice to an accountant under the rules.

12 The Law Society's right of waiver of the rules.

5.3 Similarity of the work to an audit

The accountant's work is prescribed in detail in the above rules. Although it is not referred to as an audit, it does have many characteristics of an audit and, in general, accountants in practice refer to 'SAR audits.' The similarities to the audit are:

(a) ascertain the system for dealing with client money and recording costs;
(b) carry out compliance tests of the system for dealing with and recording transactions;
(c) carry out substantive tests of transactions on, for example, the client account balance extraction; and
(d) reporting to the Law Society.

It will be noted that in some cases the rules specify the amount of testing, and in others the accountant is required to test a sample. No further guidance is given in the ARR91, other than for the need to extend testing if errors are found. Guidance on sampling sizes is given in Chapter 6, which uses standard audit sampling techniques.

However, in terms of reporting it must be noted that the format of the report does not resemble a true and fair certificate on a set of limited company financial statements. The report is on the treatment of transactions, rather than on the view shown by a set of accounts. The judgement which the accountant is allowed to use is severely limited. Again, guidance on reporting is given in Chapter 6.

5.4 Suggested audit approach

Chapter 6 contains a suggested audit approach which covers:

(a) audit planning;
(b) evaluation and review of internal control;
(c) audit tests to satisfy certain objectives; and
(d) test sheets to record the posting tests.

These test schedules should enable the accountant to carry out all of the requirements of the ARR91 prior to reporting.

Chapter 6 – Solicitors accounts audit assignment programme

6.1 Introduction

The intention of this chapter is to provide a comprehensive guide to executing the work required to make a report under the ARR91. It is designed to cover all stages of the assignment, from the initial engagement to reporting to the Law Society. Reference is made to various other chapters in this book where ideas relevant to an SAR audit have been developed.

6.2 The letter of engagement

It is recommended that the accountant drafts a letter of engagement setting out the terms of appointment drawing attention to the relevant responsibilities. The accountant must ensure that the client's acceptance of those terms is obtained. It is also recommended that the accountant updates the letter of engagement where there is an alteration to the work to be undertaken as a result of, say, a change in the SAR, and at least once every three years.

A suggested format for a letter is set out in Appendix 4. This letter also deals with the scope of any non-SAR reporting work carried out by the accountant as well as the provision of partnership and personal taxation services.

6.3 Permanent information

The accountant should keep the following permanent information in respect of solicitor clients:

(a) copy of the ARR91, the SAR91 and any guidance notes issued;
(b) list of partners and branches;
(c) list of specimen signatures of those persons authorised to sign cheques and other withdrawals from the client account;
(d) list of banks and building societies where any money handled by the solicitor is held;
(e) copies of mandates signed by the solicitor authorising the bank or building society to disclose information;
(f) organisation charts and systems notes or other documentation;
(g) engagement letter;
(h) copies of previous years' reports.

For many clients it may not be necessary to have a separate permanent file and the permanent information can be transferred to each new audit file. It is, however, recommended that the accountant updates the permanent information on a regular basis and evidences this by the use of a checklist such as the one contained in Appendix 5.

6.4 The planning document

At the commencement of every assignment it is recommended that a planning document is produced. The size and sophistication of the planning document will be determined, in general, by the size and sophistication of the client, although a high possibility of error will of necessity demand a more detailed document.

Each document should have all of the following:

(a) *Objective of the assignment.* This will be at a minimum the reporting to the Law Society under the ARR91 for the relevant practice year. However, it may also include other work such as a limited review of the financial statements and a review of all of the systems of the practice.

(b) *The firm's business and personnel.* While it is not necessary to investigate the firm and its business in the detail which would be required for a Companies Act audit, the activity of the firm should be considered. It may have a bearing on the risk assessment to be carried out and will indicate whether population sizes have changed from the previous year. In addition, the document should list key personnel and note any changes during the year which may have a bearing on the audit work.

(c) *On a continuing assignment the planning document should note the assessment of the system in the previous year together with any changes to the system since then.* The systems review itself is one of the main items of work which the accountant is required to carry out under the ARR91.

(d) *Reconciliation.* The accountant should already have chosen the dates at which the two reconciliations are to be carried out. These should be noted in the planning document. He should also have requested directly from the banks and building societies the audit confirmation of bank balances and these should be received before he starts his fieldwork.

(e) *Problems or issues raised on previous audits.* These should be summarised together with a note of how they were dealt with, and whether they are likely to be significant in the current year.

(f) *Staffing and timing.* These should be noted, including the dates of any deadlines.

(g) *Assessment of risk and sample sizes.* The accountant should carry out an assessment of the risk of a breach of the rules occurring. Having done this assessment of the risk, an initial estimate may be made of sample sizes. These will be subject to change as a result of the systems review.

The accountant should discuss his planning with his client, even if it is just to find out whether there have been any changes to the system or to agree the dates of the audit. The accountant should also formally approve his planning document.

6.5 Analysis of risk

Risk in the context of an audit under the SAR91 can be defined as the risk of a breach of the rules occurring which is not reported by the reporting accountant.

This consists of three components: detection risk, inherent risk and control risk.

6.5.1 Detection risk

Rule 4 of the ARR91 specifies, in most instances, that the accountant is to undertake test examinations or check samples, that is, there is no requirement in the majority of examinations and tests under Rule 4 to carry out 100 per cent tests. This means that there will be a risk in carrying out the tests of a breach not being picked up in a sample; this risk is called detection risk.

A further element of detection risk arises if the accountant applies the wrong audit procedures.

There is also a detection risk that the reporting accountant, or his staff, find a breach as a result of a test check, but do not recognise it as such, or if a conclusion is reached which is inconsistent with the evidence.

6.5.2 Inherent risk and control risk

Inherent risk can be defined as the susceptibility of types of transaction to a breach of the ARR91. Control risk is the risk that the controls do not prevent or detect a breach of the Rules.

The accountant should undertake a thorough review of the risk of a breach, either by mistake or deliberately, having occurred.

The risk of inadvertent breaches taking place can be assessed by considering the following:

(a) previous breaches discovered;
(b) the effectiveness of the internal control system;

(c) the ability of partners or staff to override the internal control system;
(d) unusual transactions;
(e) volume of transactions;
(f) understanding of the SAR91 by client and staff;
(g) regularity of the production of accounting information;
(h) management control system.

The accountant also needs to consider the risk of deliberate breaches which may have been concealed. In this area one is thinking primarily of default by the solicitor leading to a loss of client money. This is obviously extremely difficult for the accountant because it can involve considering whether the client or any of his staff have undertaken actions that may be criminal. There may be little in the way of guidance to help the accountant other than his own commercial awareness, his knowledge of the client and his judgement.

In 1991 the Law Society published a study on default by solicitors (*Default by Solicitors*, E. Skordaki and C. F. Willis). This was based on a study of defaults by solicitors which gave rise to claims on the Solicitors Compensation Fund in 1987. Because the Fund only deals with dishonesty by sole practitioners or by all of the partners in a firm, its findings are of limited application and cannot be said to be representative of the legal profession as a whole. In addition, changes since 1987 in both regulation and the economy would probably result in different findings if the study were undertaken now. However, it may give some insight into matters which indicate additional risk.

The most interesting finding for the accountant is that the majority of defaulters had a history of submitting late Accountant's Reports to the Law Society. Late submission should always be an indicator of increased risk, even if there is no possibility of default.

The study also found that defaulters had shown considerable mobility between practices, were solicitors of between 10 and 20 years standing and had personal problems as well as work and financial worries. The majority of defaults arose from an appropriation of money for property transactions, although this presumably reflects the prevalence of such a source of client money.

Separate research by the Law Society of claims against the Solicitors Indemnity Fund involving dishonesty, by an employee in a sole practitioner's office or by fewer than all of the partners in a partnership shows that of, the 58 firms who caused such claims between 1986 and 1989, 22 were sole practitioners and 22 were firms of between two and four partners. For the period 1988 to 1991, 50 per cent of the payments by the Fund were for claims by sole practitioners or two partner firms.

If the studies can give any further guidance to the accountant, they stress the importance of having an understanding of the client and the client's business when planning work. It also means that the accountant must have a passing familiarity with methods of perpetrating certain types of fraud, such as mortgage fraud.

6.5.3 Assessment of risk

It is suggested that the accountant undertakes an assessment of risk in a structured manner, and documents the findings. The accountant will carry out an assessment of the internal control environment while documenting the accounting system and assessing its adequacy. The accountant should also carry out a review of the business of the solicitor and, for example, the financial position of the firm.

In addition, the accountant should also be aware of some of the non-financial indicators of higher risk, for example a lack of a structured management, or an overbearing senior partner. The reports of some large defalcations as published in the Law Society's *Gazette* make for fascinating reading and do show the circumstances in which frauds were carried out.

For many firms of solicitors the risk assessment should not be an onerous task, but the accountant does need to record that it has been undertaken.

6.5.4 Staff

One of the serious components of risk is that the accountant's staff find a breach but do not recognise it as such, or that they do recognise it but fail to report it, or that the procedures adopted by the audit team are inappropriate. In discussing any breaches found with the solicitor, the solicitor may convince the accountant that they need not be reported on, or the accountant may be averse to 'upsetting' his client. The accountant should be aware that the risk of this is greatly increased by any of the following factors:

(a) lack of suitably trained or experienced staff carrying out the audit;
(b) lack of suitably trained or experienced staff reviewing the work of the audit;
(c) inexperience of the accountant who has only carried out one or two SAR audits;
(d) the reporting accountant and his staff failing to keep up to date with changes in the SAR, or developments in the legal profession.
(e) overly close relationship between the accountant and the client because of, for example, significant referrals of work from the solicitor to the accountant.

6.6 Systems, controls and records evaluation

On a new assignment the accountant must ascertain the system used by the client to determine how the solicitor records the movement of client money, accounts for costs, complies with the Solicitors' Investment Business Rules 1990 (SIBR90) and accounts for controlled trust money. In addition, the accountant will probably want to gain an overview of the client's accounting and internal control system. On a continuing assignment the accountant should obtain details of any changes to the system. The accountant is primarily seeking to examine whether the system is sufficient to ensure compliance with Rule 11 of the SAR91 and Rule 13 of the SIBR90, and therefore he must document the following points:

6.6.1 Post opening procedures

These are necessary to ensure compliance with the requirements to pay client money into the client bank account promptly. The accountant should therefore, ascertain:

(a) whether the post is opened by a responsible person;
(b) whether there is segregation of duties between the persons opening the post and the cashier and/or accountant;
(c) whether duties are rotated;
(d) whether all cheques received are immediately crossed in favour of the firm;
(e) whether a record of all money received by post is made immediately, which is then reconciled to the day's postings.

6.6.2 Authority for withdrawals from the client account

The accountant must enquire into the system not just for the signing of cheques but also for authorising withdrawals by electronic transfers. He should therefore ascertain:

(a) how a cheque comes to be raised, and what documents are produced, such as cheque requisition forms;
(b) how an electronic withdrawal is made, and what documents are produced;
(c) who authorises a withdrawal to be made and where the signed authorisations are kept;
(d) what controls there are to ensure that unauthorised access to terminals through which withdrawals are effected cannot occur, for example passwords which are regularly changed.

6.6.3 Postings to and from client accounts

The accountant must ensure that postings are correctly made and that adequate controls are in place. He should therefore:

(a) enquire how a posting comes to be made to a client account, and how this is authorised;
(b) find out what controls exist over the posting process, for example, where there is a computer based system, whether batch control totals and reconciliations are used;
(c) what controls exist to ensure that postings are not made which lead to an overdrawn client account by, for example, a posting to the wrong account. A computer system might produce an exception report or refuse to process a batch which includes a posting which would lead to an overdrawn client account.

6.6.4 Cost recording system

The accountant is required by the ARR91 to ascertain the cost recording system, and he should again look at what controls exist regarding the incurring of costs on behalf of clients, and how they are split between profit costs, professional disbursements and other costs.

6.6.5 General controls

Where there is a computer system it is vital that the accountant ensures that there are general controls in place to protect data. These may include:

(a) ensuring that the opening or closing of client accounts is only carried out on the proper authority;
(b) ensuring reports are produced and maintained on the opening or closing of any accounts and that these are in a complete sequential order;
(c) ascertaining how software programmes can be altered;
(d) ascertaining how back up copies of records are kept, for example, how often, whether hard copies exist and whether these are secure;
(e) finding out what controls exist over passwords and the ability for unauthorised individuals to access prohibited areas of the system.

6.6.6 Other areas of the system

Within the SAR91 there are specific rules for certain types of transaction, and the accountant should determine first of all whether those transactions have taken place, and secondly what procedures there are to control them. For example, the accountant should enquire of the following:

(a) whether the firm takes on legally aided clients;
(b) whether the firm handles controlled trust money outside of the client accounts;
(c) whether the firm undertakes conveyancing transactions where it acts for both borrower and institutional lender;
(d) whether the firm gives investment advice;
(e) how the firm deals with the rules regarding unpaid professional disbursements;
(f) whether the firm pays settlements of bills of cost into client accounts under Rule 5A;
(g) whether the firm has handled client money which has not been paid into the client account, for example, because it is paid into a separate account in the name of a client, or because the money has been paid direct to a third party.

6.6.7 Client branches

Where the practice has more than one office, the accountant needs to determine whether client money is accounted for separately at each of those branches or whether there is a centralised accounting system.

For autonomous branches the accountant will need to carry out a systems evaluation for each branch if the systems differ, or confirm that the systems are the same. In addition, the accountant should determine what systems are in place to control transfers of money between branches or clients handled by more than one branch. Where there is centralised accounting, the accountant needs to determine the arrangements for local banking of money received and, if necessary, the controls over local payments of client money. For both types of branch the accountant should look into the degree of head office supervision of branches.

The accountant may consider testing a sample of branches each year, covering all branches over the course of a few years.

6.6.8 Books and records

Finally, the accountant should determine what books and records are maintained in respect of client money to ensure compliance with the SAR91, as follows:

(a) clients' cash account or clients' column of cash book;
(b) clients' ledger or clients' column of a ledger;

(c) office cash account and ledger or office columns of cash account and ledger;
(d) five weekly reconciliations of total of client ledger balances and balance on client bank account, and the client cash account balance and the bank and building society statements.

6.7 Audit work

The audit work required under the ARR91 consists in the main of a series of compliance tests and the substantive test of performing the two client ledger balance reconciliations. Therefore, the majority of the work is testing the operation of controls or the presence of documents. By structuring the testing it is possible to carry out a series of in-depth tests from certain prime documents, such as the bank statements, which will fulfil more than one of the objectives of the ARR91. In addition, some of the tests will be capable of being satisfied as a result of the accountant undertaking the above systems evaluation. The audit programmes set out in Appendix 6 have a number of objectives as follows.

To ensure that:

(a) the client bank accounts have been properly maintained;
(b) client money has not been incorrectly paid into office or other non-client bank accounts;
(c) client money has been correctly paid into the client bank account;
(d) any withdrawals of client money are in accordance with the Rules;
(e) the client account reconciliations have been correctly carried out and maintained;
(f) there is an adequate system for recording costs;
(g) Rule 11(3) has been complied with;
(h) interest is correctly accounted for under the SAR91;
(i) the client's bookkeeping system complies with the SAR91;
(j) the client's bookkeeping system complies with Rule 13 of the SIBR90;
(k) controlled trust accounts have been maintained in accordance with the SAR91; and
(l) branch records are properly maintained and proper returns are made to Head Office.

There is also a series of test sheets which provide a method of recording the results of certain of the tests, with the starting point taken as one of the prime documents, and with each of the tests cross-referenced back to one of the audit programmes as follows:

(a) tests on sample taken from office bank statements;
(b) tests on sample taken from client bank statements (client money in);

(c) tests on sample taken from client bank statements (client money out);
(d) tests on sample taken from bills delivered book (non-investment business);
(e) tests on sample taken from bills delivered book (investment business);
(f) tests on sample taken from controlled-trust bank statements (controlled trust money in); and
(g) tests on sample taken from controlled-trust bank statements (controlled trust money out).

6.8 Sample sizes

It should be noted that, unlike the audit requirement of 'true and fair', the ARR91 requirement is,

> 'In so far as an opinion can be based on this limited examination . . .'

There is, therefore, an expectation that the accountant will carry out his testing on samples. The ARR91 do not give guidance on the determination of what is an adequate sample for any of the tests and this, therefore, is the responsibility of the reporting accountant.

When faced with this problem the accountant has a number of decisions to take, some of which involve varying degrees of judgement. The main decisions are:

- what is the objective of the test;
- how many items to test;
- how to choose those items;
- what do the results mean.

6.8.1 Objective of the test

For an Accountant's Report the test normally aims to conclude on whether a system is in operation which is sufficient to allow compliance with the SAR91. An additional objective will be to identify breaches and to conclude whether or not they are trivial etc. (see below). The conclusion of the test will normally be either that there is an acceptable or unacceptable level of error in the system, or that specific instances of error have occurred.

It is not the intention to conclude in monetary terms, for example, that there were errors of £x during the period.

6.8.2 How many items to test

This will depend on how much confidence the accountant will want in the results of the testing. In general the greater the proportion of the population that is tested, the greater the level of confidence that the sample will reflect in the results.

The risk that the sample will not reflect the results of the population is called 'sampling risk'. The accountant will seek to reduce sampling risk to the extent that it is compatible with the cost of the examination.

To achieve an acceptable level of sample risk, sample size could be chosen purely on a judgemental basis. This has the disadvantage that it can lead to inconsistencies in approach within a firm. Alternatively it is possible to use statistical or quasi-statistical means to arrive at such a figure. Statistically sampling can allow such judgements to be made in a consistent framework.

One form of sampling which it is possible to use for this purpose is 'error rate' sampling. This is a form of 'acceptance sampling' which is designed so that the population is rejected if a stipulated number of errors is found. It involves the accountant determining the level of confidence that is required for the results (or the sampling risk the accountant is prepared to accept) and the precision or level of error that is acceptable. The higher the confidence and the lower the precision the larger the sample size. The figure below shows the size of samples given certain assumptions.

Confidence Level

Precision	*95%*	*92%*	*86%*	*78%*	*63%*
2%	150	125	100	75	50
5%	60	50	40	30	20
10%	30	25	20	15	10

The level of precision is normally a matter of judgement for the firm. Many firms use a level of five per cent for tests of this nature. The confidence level is also a matter of judgement, many firms using 95 per cent as a basic level but reducing it for assurance gained from other procedures and areas. For example, if it is concluded as a result of an assessment that there is a strong control environment and therefore there is not a high risk of error the confidence level required from detailed sampling may be reduced thus lowering the sample size. What levels are applicable will depend on the circumstances of the case.

6.8.3 How to choose those items

Samples should be chosen as a representative basis so that every item has a chance of selection. This normally involves the use of a 'random' selection method or a method such as interval sampling which uses some random element in selection.

Although each item should have a chance of selection it need not necessarily have an equal chance of selection. It is often desirable to ensure that a number of different types of business carried out by the solicitor are examined. It may also be desirable to bias samples towards the larger and more complex transactions where the chance of error is greater.

The accountant also needs to consider what the results of his testing on a sample mean.

6.9 Error evaluation

Each of the audit programmes and the test sheets has a column for recording all errors and breaches of the Rules; because all errors and breaches must be reported on it, it is recommended that error evaluation is undertaken in a systematic manner. The accountant should therefore transfer each error as it is found onto a separate error evaluation sheet, and proceed to evaluate the significance of that error according to the ARR91. A suggested format for an error evaluation sheet is included in Appendix 8. The sheet asks the accountant to consider, in respect of each error:

(a) date of discovery and rectification;
(b) whether there was any loss to any client;
(c) the reason for the error; and
(d) whether the error is trivial.

The evaluation therefore follows the considerations in determining the method of qualification as set out in the ARR91.

In addition, the sheet enables the accountant to consider the results of any further testing carried out and whether there is a weakness in the system. The need for further testing should be determined in the light of the arguments set out below.

6.10 Evaluation of errors and the need for further testing

Every error found must be noted on the audit programme and then transferred to an error evaluation sheet. The objective in assessing the error at this stage is to determine whether it is an isolated error, or whether it is symptomatic of a problem in the system.

If only one or two errors have been found then the cause needs to be thoroughly investigated and, once the cause is known, then an assessment must be undertaken of whether that cause could have given rise to further errors, not necessarily in the same population. For example, if the error was one of a posting to the wrong client ledger account due to a member of staff covering for the accounts clerk's absence during sickness, then the accountant should consider the testing of other transactions during the absence, and perhaps enquire whether the member of staff providing the cover substituted at any other times during the year. Further, if the review of the accounting system showed that there were controls in operation which should have prevented or detected the error, then the accountant needs to consider why the error was not prevented, or if and when it was detected. If acceptable reasons cannot be found then the accountant needs to consider extending the sample.

Where more than two errors are found then the accountant must conclude that there is a systematic problem and carry out detailed testing to find out the causes and the extent of the problem.

6.11 Evaluation of errors and reporting to the Law Society

On finding an error, as well as carrying out the further work to assess its incidence in the population as a whole, the accountant has to consider how he describes the error in his report to the Law Society. That he does need to report to the Law Society is absolutely clear. Each error is a breach of the relevant Rules and a failure to report renders the accountant liable to disqualification.

There are two possible disclosures that the accountant can make. First of all the accountant is allowed to say that the solicitor has complied with Parts I and II of the SAR91 and Rule 13 of the SIBR90 except in certain trivial breaches due to clerical errors or mistakes in bookkeeping, all of which were rectified on discovery and none of which resulted in any loss to any client.

This is one area in the ARR91 which gives the accountant particular difficulty. The accountant must consider each error under the following four headings.

(a) *Trivial.* There is little guidance from the Law Society as to what is trivial, and therefore the accountant must use his judgement. This is one of the few areas in the ARR91 where the accountant can use his discretion, and it is the only area where judgement can be exercised in considering the type of qualification in the Report. The Law Society has issued certain guidance notes on what may be considered an indication of non-trivial breaches, as follows:

> 'A reporting accountant is not required to report on trivial breaches of the Accounts Rules due to clerical errors or mistakes in book-keeping provided they have been rectified on discovery and that the accountant is satisfied that no client suffered any loss as a result.

> 'A number of accountants' reports are received by the Society which are qualified only by reference to trivial breaches. Nonetheless they show a significant difference between liabilities to clients, and clients' money held in a client account and elsewhere than in a client account. Where such difference is shown it would be helpful if an explanation for this difference, from either the accountant or the solicitor, could be provided, as this explanation may obviate the need for any further correspondence on this point.'

The implication of this statement is that differences on the comparison must, *prima facie*, have arisen from a non-trivial breach and that if it is considered not to be trivial then the reasoning behind this consideration should be explained. Whether the breach is trivial will depend on the amount, whether it was isolated, the period for which the breach was undetected and the degree of error involved in the breach being made. For example, it is difficult to see that a posting of a receipt of £10,000 of client money to the wrong client account and such error remaining undetected for six months can be anything other than non-trivial. Similarly, the omission of the word 'client' from a client bank account or a non-authorised person signing a cheque drawn on a client bank account are non-trivial breaches;

(b) *Clerical errors or mistakes in book-keeping.* This explanation will not cover every breach, and therefore it is vital that the reasons for the error are thoroughly investigated. A breach due to an error by a partner in the firm acting in that capacity cannot be a clerical error. Also, if the procedures to control transactions do not exist in the first place then the breach cannot be said to have arisen from this cause. Similarly, where the breach has occurred because a control has been overridden, then the breach will not be due to a clerical error;

(c) *All of which were rectified on discovery.* A check must obviously be made to ascertain whether this statement is correct. It also applies to breaches discovered by the accountant in carrying out his tests;

(d) *None of which, I am satisfied, resulted in any loss to any client.* This statement also requires positive verification.

If the accountant requires further help on determining the significance of a breach then he always has access to the Guidance Section of the Professional Ethics Directorate of the Law Society as noted in Chapter 2.

If the accountant does not consider the breach to have been trivial then he must report this using the form of words:

> the matters set out in Section F, in respect of which it appears to me that the solicitor has not complied with the provisions of Parts I and II of the SAR91 and, where he is authorised in the conduct of investment business by the Law Society, Rule 13 of the SIBR90.

He must also, therefore, set out the full circumstances of the breach in the report to the Law Society.

In making his decision concerning the reporting of breaches it is critical that the accountant sets out his judgement and consideration of the triviality of each breach in his working papers.

Having completed his work, the accountant should summarise his findings, his proposed qualification and his judgement underlying that qualification. He should then draft his qualification together with any accompanying explanations to be attached to the Report. This last aspect is particularly important. The Law Society is far less likely to revert to either the solicitor or the accountant for information concerning a qualification if a full explanation has already been sent to them with the Accountant's Report. In addition, if appropriate, the accountant should draw up a management letter of his findings for presentation to the client.

6.12 Discussions with the solicitor

It is important, both for continuing good relations between the accountant and his client and for that client to be aware of any problems in his accounting system that the accountant discusses with him breaches of the SAR91. Trivial breaches can be left until, say, the end of the day or the week, but non-trivial breaches must be notified to the client as soon as they are found to be non-trivial. Further, the accountant should discuss his proposed Report and any explanatory notes with his client at the end of the fieldwork. Where there is a partnership the accountant should ensure that his Report is communicated to each of the partners in the firm. It will be necessary to ask that certain qualifications are discussed by the partners as a whole so that each is aware of the seriousness of the breach.

It is also important that any changes to the system to prevent further breaches are put in place quickly, and therefore the management letter should be discussed with the client and issued immediately after fieldwork finishes.

6.13 Report to the Law Society

The accountant should complete the various sections of the Accountant's Report as set out in Appendix 2. The accountant should ensure that:

(a) the names of all of the partners are set out in Section A or on an attached sheet;
(b) the addresses of all of the practice offices are set out in Section A;
(c) the Report has been sent to all partners or to one partner on behalf of all of the partners;

(d) he makes his Report being either a qualification due to a trivial breach of the Rules, or a non-trivial breach, or a qualification due to a restriction in the scope of his work;
(e) he sets out the client ledger and bank balances at the two dates selected for reconciliation;
(f) where he relies on the waiver in respect of mechanical systems under ARR91, Rule 4(3)(f) he specifies that he has done so;
(g) he completes the details required in Section D in respect of any partner who has retired or ceased to hold client money; and
(h) he completes Section G regarding his name, qualification and the name and address of his office, and then signs the report, either in his own name or that of his firm.

Although many accountants send the completed Report to the Law Society themselves, the responsibility for delivery remains that of the firm of solicitors to whom the Report relates.

Chapter 7 – Areas of difficulty in carrying out an audit under the ARR91

7.1 Introduction

The aim of this chapter is to give guidance on dealing with some of the more common problems accountants encounter in carrying out an ARR audit.

7.2 Interest

As noted in Chapter 2, the most common enquiry regarding the SAR91 and the ARR91 received from accountants concerns interest. As noted in Chapter 4, apart from interest arising on designated deposit accounts, the accountant does not have any responsibility under the ARR91 regarding the compliance of the solicitor with Part III of the SAR91 (accounting to clients for interest).

This would seem at first difficult to understand. Interest on a client's money, subject to the *de minimis* rules, would appear to be that client's money and if the amount has been wrongly calculated or not calculated at all, *prima facie*, there would appear to be a clear breach of the rules in Part I, let alone Part III. In addition, it is likely that clients would complain if they did not feel they were receiving compensation for leaving money with their solicitor. The term compensation is operative here in that the Law Society would seem to take the view that the interest due is not client money until it is credited to the client's ledger; if it is not then it remains a liability.

The Solicitors Act 1974 would appear to give the Law Society power to monitor the regulation of this area through an Accountant's Report and the accountant may consider it in his client's interest that he check compliance with Part III. However, there is no such requirement, other than for interest on separate designated accounts, and many accountants may be glad to be relieved of an additional burden which can be difficult to discharge.

Finally, it should be noted here that interest received on the general clients' deposit account should be credited to the solicitor's office account, not being client's money, and any interest due to clients recredited to the individual client ledgers if a notional amount of interest has not already been credited before actual receipt.

7.3 Reconciliations

As noted in Chapter 2 the second most frequent enquiry accountants concerns the reconciliations, although here it wo to be that there is an unexplained difference and the accoun avoid qualifying on other than a non-trivial breach. As also n 2, the Law Society treat differences as a full qualification any the difference is large, require an explanation.

It is obvious that any difference on reconciliation must have breach of the Rules. The accountant's responsibility is to reason for the difference, not to attempt to cover it up. By five-weekly reconciliations the accountant may be able to isolate the difference and assess the cause behind it.

A particularly onerous task is the checking by the accountant of the extraction of every single client ledger balance in the two reconciliations to the client ledger account. However, this is the requirement and cannot be avoided unless the solicitor has a computerised system. In this case the accountant need only check a sample of balances if he is satisfied that there is a satisfactory system of control in operation and the books balance. There are therefore two specific tests which must be carried out if the accountant wishes to rely on the system. If, however, in his test checking of a sample of balances to the ledger accounts the accountant finds an error it would appear to be the case that he can no longer rely on the system and therefore a full check has to be carried out.

7.4 Bulk payments from the Legal Aid Board

Bulk payments can provide particular difficulties for the accountant. The Rules provide that such amounts can be paid into the office account and only paid into client accounts if any professional disbursements to which the legal aid payment relate have not been paid by the solicitor. It does appear extremely unfair if the solicitor holds onto money which is in respect of bills submitted by professionals. However, it is often the case that the Legal Aid Board receipts cannot be reconciled to the various forms submitted by the solicitor in respect of professional costs. The solicitor may not be aware of to whom the legal aid payment relates. Additionally, the solicitor may not wish to pay all of the money destined for the professional because of the possibility of taxation of the professional's fees on conclusion of the case. It has been known for unapproved professional fees to be substantially reduced on taxation and if the solicitor has made a payment prior to agreement of the fee he may be forced to try and recover the excess from the professional.

Additionally, it may be thought that the Rules are unrealistic in requiring amounts not disbursed within 14 days to be paid into the client account, because the solicitor may not set up a client account for a legally aided client; in any case, why should he get any interest due? The correct approach would appear to be to treat the Legal Aid Board as the client, and set up a client account in its name. Any interest due would appear to belong to the Legal Aid Board rather than the client.

7.5 Controlled trusts

Since the introduction of the Rules requiring the accountant to test controlled trusts in 1992, a number of accountants have queried their responsibilities in this area. First of all, it will often be the case that a solicitor has no controlled trust clients. Secondly, guidance issued by the Law Society emphasises that the new Rules should not increase the workload of the accountant materially. It mentions that, where an accountant has previously tested, say, 20 client files, he might now include a couple of controlled trusts.

7.6 Professional disbursements

One of the major changes introduced by the SAR in 1991 is the requirement to leave on client account the settlement of a bill of costs, to the extent that the settlement relates to professional disbursements which have not been paid. It was not unknown for solicitors to bill a client for counsel's fees, receive the money and then wait a substantial period of time before paying counsel. It is well known that counsel cannot sue a solicitor for his fees; he can only complain to the Law Society.

Section 67 of the Solicitors Act 1974 states that a solicitor's bill of costs may include costs payable in discharge of a liability incurred by him on behalf of the client notwithstanding that costs had not been paid before delivery of the bill. The rules have always restricted the payment of money in settlement of a solicitor's fees into the client account (the current rules allow such payment to be paid into the client account for up to seven days only). The problem was resolved by changing the definition of costs to be used in interpreting the SAR91, which effectively now excludes the fees of counsel or other lawyers, professionals or other agents, translators and interpreters and experts instructed by the solicitor for the interpretation of certain of the SAR regarding withdrawals from the client account and payments of money to the solicitor in respect of bills of cost.

A number of firms thought that this provision would give them problems with regard to the accounting treatment of the settlement of bills which included, say, profit costs, unpaid non-professional disbursements and unpaid professional disbursements. Indeed, the solicitor would be unwilling to pay a disbursement unless money had been received from the client. To avoid the problem of splitting receipts of money into office account (for settlement of profit costs, non-professional disbursements and paid professional disbursements) and client account (for unpaid professional disbursements) on receipt, changes in 1992 allow the solicitor to pay all of the remittance into the client account for up to seven days. The seven day period allows the solicitor to pay the professional disbursements and pay the whole of the amount into the office account thereafter.

The view of many directors of finance or finance partners is that the change and the subsequent amendment will still provide substantial problems for accounting systems. It can double the number of transactions. The accountant must view this area as one of high risk. As well as understanding the reasons for the rule regarding professional disbursements, the accountant must take the time to ensure that the solicitor's procedures deal with this area effectively.

7.7 Rule 11(3)

Rule 11(3) of the SAR91 is seen by a number of accountants as a problem area, probably because the SAR91 require the accountant to carry out a specific test in respect of it and the accountant has difficulty in determining whether the Rule has been applied. The rule covers the situation where the solicitor acts for both lender and borrower in a conveyancing transaction. However, the required test is quite specific, and some accountants will not come across Rule 11(3) situations in practice. The probable reason for the difficulty is that the accountant may be looking for a problem which does not exist.

The accountant should note that by Rule 6 of the SPR90, a solicitor is not allowed to act for both borrower and lender in a private mortgage, that is one which is not provided by an institution in the normal course of its activities.

7.8 Withdrawals

The SAR91 require that withdrawals of money from a client account can only be made by persons where at least one of those persons is specifically authorised under the Rules, that is solicitors with practising certificates, certain legal executives and certain licensed conveyancers. The problem for the accountant here is that many transactions will be by way of transfer rather than cheque, and that the transfer may be effected by an instruction over the telephone, or by way of a terminal.

The accountant must ensure that first of all there is a system which controls the effecting of transfers by means of, for example, passwords similar to those used to control transfers effected by telex such as test keys. Thus, passwords would identify not just the firm but also give an indication of the amount of the transfer. Secondly, in order to comply with the SAR91, the transfer must have received a specific prior authority by one of the persons named under the Rules as noted above and that means there must be a document evidencing the authorization.

Some accountants think that their responsibilities are limited to the examination of returned cheques; this is obviously not the case.

7.9 Overdrawn client accounts

In computerised systems a common error which arises from clerical mis-postings is that an entry is posted to the wrong client account thereby causing either the correct or the incorrect account to become overdrawn. The length of time between mis-posting and discovery will vary depending on how often postings are made and when the reconciliation is carried out. The accountant will need to assess the frequency and magnitude of these mis-postings and should consider recommending the use of regular default reports of any overdrawn accounts.

7.10 Bank and building society accounts

The accountant needs to be aware of the definitions of 'bank' and 'building society' to ensure that money is not being paid into non-authorised institutions. If there is any doubt on this point then the accountant must contact the Law Society for guidance. For example, the Jersey bank of a UK high street clearer does not come within the definition and therefore the use of such a bank is a clear breach of the Rules.

In addition, the Council of the Law Society regard it as essential that money held in a client account should be immediately available even though this may be at the sacrifice of interest. This means that certain types of account, for example trust or share accounts, are not suitable.

If there has been, *prima facie*, a breach of the Rules regarding banks or accounts, the accountant must consider whether the use of say a Channel Islands bank account has been at the instruction of the client. The accountant should, in these circumstances, ensure that such instructions are in writing or are acknowledged by the solicitor in writing.

Finally, accountants are reminded that banks do make mistakes, and that they must check the accuracy of certificates received from banks and building societies and follow up any errors or inconsistencies.

Chapter 8 – The effectiveness of work carried out under the ARR91, possible future developments and the liability of the reporting accountant

8.1 Introduction

With the rising incidence of default, the work of the accountant reporting under the ARR91 is increasingly coming under scrutiny. This chapter looks at the possible reasons for putting the blame for default onto the accountant, the way in which the effectiveness of an ARR audit may be improved by regulation, and the liability of the accountant for negligently prepared reports.

8.2 The effectiveness of work carried out under the ARR91

As mentioned in Chapter 2, there is a widespread belief that the number of qualified reports received for breaches other than trivial breaches is low. There is also a belief that this is because in many cases non-trivial breaches of the Rules are treated as trivial, or that many breaches of the Rules are being missed in the audit testing, either deliberately or by inappropriate audit work.

The reason would seem to be that SAR audits are not taken seriously by many accountants. They have traditionally been regarded as low risk, and the most junior of staff have been assigned to them. This assessment, if it can called that, of risk is due to an empathy between accountants and solicitors as fellow professionals. Additionally, solicitors have other work requirements in the form of tax advice, and do themselves provide significant levels of referral work to accountants. There is therefore often a reluctance to upset a close relationship based on a combination of friendship, trust and work referral. Obviously this is exactly the situation in which a breach, if detected, is unlikely to be reported on.

The use of junior staff is combined with a lack of any effort at providing proper training for staff involved on a solicitor's audit. Where testing is carried out, it may be based on old rules, or tests which have become wholly inappropriate. This will mean that there is no rigorous consideration of the function of the SAR work, and therefore a lack of critical analysis of the work required to meet the objectives of the ARR91. In short, many accountants think that the Rules are more honoured in the breach than in the observance.

It has been reported that some firms of accountants will not carry out any testing at all, and will just sign the certificate when it is presented by the solicitor. This attitude, and the increasing incidence of default by solicitors, will inevitably have the effect of tightening the ARR91 requirements.

8.3 Improving the effectiveness of the SAR91 and the ARR91

In 1992 the Law Society published a consultative paper entitled, *The Cost of Default*. This raised a number of possible measures to deal with the increasing incidence of default by solicitors and the increasing cost of such default to the solicitors' profession. The Institute of Chartered Accountants in England and Wales raised a number of issues which have a bearing on the participation of the accountancy profession in the system of the supervision of clients' money by the Law Society (Financial Reporting and Auditing Group, ICAEW, September 1992). The response may give an indication of the future work programme of the reporting accountant.

Proposals with which the Institute found favour were as follows:

(a) that a solicitor who intends to practise as a sole practitioner and hold client money should, prior to starting in practice, obtain an Accountant's Report regarding the adequacy of the solicitor's accounting arrangements;
(b) the use of Accountants' Reports at more frequent, say six monthly, intervals;
(c) that greater use should be made of the five-weekly reconciliations by, for example, the accountant receiving copies of the reconciliations when they are produced to ensure that they are produced at the correct time;
(d) reducing the period between the end of the accounting period and the latest date for submission of the report from six months to three months;
(e) solicitors' practices having a nominated partner as compliance officer;
(f) requiring the accountant to report on the existence of a record of undertakings given by the solicitor to banks, building societies and third parties in conveyancing transactions, an area where default is common.

It should be noted that the Institute was conscious of the Law Society's dissatisfaction with reports from certain accountants and confirmed that on receipt of a complaint by the Law Society investigation and disciplinary proceedings would follow.

Even without tightening the ARR91, there are ways of improving the manner in which accountants carry out their work. One proposal that is likely to become effective in the next year is to restrict the signing of Accountants' Reports to registered auditors. It would therefore seem possible that Joint Monitoring Unit inspectors could be required to include in their visits to firms of accountants an inspection of the files of SAR audits. An additional responsibility could be placed on firms requiring them to demonstrate suitable expertise in SAR audits, for example already carrying out SAR work, prior to commencing any new work. It is very common for large numbers of firms of accountants to carry out just one SAR audit. There is, therefore, a real possibility of SAR work being restricted to a smaller number of firms if the quality of SAR audits does not improve.

A further possibility which could be considered in greater detail by the Institute and the Law Society is to take disciplinary action against firms for a breach of procedures or negligent work as well as the partner at the firm responsible for an unsatisfactory SAR audit. Currently the sanction of disqualification from carrying out future SAR work attaches to the individual partner only.

As well as the proposals noted above, it is likely that certain types of firm will be required to deliver financial reports such as accounts, statements of net worth and liquidity reports to the Law Society, and to have those reports subject to an accountant's review. The Law Society can also be expected to produce a checklist for completion by accountants similar to that introduced by the New South Wales Law Society which is reckoned to have reduced fraud by 50 per cent in four years. It should be noted that many accountants have difficulty in interpreting the SAR91 and the ARR91, and this type of measure may go some way to assist them in their difficulties.

In summary, the future responsibilities of the accountant with regard to solicitors' accounts can only become more onerous.

8.4 Liability of an accountant reporting under the ARR91 in respect of a negligently prepared Report

Accountants who prepare negligent Reports are liable to disqualification from carrying out further work under the ARR91. As noted in Chapter 2, a large number of inspections by the Law Society's investigation accountants are not triggered by a qualified Report; therefore, an unqualified report may be the start of serious problems for the accountant concerned. Following an inspection the Solicitors Complaints Bureau may seek observations from the accountant and, depending on their adequacy, this may lead to a disqualification of the accountant from delivering further Accountant's Reports. The matter will then be referred to the relevant institute for disciplinary action. The ICAEW has assured the Law Society that it takes such referrals very seriously and there is a strong possibility of an accountant having to stand before a disciplinary committee, the results of which could include fines and exclusion.

As well as the strong possibility of disqualification from future ARR work by the Law Society and disciplinary action by his institute, the accountant who prepares a negligent report runs the risk of an action for professional negligence. If any loss is suffered which can be attributed to the accountant's negligence then he faces an action from a number of potential claimants.

First of all, if a claim on a firm by clients has been met by the Law Society through the Solicitors Compensation Fund, then the Law Society may attempt to bring an action in tort against the accountant for negligent mis-statement. The conditions for such an action under a duty of care laid down in the *Caparo Industries* case may well be held to be satisfied when applied to a report under the ARR91 as:

(a) the statement has been given to a known recipient, the Law Society;
(b) the statement was given for a specific purpose, that is for the purpose of enabling the Law Society to monitor the compliance or otherwise of the firm of solicitors with the SAR91, and ultimately to make a decision whether to investigate the firm, allow it to continue to hold client money or to practise;
(c) the accountant knew of this purpose, and it would be difficult for the accountant to deny this; and
(d) the recipient of the statement acted to his detriment, and this would be the case if as a result of, say, an unqualified report where there was a serious defalcation, the Law Society did not act to investigate and close down the firm.

Claims on the Solicitors Compensation Fund are made in respect of sole practitioners or where all of the partners in a firm are dishonest. Where there are innocent partners within a firm and they themselves have to settle a claim against the firm, or look to their insurers or the Solicitors Indemnity Fund then there may be an action by the firm against the accountant for loss arising from breach of contract, the breach being the failure by the accountant to carry out his duty under the contract. There would also be an action for negligent mis-statement where the firm would argue that it had relied on the Accountant's Report and thereby suffered loss.

The actual amount of the loss claimed will depend on when the accountant's negligence occurred in relation to the default, but where there has been a series of defalcations over a long period of time with a complimentary series of unqualified Accountant's Reports, the accountant may be looked to reimburse all of the missing money.

The accountant may be able to mitigate his liability in any action by the firm by pleading contributory negligence, and it is certainly the case that just as the reporting accountant has responsibilities under the ARR91, there are responsibilities under the SAR91 for each and every partner in the firm of solicitors.

Although the accountant may be able to mitigate some of his liability, given the size of some recent well publicised defaults, the final bill, with interest and costs could run into tens of millions. Many small practices are audited by small firms of accountants who may have a fairly low level of professional indemnity cover. However, recent experience indicates that large defaults do not necessarily arise only from large firms of solicitors, and the accountant may find some of the claim uncovered. There is also a risk that where there is a knowing failure to qualify because of the close relationship between accountant and solicitor, the accountant may have no cover at all.

PART III

Solicitors accounts

The form and content of solicitors' accounts and the reporting by accountants on those accounts is not regulated in the way that statutory financial statements are regulated. This lack of regulation results in a wide range of possible policies to account for transactions, causing inconsistencies between the accounts of any two practices.

Given this lack of consistency, it is doubtful whether the accounts of many practices are capable of being understood by partners within those firms, let alone third party users; the certificates issued by firms accountants do little to assist.

This section looks at the many possible accounting policies, and the different levels of reporting by accountants. Reference is made to the model set of accounts in Appendix 9.

Chapter 9 – The solicitors accounts and accounting policies

9.1 Introduction

There is no statutory requirement for a solicitor to produce accounts and consequently no requirement for accounts which are produced to follow a particular format or generally accepted accounting principles. The accounts of the solicitor are generally seen to have three main users: the partners for profit share purposes, the Inland Revenue and the practice's bankers. Given this it is surprising that there are not widespread accepted formats, or that partners in larger firms do not take more of an interest in the composition and interpretation of their firm's accounts. There can be widespread interpretation of the accounting policy and disclosure requirements of accounts subject to a statutory audit; the scope for the abuse of accounting techniques is consequently wider for the unregulated partnership.

The purpose of this chapter is to consider the various components of a set of a solicitor's accounts and to discuss the range of accounting treatments applied to them. This will lead directly on to Chapter 10 which looks at the various levels of reporting which the accountant can make on a solicitor's accounts.

9.2 Format of accounts

Appendix 9 is a suggested format for a set of accounts for a solicitor's practice, although it is recognised that smaller practices will have less information to disclose, and larger practices may show more management information and even include a commentary.

There are four main components of the accounts:

(a) income and expenditure account, balance sheet and notes thereto;
(b) list of accounting policies used;
(c) partners' information; and
(d) Accountant's Report.

The various types of accountants' reports are considered in Chapter 10. There is a split between the normal accounting information and the partners' information because of confidentiality; most partnerships will be reluctant to show a set of accounts containing information on partners' profit share to outsiders and some may even restrict this information to a favoured few within the partnership, individual partners only getting a statement of their own profit share, drawings account and capital account. Obviously this latter practice is both bizarre and impossible to defend in the context of a partnership. A suggested partners' information pack is provided in Appendix 11. Of prime importance is a statement of accounting policies used, as will become evident from the remainder of this chapter.

The suggested format for accounts in Appendix 9 contains a large number of possible accounting policies which are referred to in the text of this chapter in block capitals.

9.3 Basis of preparation

There are two possible bases for preparing the accounts, that is the accruals basis under the historical cost convention (BASIS OF PREPARATION – OPTION 1) and the cash basis (BASIS OF PREPARATION – OPTION 2). The basis must be stated.

9.4 The income and expenditure account

9.4.1 Fees

There are three methods of accounting for fee income, being the cash basis, the final bills delivered basis and the total bills delivered basis.

The cash basis is quite simply accounting for that income received by the practice in the form of cash up to the balance sheet date. It makes no allowance for work for which a request for payment has been sent by the year end, or for cash received after the year end which may relate to work carried out some time before the current accounting period. As far as the firm is concerned its only merit is that it delays the payment of tax; it can distort quite markedly the actual performance of the firm. Its use in accounts is determined by whether the Inland Revenue allows it, although it would seem to be dying out. As a way of measuring financial performance it has little merit compared to the other two methods, and may lead to inequity in a partnership experiencing change in partners or profit sharing ratios.

For some firms, however, the cash basis may be the only realistic method of accounting for fees, for example where a firm undertakes a substantial amount of legal aid litigation work in which the fees rendered may not be settled for some time and where the fee may be reduced by taxation.

The final bills delivered basis (FEES RECEIVABLE – OPTION 1) includes in fee income all final bills delivered by the year end; unlike the cash basis, there will also be included in the balance sheet an amount of debtors, being unpaid fees rendered. This is by far the most common basis for accounting for fee income, and should be readily understandable by all partners. However, it is important that the policy is followed in accordance with generally accepted accounting principles and that, for example, after date credit notes are deducted from the year end total of fees rendered.

The distinction between final bills and total bills arises from the use of progress billing. Traditionally, many solicitors only billed on the conclusion of a matter. With increasing attention paid to working capital management, the use of progress bills throughout the period of the matter is widespread. Such bills may not be taken to fees rendered, but rather set off against the balance of work in progress. The use of progress billing may allow a firm to decide what its billing for the year is, and within a partnership individual solicitors can distort their levels of fee income. This, coupled with the common practice of carrying out a very large proportion of billing in the final three months of the year, can render the fees figure meaningless at the year end or at any interim point.

There is a further problem with the use of progress bills. Depending on how the practice values its work in progress, taking progress bills to work in progress may mean that the profit or loss on such bills is not reflected in the accounts until the matter is concluded and the progress bills converted into final bills. This can be illustrated as follows:

	£
Gross value of work in progress	10,000,000
Less write down to cost-30%	3,000,000
Net value of work in progress	7,000,000
Less progress bills	2,000,000
Per balance sheet	5,000,000

If the progress bills include matters which are completed, but not finally billed and therefore cleared from work in progress, then the profit for the year and the work in progress will both be understated. Further, the profit on progress bills in respect of matters not fully concluded will be omitted from the profit and loss account.

	Scenario 1	*Scenario 2*
	£	£
Gross value of work in progress	10,000,000	10,000,000
Progress bills	1,000,000	2,000,000
Value after progress bills	9,000,000	8,000,000
Write down to cost	2,700,000	2,400,000
Per balance sheet	6,300,000	5,600,000

In scenario 1 it is assumed that on 50 per cent of the progress bills the matter is complete and the bills can be cleared from work in progress. In scenario 2 all progress bills are cleared from work in progress and on that basis the profit on each bill can be calculated. It can be seen that by controlling the issue and clearance of progress bills, the profits could be misstated.

The possible options are to include within fees receivable all final and interim bills in respect of completed matters (FEES RECEIVABLE – OPTION 2) or alternatively all final and interim bills in respect of all matters (FEES RECEIVABLE – OPTION 3) or some compromise which takes account of work where the profit can be determined.

Some firms resolve this issue by including within fee income an amount in respect of matters completed at the year end but billed after the year end (FEES RECEIVABLE – OPTION 4), or by increasing the value of work in progress to take account of the sales value of work in progress where the work is complete but unbilled (WORK IN PROGRESS – OPTION 7). Both methods will have the same effect on profit, but only the first will increase fee income.

It is therefore important that the accounts disclose exactly what method of recognising fee income is adopted and that the partners are able to make an intelligent assessment of what this policy means. Some firms may wish to distinguish between the fees in respect of time costs and those in respect of disbursements recharged. In addition, where the firm accounts for work in progress, the increase in work in progress may be shown as a separate amount after fee income. Work in progress is considered below.

9.4.2 Other income

Other income will normally comprise interest receivable only, although a number of solicitors' firms are now receiving rental income in respect of surplus accommodation. Interest is often shown after amounts paid to clients under Part III of the SAR91. All items should be shown on a receivable rather than received basis if the accounts are prepared on an accruals basis.

9.4.3 Expenses

The method of disclosure of expenses will vary from firm to firm, but should be clear enough to enable individual partners to understand what the various amounts mean. Therefore, large items in respect of sundry or general expenses are not recommended, nor is the lumping together of similar costs under one heading, such as having one figure, entitled accommodation costs which includes rent, electricity, security etc. It is also recommended that exceptional items are highlighted in the accounts, such as a large bad debt, or moving costs.

The method of taking expenses to the profit and loss account should be consistent with the fee income policy, and therefore, strictly speaking, if fees are recognised on a cash basis, expenses should be only included on a paid basis. Where the practice includes an amount in the accounts for work in progress then all disbursements rechargeable to clients should be carried forward in work in progress and not written off when paid.

There are certain expenses which should be charged to a particular year regardless of when they become payable. An example of this would be regular charges to a dilapidations reserve, or a spreading out of the rent over a lease, or up until the next rent review date where there are reduced rentals as a result of inducements to enter the lease. A further example would be charges in respect of a professional indemnity claim. Strictly, the accounting period which should bear the cost of investigating, defending and paying a professional indemnity claim should be the period in which the alleged act of negligence became known, or took place. The costs will include the payment of the excess and any uninsured amounts. It is debatable whether the firm's own time costs incurred on the investigation should be included. This latter item could well be sizeable, but it is a very real cost if the partnership is stopped in future periods from operating at its full capacity.

Bad debts are a further item which may become chargeable in one period but relate to circumstances in respect of an earlier period. The timing of the charge in respect of all of these items can be critical for profit share purposes.

9.4.4 Notional expenses

Notional expenses are those charges which take account of the partners' ownership of the practice. They will comprise a partner charge, being the estimated professional salary of an assistant solicitor and notional interest on the total of the partners' investment in the practice. They may equate to actual profit shares, but will be reversed before the profit is appropriated. Some practices will include a notional market rent if the practice owns the property, or if the actual rent is substantially below market levels (NOTIONAL EXPENSES).

9.5 The balance sheet

9.5.1 Fixed assets

Goodwill

There is no doubt that goodwill is an asset of the partnership. However, it is common practice now for most firms to exclude goodwill from transactions between partners by, for example, a clause in the partnership agreement valuing goodwill at zero. Even where goodwill does have a value firms would not normally place a value on it in the accounts of the practice (GOODWILL – OPTION 1).

However, a number of firms will account for goodwill, often after a merger where there are real differences in 'value', between the pre-merger firms. The policy concerning how the goodwill has been valued and whether or not it is amortised should be disclosed (GOODWILL – OPTION 2 and GOODWILL – OPTION 3).

Investments in other entities

As can be seen from Chapter 3 solicitors are severely restricted from setting up subsidiary companies and therefore the only investment in another company is likely to be a service company set up to carry out necessary administrative functions concerned with running the practice. There is no requirement to consolidate the results and balance sheet of service companies, but it is recommended that a set of the accounts of any service company is attached to the annual partnership accounts presented to the partners, and that the two entities have coterminous year ends. This will be necessary to enable individual partners to assess, for example, the effect of any guarantees given by the partnership in respect of the service company (CONSOLIDATED ACCOUNTS AND INVESTMENTS IN RELATED ENTITIES).

It is increasingly common for the larger firms of solicitors to set up offices outside England and Wales; Brussels, Eastern Europe or Japan being common locations. Where the overseas office is a branch then the results of that branch form part of the overall results of the partnership. However, where the offices operate as separate partnerships, there may well be an effective investment by the English firm in the overseas firm. It is obviously important that an assessment of the value of any amounts incurred in setting up or maintaining the office is made when preparing the accounts. It is also important that the method of translating foreign currencies complies with proper accounting practice (FOREIGN CURRENCIES).

Other investments

The other common investment will be life assurance policies which are taken out on the lives of younger partners to repay a loan. These should be stated at cost, rather than market value (VALUE OF FIXED ASSET INVESTMENTS). Investments taken out to pay future tax liabilities should be shown in the accounts with the reserves to which they relate (FUNDING OF TAX RESERVES).

Tangible fixed assets

All firms will have tangible fixed assets of some type, but there is a very wide range of different accounting treatment applied to them. The main types of asset which a practice will have will be as follows:

(a) freehold and long leasehold property;
(b) short leasehold property;
(c) improvements to premises;
(d) furniture and equipment;
(e) library;
(f) computer equipment; and
(g) motor vehicles.

Freehold and long leasehold property is dealt with separately in Chapter 16. For short leasehold property, such leases will be operating leases and therefore no account will be taken of the discounted future rentals in the balance sheet. However, where there is a premium paid in respect of the assignment of the lease, then this should be capitalised and written off over the remaining life of the lease; this policy is not widespread, with some firms writing the amount off over a lesser period, or immediately on the grounds of 'prudence!' (CAPITALISATION OF ASSETS – OPTION 2)

In addition, it is at least arguable that some of the costs of moving offices should also be capitalised and amortised over the life of the lease. Similarly, fitting out costs and improvements should be capitalised and written off. In assessing the rate of depreciation to apply, the partnership should comply with generally accepted accounting principles and make an assessment of the life of such assets and the length of time before they will be replaced. Some firms have in recent years spent large sums of money on improving their premises, which may have been the first major refit in 20 years. Writing such improvements off over a period of four or five years is, in many cases, going to be wholly inappropriate and for certain items, depending on the life of the lease if there is one, 15 years may be too short.

As noted in Chapter 11 a number of firms have been in receipt of substantial inducements to enter into a new lease, which may have been recognised in the form of the payment of moving expenses and a contribution towards fitting out costs. In such circumstances the capital value of fixed assets may not be correctly stated in the accounts of the partnership (LEASE INDUCEMENTS – OPTION 1 and LEASE INDUCEMENTS – OPTION 2).

As far as furniture and other office equipment is concerned, similar considerations apply. However, some firms will try not to capitalise any equipment at all, all items being written off, whereas others are written off over a blanket three or four years, without reference to their expected life. With some types of asset, such as computer software, this may be justified, but this is unlikely to be the case with most furniture and equipment.

A common practice among firms currently is to include on the balance sheet those motor vehicles which are purchased or leased in respect of staff, with partners' motor vehicles being 'owned' by the individual partners. Some firms include on their balance sheet their library, although most do not; for small firms, the cost of a library can represent a significant asset, and one, moreover, which has an extremely long life. A number of firms of solicitors only lease equipment, and treat all leases as operating leases, regardless of their terms, thereby getting rid of the issue from the balance sheet altogether (LEASES – OPTION 2), but obviously not complying with best accounting practice (LEASES – OPTION 1).

There is a widespread feeling among many firms that their tangible assets are written down over too short a period and therefore the balance sheet does not adequately reflect the capital of the firm; the annual depreciation charge will likewise not be a true measure of the use of the assets by the practice. In these circumstances, and because of the effect the differing use of the various policies can have on the profits of the practice, the capitalisation policies, depreciation rates and lease policies should be clearly set out in the accounts. This also applies where the depreciation charge is made by way of a management charge from a service company.

One method which could be adopted to overcome the problems of low asset values because of, for example, all fitting out costs being paid by a landlord, is the regular revaluation of fixed assets. However, it would seem that revaluation is rarely used. One of the main reasons for this is the difficulty of attributing surpluses and deficits between partners, and the problem of paying to a retiring partner that part of his capital account due to revaluations (REVALUATION OF LAND AND BUILDINGS).

9.5.2 Work in progress

Like fees, there are a number of differing methods of accounting for work in progress, which are based on agreements with the Inland Revenue rather than other commercial considerations.

A very common basis is not to account for work in progress in the annual accounts (WORK IN PROGRESS – OPTION 1), or to include an amount which has been at a constant value for a considerable period of time. In such a firm all professional costs incurred in the year will be written off to the profit and loss account, and the firm will only account for the profit on those fees rendered during the year. The firm may also exclude disbursements from the balance sheet. Because of the length of time that certain legal work can take, the billing regime of the firm will determine how much of a mismatch there is between fees and costs. However, where the firm is of significant size, the probable understatement of actual work in progress compared to a full cost method will be very large.

For some firms that do not account for work in progress there is not even the tax saving to justify the practice. The Inland Revenue will assess the increase in work in progress and charge tax on this notional amount. Methods used by the Inland Revenue to determine the increase in work in progress include the increase in professional salaries from one year to the next. It should be noted that, as far as the individual partners are concerned, they are being charged tax on a profit not recognised within the accounts. In these cases a compensating asset should be created within the balance sheet.

Because a firm does not recognise work in progress in its balance sheet, it does not mean to say that it does not take account for time costs and disbursements at all; however, where a firm does have a time recording system it exists outside of the accounts.

Another common method of accounting for work in progress, which is not based on a time recording system, is to calculate it as the last two or three months professional salaries in the accounting year (WORK IN PROGRESS – OPTION 2). Again, this is only a notional figure, reached by agreement with the Inspector of Taxes. Alternatively, the increase in work in progress may be agreed with the Inspector to be the increase in professional staff costs from year to year (WORK IN PROGRESS – OPTION 3).

It is becoming increasingly common for firms to use a figure for work in progress which has a basis in reality, by reference to a time costing system.

The most common is the value of non-partner professional costs, excluding the profit element included within the professional's charge out rate (WORK IN PROGRESS – OPTION 4). Partner time is excluded because it is not considered to be a cost for tax purposes. Where the work in progress is measured on the basis of work actually carried out, then it is important that a full assessment is undertaken of the value of work in progress by reference to its likely billing and collection. Because a partnership's accounts do not need to be filed, and because there can be a delay in agreeing accounts with the Inspector, there can be a long period between the date of a set of accounts and the need to finalise them. In such circumstances a very accurate assessment can be made concerning the net realisable value of work in progress by the time the accounts are finalised.

As noted at 9.4.1 above, where progress bills are deducted from work in progress, when they are deducted, that is before or after the mark down to cost, can have an effect on the level of work in progress and therefore profit (WORK IN PROGRESS – OPTION 5 and WORK IN PROGRESS – OPTION 6).

There are other methods of accounting for work in progress on a time cost basis, but these are unpopular because they would result in an overall increase in the level of work in progress and would therefore accelerate the payment of tax. These would involve taking, in respect of all work carried out at the balance sheet date, an element of the profit where it could be seen that work was validly billable and on which a profit could be justifiably taken. For example, where the firm does not actually complete work on a matter until just after the year end, but where there is a substantial amount of unbilled work in progress at the year end, there is a strong argument that a substantial part of the profit could be taken before the final billing. This is underlined by the general conceptual point that what solicitors generally sell is time, rather than products. This idea is similar to the taking of profits on interim billings. The accounting policies for firms which do use a method such as this would be that work in progress includes the selling value of all work which could have been billed at the year end. In this case, there may be an inclusion of not just non-partner profit, but also the full charge out rate of partner time incurred on the work.

In certain cases the final bill rendered in respect of work includes a success element, or alternatively there is an agreement that not all costs will be rendered should a transaction not go forward. In such cases it would not be appropriate to account for the full value of work in progress at the year end.

9.5.3 Debtors

Whether a firm has any debtors will depend on whether it accounts for fees on a bills delivered or cash basis. As with work in progress included on a time cost basis, it is important to determine whether any provision needs to be made against bills which may be doubtful or bad. Some firms as a matter of policy make a general provision in addition to any specific provisions against bad debts. In addition, others will make full provision for all debts outstanding after, say, six months (BAD DEBTS). Given the flexibility many firms have regarding the finalisation of accounts, it should be possible to identify all bad debts by the time the accounts are signed. Firms which do not maintain a work in progress ledger, and some which do, may include as part of debtors disbursements incurred on behalf of clients. Again, these should be reviewed for recoverability.

It was noted in the section on work in progress above that where a firm recognises profit on unbilled work in progress at the year end, it may include the selling value as part of work in progress. Alternatively, some firms include within debtors an amount entitled either work capable of final billing as at the year end, or bills delivered after the year end in respect of matters completed before the year end (DEBTORS – OPTION 2). In these cases an appropriate amount will be included in fee income.

9.5.4 Cash and current asset investments

Cash should obviously be included on the balance sheet, but where it is in respect of money held on behalf of clients there is a very wide treatment. Some firms will include cash held on behalf of clients within the overall cash figure, the corresponding liability to clients being shown as part of creditors. This practice is not recommended because it gives a false view of the amount of cash owned by the partnership and ratios based on balance sheet figures may be materially misstated. Other firms ignore all reference to client money and the liability to clients. The best treatment is to include, either by way of note or on the face of the balance sheet, the total of the client balances less the total liabilities, and the difference between the two, which should equal zero.

Some firms maintain large cash balances and other investments to represent the future tax reserve. As noted in Chapter 14, many firms use tax reserves to fund the business generally, but a few set aside specific amounts to pay the future tax. Where this is the case, and those tax reserves are considered by the firm to be inviolable, it should be noted on the balance sheet (FUNDING OF TAX RESERVES). Indeed, there is an argument that such amounts should be included on the balance sheet as a specific asset, 'amounts set aside to pay tax'.

9.5.5 Creditors

The inclusion of creditors within the balance sheet is relatively straightforward except for the issues of taxation, deferred taxation and contingencies.

Regardless of the method of provisioning (see generally Chapter 13), many firms will make a transfer from the tax reserves or, if there is no tax reserve, from the capital accounts, to create a liability for the next payment of the tax due, generally the next 1 July payment. This is the tax payment which can be assessed with the most accuracy. Other firms will provide for the next two payments, that is those falling due within one year, and some will provide for whatever the total tax provision is, thereby removing it from the partners' accounts (TAXATION – OPTIONS 1,2,3,4 and 5).

It is recommended that whatever method is chosen, the choice is clear from the accounts, and that partners are left in no doubt as to how the various components of the tax provision are shown in the accounts. It would seem, though, that if the tax reserves within the partners' accounts show enough information on the dates tax is due, then there is little point making transfers to creditors in respect of the next one or two payments.

The issue of deferred tax is dealt with in full in Chapter 13. It is sufficient to state here that there will be instances when a provision for deferred tax should be made by a firm. The various options in the accounts are to ignore deferred tax altogether (DEFERRED TAX – OPTION 1), not to provide for it but to disclose the unprovided amounts (DEFERRED TAX – OPTION 2), or to account for it in accordance with normal accounting principles (DEFERRED TAX – OPTION 3).

Contingencies provide the most difficulty because, although lawyers may be dealing with issues arising from claims every day, they do not normally make any provision or indeed any reference to an unprovided amount in their accounts. Firms might consider disclosing liabilities or possible liabilities in respect of the following:

(a) *Leases*. Where a firm has operating leases it would be of help to provide the information in respect of future lease commitments as required under SSAP 21. Many firms do not purchase their equipment, but lease it, causing a significant ongoing burden which the partners should be aware of. There is also a potential liability for those firms which have sold leases or have had them taken over prior to moving into new premises. Privity of contract will put the commitment to pay the rent under the lease back on to the firm should the assignee fail, and this is a real problem faced by some firms. It is recommended that partners are made aware of this potential liability in the accounts. Other liabilities which may arise under leases include dilapidations reserves, although the firm should be making regular provisions for this throughout the term of the lease;

(b) *Professional indemnity claims*. It is vital that partners should be aware of any potential professional indemnity claims, as well as those claims of which the firm has been formally notified. Where possible, provision should be made for the likely costs of the claim which are uninsured as well as those internal costs which the firm will incur in investigating and defending the claim. It may be difficult to make estimates with any accuracy, and some firms will provide round sum amounts on an annual basis to build up a claims reserve;

(c) *Pensions liabilities*. Pensions in respect of staff are increasingly provided by way of an externally funded pension scheme to which the firm may contribute; there are therefore unlikely to be any ongoing commitments to pay pensions to former employees, but to the extent that there are, then these should be disclosed. However, where a defined benefit scheme is operated, it is recommended that the normal disclosure rules which apply to limited companies are adopted. If there is an actuarial deficiency then this must be provided for in the accounts. Firms may have an ongoing liability to pay pensions or annuities to former partners. Although most partners will now fund their own pensions, there are some partnership agreements which provide for an annuity to be paid to former partners. Whatever the terms of these, and they are considered in detail in Chapter 17, the accounts should disclose this future liability although there is no need to provide for this amount (PENSIONS);

(d) *Guarantees and indemnities*. These should be noted and quantified. They may include guarantees given in respect of the borrowings of a service company, or the borrowings of an overseas partnership.

9.5.6 Other disclosures

The above contingencies may be considered too sensitive to disclose within the partnership's accounts; if this is the case thought should be given to disclosure in a separate pack given to the partners (see below). Other information which might be included within the separate pack, but which should certainly be shown to the partners in some form, would include the following:

(a) *Terms of finance*. Where the firm has external borrowings, for example a medium term loan, the terms of that loan, including details of security, interest rate and especially any covenants should be made available to all partners. It is difficult to see the spirit of partnership operating if these facts are not made available to all of the individuals who are liable under a loan agreement;

(b) *Transactions in which partners have an interest*. The firm may rent premises owned by any number of partners, or undertake transactions with companies in which a partner, through connected persons or indeed personally, has an interest. It is in the interests of the partnership as a whole that any such contracts are disclosed, and that any transactions undertaken at other than market value have such entities clearly identified. The Companies Act provisions applying to transactions with directors are a good guide to what should be disclosed.

9.6 Accounting policies

Given the wide range of accounting policies possible, and the fact that those used may not comply with best accounting practice, it is imperative that the accounts disclose comprehensively those accounting policies used in the preparation of the accounts. The list and description of accounting policies should cover the following:

(a) *fees and expenses* – basis used (as noted above);
(b) *notional expenses* – whether there are any and the method of calculation;
(c) *related entities* – how any investments in or results of other entities are treated; if there are overseas entities then the treatment of foreign currency transactions should be disclosed;
(d) *tangible fixed assets* – capitalization policy and depreciation rate;
(e) *leases* – how finance and operating leases are treated;
(f) *work in progress* – basis of calculation or statement that not included;
(g) *debtors* – method of inclusion in accounts and how bad debts are calculated;
(h) *taxation* – provisioning method and if deferred tax is calculated, how;
(i) *pensions*.

9.7 Partners' information

Whether the information is included within the main body of the accounts, or is contained within a separate pack, the partnership should, on an annual basis, provide information concerning the following:

(a) *Summary of movements on partners' accounts*. Some firms do not distinguish between capital and current accounts, whereas others do. In any case, information regarding capital introduced and withdrawn, drawings, pension payments and taxation deductions should be provided. For individual partners a full breakdown of their drawings and pension payments should be given. As well as showing the balance on capital and current accounts at the end of the year, where capital is to be provided in certain ratios or amounts, then a comparison of required capital and actual capital should be shown.
(b) *Calculation of profit share*. The accountant may be asked to provide the detailed calculation of notional interest and other allocations of profit, and a schedule setting out the calculations should be given to partners.
(c) *Movement on and composition of partners' tax reserves*. Tax is one of the least understood areas of a firm's accounts and there should be a full disclosure of the breakdown of the tax reserve by year, details of

equitable adjustments in respect of tax between partners, and a note of agreement and payment of liabilities in respect of open years.

As well as the above minimum information, firms are starting to provide more information of a management nature, which can enable the individual partners to assess the financial contribution of individual partners or departments to the firm's performance. Such information may include the following:

(a) billings for the year;
(b) cash collections for the year;
(c) profitability as measured by profits or losses on bills, together with the detail of any large variances or bad debts;
(d) debtors and work in progress at the year end and average debtors and work in progress throughout the year.

The provision of such information can be divisive, and its presentation needs to be carefully considered. As noted in the first part of this chapter, manipulation of various accounting practices can enable the firm to 'create' its performance. The same is true for individual departments and partners within the firm. Such information could be dangerous in an environment where there is no meritocratic culture, and in these cases is probably best left out altogether. Indeed, in some partnerships there is no attempt even to allocate billings by partner for fear of causing precisely these sorts of problems.

The final part of the accounts is the Accountant's Report and this is dealt with in the next chapter.

Chapter 10 – Reporting on the solicitors accounts

10.1 Introduction

It is probably fair to say that the majority of firms of solicitors have little if any work carried out by their accountants on their accounts, other than their preparation and analysis for the tax computations. Further, although most firms' accounts will be set out in a broadly similar manner, the information contained therein may not be in compliance with generally accepted accounting principles, or in the most understandable format; this is clear from the previous chapter. For the majority of firms, sole practitioners and two partner firms, this may not matter much to the partners. However, for partners in larger firms it may be a very real problem indeed, and those partners not directly involved in the financial management of the practice may misinterpret the restricted Accountant's Report attached to the annual accounts as a clean bill of health on the partnership's financial practices overall; the expectation gap between the user and the accountant may be wider than that between auditors and shareholders in a corporate situation.

The previous chapter looked at the way solicitors commonly account for transactions, and suggested improvements which can be made and on which the accountant can advise. This chapter looks at the various levels of reporting which the accountant can undertake and gives guidance on the audit and review procedures which will underlie the ability to make such a Report.

10.2 Preparation of accounts

The first report is set out at Appendix 10 and deals solely with the preparation of the accounts. Reports such as this are probably the most commonly used and, read in a very strict sense, seem designed to absolve the accountant from any responsibility whatsoever for the accounts which he has prepared. The actual level of preparation may vary from writing up the books, to preparing accounts from a trial balance, to merely putting a certificate on a set of accounts prepared by the solicitor. Clearly, the degree of preparation will have a direct impact on the level of the accountant's understanding of the composition of the accounts and therefore the somewhat bland certificate will tend to hide the actual level of work carried out.

Where the certificate increases the accountant's responsibility is in the use of the word 'explanation". Explanation indicates that the accountant has asked the solicitor questions, and from this it can be inferred that the accountant will have advised his client; if this is not the case then the accountant could give his certificate on a set of accounts which were wholly wrong. The point here is that the accountant must always bear some responsibility for the accounts, and to give the certificate at this level the accountant must at least ensure that:

(a) the accounts can be reconciled to the books of account;
(b) any adjustments to the books are reasonable;
(c) the various control accounts and the nominal ledger are in balance; and
(d) the financial performance and position of the firm appear reasonable, are consistent with previous periods and the market as a whole or can be explained.

This last point is of fundamental importance given the principle users of the accounts and the use of the accounts to assist decisions which may be taken on drawings and funding.

10.3 Certification that accounts are in accordance with accounting policies adopted by the firm

The wording of the Report that certifies whether the accounts are in accordance with the accounting policies adopted by the firm is the first report on page 268. It is important to note that the accountant is not giving a certificate regarding how appropriate the accounting policies are, or even if they make commercial sense; he is merely stating that, given the accounting policies adopted by the firm, the accounts have been prepared using those accounting policies. This is obviously open to misinterpretation by individual partners as well any third parties who may see the accounts. It is therefore suggested that in the letter of engagement the accountant stresses that he is not confirming whether or not the policies are appropriate.

In carrying out the minimum work necessary to give such a certificate, the accountant will need to undertake the work as set out above for the preparation of the accounts certificate, and then formally confirm whether for individual balances and transactions the stated policies have been used. Therefore, the accountant will confirm that fees comprise all bills rendered to the year end if the policy for accounting for bills is on a bills delivered basis; or that all leases are written off to profit and loss account if the policy is to treat finance leases in the same manner as operating leases.

It is doubtful whether the accountant's responsibilities stop at this point. To enable a user of the accounts to make any sense of them, the accountant must ensure that the accounting policies as adopted by the firm are stated in the accounts. For example, if the policy is to treat finance leases as if they were operating leases, and this is not stated in the accounts, then if there were to be a material amount of finance leased assets a user of the accounts could be misled. The same considerations would apply if there were significant accelerated capital allowances, but the practice did not provide for deferred tax. If the accounts did not state the amount of deferred tax that was not provided for then, similarly, a user could be misled.

Concepts of materiality and significance indicate that the accountant is doing more than just drafting up a set of accounts, and has a wider responsibility than he might initially believe.

10.4 Certification that accounting policies are appropriate

This certificate goes a stage further, but is not a full audit certificate. It is probably the most confusing of all of the certificates because it raises an expectation in the user regarding the suitability of the accounting policies which may not be justified; it is the first report on page 269. Some accountants will interpret this to mean that the policies used are in accordance with generally accepted accounting principles; others will read into this that the policies are similar to those used by solicitors' firms. If the latter interpretation is used, then such a certificate could be used for a firm which operated on a cash basis, or did not account for work in progress. If the former interpretation is used then it obviously could not. Whichever policy is used there should be a clear statement as to the level at which the policies would be considered appropriate.

The second example on page 269 is a certificate that would be appropriate if the policies were in accordance with those used by solicitors' firms generally. The third example on page 269 would be appropriate for policies which were generally acceptable.

Whichever interpretation is used, it does involve the accountant in considering, to a certain extent, the commercial background to the policies, such considerations requiring documentation on his files.

10.5 'Audit' certificate

Because the word 'audit' is most often used in the context of a set of statutory financial statements, when applied to a set of partnership accounts it must be used with great care.

Where the accountant is asked to prepare an audit certificate, he must be aware that any user of the accounts may have in mind the work which goes into preparing a statutory audit certificate, and will be relying on a similar type of work on the partnership accounts. For this reason it is recommended that the word audit is only used if a full statutory type audit is carried out, and an opinion is given on the truth and fairness of the accounts. The use of the word 'audit' in any other circumstances would be potentially misleading unless the accountant sets out in considerable detail in his Report exactly what his terms of reference are and what work he has carried out.

10.6 Additional paragraphs of the Accountant's Report

10.6.1 Certification of profit share

In addition to his work on, for example, the preparation of the accounts, the accountant may be asked to calculate or certify the allocation of profit. In this case he should make his calculations and set out in his Report in a separate paragraph the sources of information he has used in reaching the allocation. These will comprise the partnership agreement, or the pronouncements of any remuneration committee. Given the importance individual partners place on profit share, it is vitally important that these sources are clearly stated.

A suggested format for a paragraph is given in Appendix 10.

10.6.2 Commentary on the accounts

It has already been noted that a commentary on the accounts provided by the partnership is most useful in understanding the performance and financial position of the firm. It is important that this is prepared by the firm, and not the accountant. Where the commentary is attached to the accounts, it is important that the accountant states that he takes no responsibility for the commentary, and that his certificate on the accounts, whatever its form, does not extend to any commentary. However, the accountant probably has a duty to the partners to ensure that any commentaries issued with the accounts are not misleading.

A suggested format for a disclaimer paragraph is given in Appendix 10.

PART IV

Financial management practices of solicitors practices

This section sets out the types of financial management practices which solicitors' firms adopt in the areas of determination of profit share, setting drawings levels, financing, tax provisioning, ownership of property, the admission and retirement of partners and working capital management. This section is primarily based on the author's discussions with the senior partners, finance partners and directors of finance of over 60 firms of solicitors and with a number of bankers. It therefore aims to give an insight into the ways in which firms approach financial management.

Throughout the section the author gives some recommendations, but would draw the attention of the reader to the importance that culture plays in the practices developed by firms. The section should therefore be used more of a guide to the options available to firms, and the reasons why these are adopted, rather than as a statement of best practice.

Chapter 11 – Profit sharing arrangements

11.1 Introduction

The way in which a partnership shares its profits provides one of the clearest insights into the culture of that partnership. It can also indicate at which stage of development the practice is. Profit sharing arrangements are dynamic, not static; one expects to see, in a well run (and well balanced practice) a continual appraisal of those arrangements. In the badly run partnership there will also be a constant discussion of profit share, but it is likely to be divisive rather than consensual. Indeed, profit sharing arrangements which do not reflect the culture of the firm and the way the partners wish to work together will be a principle cause of a fractious partnership.

It will also be seen throughout this chapter that profit sharing is inextricably linked with the management of a firm; for example a radical change in the management practices of a firm will often be accompanied by a change in the profit sharing arrangements.

The accountant who advises a solicitor's practice on its profit share therefore has potentially a great deal of power, and certainly a heavy responsibility. Profit sharing arrangements that are successful, notwithstanding the need for regular monitoring, can have a long life. A poorly advised partnership may well have a very short life.

In the author's experience of partnership disputes, profit share is commonly seen as the offender.

11.2 Types of profit sharing arrangements and the evolution of a practice

Partnerships which do not arise from a merger or demerger commonly start life with two or three partners. Profit share will normally be equal as between partners. Equality partnerships can be very stable but where there is growth in the numbers of partners there are two possible changes and one unlikely one.

It is unlikely that it will remain an equality partnership; by the time the third or fourth candidate is up for partnership, one of the senior partners will object to him receiving a full profit share. However, the author is aware of equalities in excess of ten partners.

It will either become a 'lock-step' partnership, or a 'proto-meritocracy'. Lock-steps, the classic type of legal practice, are discussed in great detail below, but essentially represent a method of increasing a new partner's profit share over time. Equality based on seniority is the aim. Proto-meritocracies can only exist up to about 15 partners. They involve the partners sitting round a table once a year and deciding what the profit share will be. Profit share is based on what is best expressed as 'contribution to the practice.'

A proto-meritocracy that grows will develop into a full meritocracy, that is where contribution to the practice is not decided at a plenary session of the partners but by an elected, or self-appointed, committee. Lock-steps can remain lock-steps no matter how large they grow; indeed the largest legal practices tend to be lock-steps. However, it is becoming increasingly common for lock-steps to be tinged (some would say contaminated) by meritocratic practices and there are a large number of possible lock-step/meritocratic hybrids until the fully-formed meritocracy emerges.

The move to a meritocracy is by no means definite. However, full meritocracies exert a gravitational pull on the hybrids. Further, lock-steps have been attacked at a more fundamental level, that of what a partnership should be, and this is also considered below. Finally, it is possible for a meritocracy or a hybrid to lurch back towards a pure lock-step and some medium sized firms may consider scrapping their meritocratic principles and becoming a rigid lock-step when a certain size is reached.

11.3 Equalities

Of the 8,000 firms of solicitors in England and Wales, over 40 per cent have between two and four partners. Given that just under 40 per cent of firms are sole practitioners the vast majority of solicitors' practices are small partnerships; most of these will be equalities.

Equalities work in these practices because they are small, and because each partner is making a definite choice in wanting to be in practice with the other partners. Clients will be loyal to the partner, rather than the firm, and any dispute is capable of resolution by dissolution. Where a new partner is introduced, he will commonly be an established solicitor with a client list. A new partner by way of elevation may be on a lower profit share, but this is often a temporary position before equality.

However, equalities are not immune to problems over profit share due to differing perceptions of contribution. A common situation is for one partner to make a conscious decision to restrict his input to the firm, for example due to age. In these situations a fixing of that partner's profit share solves the problem rather than that partner leaving. If the fixed profit share partner and the other partner or partners understand and appreciate what is being given up, then these arrangements can work very successfully.

11.4 Proto-meritocracies

Proto-meritocracies can be a source of wonder to those who have not experienced them; how can 15 partners agree between themselves on something as emotive as the worth and contribution of each individual to the practice? Yet they do work, and often decisions are reached in a very short time.

This type of arrangement shows a practice working as a partnership, with consensus regarding the final result. It is possible that one individual may dominate the proceedings, but each partner gets the chance to comment on everyone else. As important is that plans for the future development of the practice are a natural by-product of these discussions. A further feature is that, for under-performers, peer pressure plays as important a role in motivation as monetary reward. These two strengths can become diluted in a full meritocracy.

The issue of the dominant individual or individuals is often found in these firms. Such a partner will invariably be the founding partner (the firm may carry his name) and for a substantial period of time, because the founding partner's profit share is so high compared to his fellow partners, the other partners may be, in profit share terms, little more than salaried partners. The profit share may only be meritocratic to the extent that the founding partner ultimately decides who, in his view, has made what contribution.

The founding partner will also tend to manage the firm, often with little or no help from the other partners. The problem of succession is therefore strongly linked with that of profit share. Attempts to change either or both, especially before the founding partner is ready to go, often appear to be part of a *coup d'etat*. The accountant is therefore advised to be very careful in offering his services in these situations.

It is the author's experience that partners in proto-meritocracies are generally satisfied with the way they work, (although where there is one dominant individual there can be a high level of dissatisfaction). However, a growing practice needs to be aware that over a certain size, the practice will start to break up into factions. This will often coincide with a realisation that there needs to be a formalisation of management practices or a change away from, say, a senior partner undertaking all management, to a management committee with defined responsibilities.

11.5 Lock-steps

The lock-step is thought by a great many people to epitomise the ideals of partnership. Terms such as equality, loyalty, bringing-the-new-chaps-on, ownership as a function of age and seniority are utilised.

Other commentators think that the lock-step is an outmoded practice that has held back many partnerships in their development. The link in a lock-step between seniority/profit share/ownership and therefore an individual's 'right' to be involved in the management of the firm takes little account of that person's ability. Management is once again tied to profit share. Lock-steps are also thought to act as a dis-incentive to the younger and hungrier partners. Culture is therefore also a critical factor.

The cultural reasons for the development of lock-steps are as follows. New partners are introduced to a partnership because there is a need to establish a succession and to ensure, first of all, continued existence and, secondly, growth. Existence is critical because it allows the founding or senior partners a source of profit shares in the final years up to retirement, and perhaps an annuity from the partnership thereafter. However, if a partnership is developing its new partners internally, those candidates may not have an established client base of their own, will have little experience in the management of the firm and might not have the financial resources to inject capital at the same level as the existing partners.

The lock-step means that over a period of, perhaps, ten years a partner will see his partnership profit share increase every year from, say, one quarter of the senior partners' profit share to a full share. His capital in the firm should increase at the same rate, perhaps by a capitalisation of a certain level of undrawn profit share each year.

One of the primary features is that, in the first years of the new partner's partnership, the existing partners will have to give up only a small amount of their own profit share; by the time the new partner has completed his ten years, he will, hopefully, be generating enough of his own profits to pay for his own profit share and for some of his partners' profit shares, both those coming up to retirement and those newly elevated. In the early years the older partners subsidise and therefore encourage the new partners. A steady development of the firm takes place; younger partners are not encouraged to be overly risky in their development of new work, because it makes no difference in their progression up the lock-step, but are given time for that development.

Lock-steps are an extremely common feature of medium- and large-sized firms of solicitors, but there is a surprising variation between firms as to the actual mechanics. In the past, the time element of the lock step has been as much as 20 years, but now ten years is the generally quoted upper limit. However, some firms do go above this figure. Medium-sized firms will often be below this, quite often seven or five years, and time gaps of only three years do exist.

The other mechanical feature is the equity- or points-gap, that is the difference between the profit share which a new partner gets and that of a senior or full equity partner. Again there is a wide variation between firms, with ratios between the new partner and the full equity partner of 150 per cent to 500 per cent. This, coupled with the time element can mean a substantial variation between the potential profit shares of partners moving up a lock-step, even before the firm's level of profits and number of partners are considered. These variations are shown numerically at pages 100 to 103. The tables take three firms, with five, 20 and 50 full equity partners respectively, each with profits per partner of £200,000 per annum. The tables then consider the various profit shares which a new partner would receive over a 13 year period, at a number of different time intervals, and points-gaps. The average profit share which the individual would receive over the 13 year period is summarised and expressed as a percentage of his profit share as a full equity partner. Profits of each of the firms are assumed not to change from year to year.

11.5.1 Points-gap

The tables show the large variation between initial profit shares depending on the size of the points-gap. This therefore means that, for a practice with a very large points-gap, initial profit shares will be very low, or final profit shares very high.

The initial profit share may in practice be fixed by reference to, for example, a mark up on the new partner's salary as an employee. Firms will have different views as to what the mark up should be and one firm may place a very large premium on elevation, whereas another will take the view that elevation is reward enough for a partner. The most common practice among legal firms is to base the first year profit share on an assistant solicitor's salary, as adjusted for a loss of benefits such as car, pension etc. An alternative is to look first of all at drawings, and ensure that the new partner's fixed drawings are equivalent to his take home pay as an employee. The setting of a benchmark has implications for firms where profits are falling, and this is considered below. This has the effect of linking initial profit shares to market rates of pay, and thus the maximum possible size of the points-gap will be dependent on the overall profit level of the firm.

Year of partnership	0	1	2	3	4	5	6	7	8	9	10	11	12
5 full equity, 1 new profits £1 million													
12 year gap new partner's profit share at:													
100 to 150 points	117647	121951	126214	130435	134615	138756	142857	146919	150943	154930	158879	162791	166667
100 to 200 points	90909	97744	104478	111111	117647	124088	130435	136691	142857	148936	154930	160839	166667
100 to 250 points	74074	82569	90909	99099	107143	115044	122807	130435	137931	145299	152542	159664	166667
100 to 300 points	62500	72165	81633	90909	100000	108911	117647	126214	134615	142857	150943	158879	166667
100 to 500 points	38462	50633	62500	74074	85366	96386	107143	117647	127907	137931	147727	157303	166667
10 year gap new partner's profit share at:													
100 to 150 points	117647	122807	127907	132948	137931	142857	147727	152542	157303	162011	166667	166667	166667
100 to 200 points	90909	99099	107143	115044	122807	130435	137931	145299	152542	159664	166667	166667	166667
100 to 250 points	74074	84249	94203	103943	113475	122807	131944	140893	149660	158249	166667	166667	166667
100 to 300 points	62500	74074	85366	96386	107143	117647	127907	137931	147727	157303	166667	166667	166667
100 to 500 points	38462	53030	67164	80882	94203	107143	119718	131944	143836	155405	166667	166667	166667
7 year gap new partner's profit share at:													
100 to 150 points	117647	125000	132231	139344	146341	153226	160000	166667	166667	166667	166667	166667	166667
100 to 200 points	90909	102564	113924	125000	135802	146341	156627	166667	166667	166667	166667	166667	166667
100 to 250 points	74074	88542	102564	116162	129353	142157	154589	166667	166667	166667	166667	166667	166667
100 to 300 points	62500	78947	94828	110169	125000	139344	153226	166667	166667	166667	166667	166667	166667
100 to 500 points	38462	59140	78947	97938	116162	133663	150485	166667	166667	166667	166667	166667	166667
5 year gap new partner's profit share at:													
100 to 150 points	117647	127907	137931	147727	157303	166667	166667	166667	166667	166667	166667	166667	166667
100 to 200 points	90909	107143	122807	137931	152542	166667	166667	166667	166667	166667	166667	166667	166667
100 to 250 points	74074	94203	113475	131944	149660	166667	166667	166667	166667	166667	166667	166667	166667
100 to 300 points	62500	85366	107143	127907	147727	166667	166667	166667	166667	166667	166667	166667	166667
100 to 500 points	38462	67164	94203	119718	143836	166667	166667	166667	166667	166667	166667	166667	166667

Year of partnership	0	1	2	3	4	5	6	7	8	9	10	11	12
20 full equity, 1 new profits £4 million													
12 year gap new partner's profit share at:													
100 to 150 points	129032	134228	139410	144578	149733	154873	160000	165113	170213	175299	180371	185430	190476
100 to 200 points	97561	105477	113360	121212	129032	136821	144578	152305	160000	167665	175299	182903	190476
100 to 250 points	78431	88020	97561	107056	116505	125908	135266	144578	153846	163070	172249	181384	190476
100 to 300 points	65574	76294	86957	97561	108108	118598	129032	139410	149733	160000	170213	180371	190476
100 to 500 points	39604	52632	65574	78431	91205	103896	116505	129032	141479	153846	166134	178344	190476
10 year gap new partner's profit share at:													
100 to 150 points	129032	135266	141479	147673	153846	160000	166134	172249	178344	184420	190476	190476	190476
100 to 200 points	97561	107056	116505	125908	135266	144578	153846	163070	172249	181384	190476	190476	190476
100 to 250 points	78431	89932	101365	112731	124031	135266	146435	157541	168582	179561	190476	190476	190476
100 to 300 points	65574	78431	91205	103896	116505	129032	141479	153846	166134	178344	190476	190476	190476
100 to 500 points	39604	55227	70727	86106	101365	116505	131528	146435	161228	175908	190476	190476	190476
7 year gap new partner's profit share at:													
100 to 150 points	129032	137931	146789	155606	164384	173121	181818	190476	190476	190476	190476	190476	190476
100 to 200 points	97561	111111	124567	137931	151203	164384	177474	190476	190476	190476	190476	190476	190476
100 to 250 points	78431	94840	111111	127248	143251	159122	174863	190476	190476	190476	190476	190476	190476
100 to 300 points	65574	83916	102088	120092	137931	155606	173121	190476	190476	190476	190476	190476	190476
100 to 500 points	39604	61885	83916	105702	127248	148556	169631	190476	190476	190476	190476	190476	190476
5 year gap new partner's profit share at:													
100 to 150 points	129032	141479	153846	166134	178344	190476	190476	190476	190476	190476	190476	190476	190476
100 to 200 points	97561	116505	135266	153846	172249	190476	190476	190476	190476	190476	190476	190476	190476
100 to 250 points	78431	101365	124031	146435	168582	190476	190476	190476	190476	190476	190476	190476	190476
100 to 300 points	65574	91205	116505	141479	166134	190476	190476	190476	190476	190476	190476	190476	190476
100 to 500 points	39604	70727	101365	131528	161228	190476	190476	190476	190476	190476	190476	190476	190476

Year of partnership	0	1	2	3	4	5	6	7	8	9	10	11	12
50 full equity, 1 new profits £10 million													
12 year gap new partner's profit share at:													
100 to 150 points	131579	136986	142388	147783	153173	158557	163934	169306	174672	180033	185387	190736	196078
100 to 200 points	99010	107172	115321	123457	131579	139688	147783	155865	163934	171990	180033	188062	196078
100 to 250 points	79365	89197	99010	108803	118577	128332	138067	147783	157480	167158	176817	186457	196078
100 to 300 points	66225	77178	88106	99010	109890	120746	131579	142388	153173	163934	174672	185387	196078
100 to 500 points	39841	53050	66225	79365	92470	105541	118577	131579	144547	157480	170380	183246	196078
10 year gap new partner's profit share at:													
100 to 150 points	131579	138067	144547	151018	157480	163934	170380	176817	183246	189666	196078	196078	196078
100 to 200 points	99010	108803	118577	128332	138067	147783	157480	167158	176817	186457	196078	196078	196078
100 to 250 points	79365	91161	102930	114670	126382	138067	149724	161354	172956	184531	196078	196078	196078
100 to 300 points	66225	79365	92470	105541	118577	131579	144547	157480	170380	183246	196078	196078	196078
100 to 500 points	39841	55688	71485	87232	102930	118577	134175	149724	165224	180676	196078	196078	196078
7 year gap new partner's profit share at:													
100 to 150 points	131579	140845	150094	159325	168539	177736	186916	196078	196078	196078	196078	196078	196078
100 to 200 points	99010	112994	126939	140845	154712	168539	182328	196078	196078	196078	196078	196078	196078
100 to 250 points	79365	96208	112994	129724	146396	163013	179574	196078	196078	196078	196078	196078	196078
100 to 300 points	66225	84986	103676	122295	140845	159325	177736	196078	196078	196078	196078	196078	196078
100 to 500 points	39841	62465	84986	107405	129724	151941	174060	196078	196078	196078	196078	196078	196078
5 year gap new partner's profit share at:													
100 to 150 points	131597	144547	157480	170380	183246	196078	196078	196078	196078	196078	196078	196078	196078
100 to 200 points	99010	118577	138067	157480	176817	196078	196078	196078	196078	196078	196078	196078	196078
100 to 250 points	79365	102930	126382	149724	172956	196078	196078	196078	196078	196078	196078	196078	196078
100 to 300 points	66225	92470	118577	144547	170380	196078	196078	196078	196078	196078	196078	196078	196078
100 to 500 points	39841	71485	102930	134175	165224	196078	196078	196078	196078	196078	196078	196078	196078

Average profit share as a total of final profit share over 13 year period	*5 partner firm*	*20 partner firm*	*50 partner firm*
12 year gap			
new partner's profit share at:			
100 to 150 points	86%	84%	84%
100 to 200 points	78%	76%	75%
100 to 250 points	73%	71%	70%
100 to 300 points	70%	68%	67%
100 to 500 points	63%	61%	60%
10 year gap			
new partner's profit share at:			
100 to 150 points	88%	86%	86%
100 to 200 points	81%	80%	79%
100 to 250 points	77%	75%	75%
100 to 300 points	74%	73%	72%
100 to 500 points	69%	67%	66%
7 year gap			
new partner's profit share at:			
100 to 150 points	91%	90%	90%
100 to 200 points	86%	85%	85%
100 to 250 points	83%	82%	82%
100 to 300 points	81%	80%	80%
100 to 500 points	77%	76%	76%
5 year gap			
new partner's profit share at:			
100 to 150 points	93%	93%	92%
100 to 200 points	90%	89%	89%
100 to 250 points	88%	87%	86%
100 to 300 points	86%	85%	85%
100 to 500 points	83%	82%	82%

11.5.2 Time-gap

At relatively low points-gaps, the differing time gaps do not lead to great variations in profit share levels along the lock-step. However, where they are combined with wide points gaps, the difference between initial and final profit shares becomes even more marked.

11.5.3 Size of firm

The size of a firm can have a substantial effect on its initial profit shares, and therefore on the profit shares taken by the full equity partners, or the amounts which they have to 'give up' to new partners. One would expect to see the widest time-gaps and points-gaps in the smaller firms, although this is not usually the case.

In the table above, the greater the percentage, the 'steeper' the lock-step is. The partner's actual profit share will also be affected by actual profit levels and changes in partnership numbers due to elevations and retirements.

However, the steepness of the lock-step gives an incoming partner an impression of his likely rewards to full equity.

Variations reflect the culture of different partnerships, their size and also their age. For example, smaller partnerships often have shorter time and point-gaps in their lock-steps and because of their size a smaller partnership will have a markedly steeper lock-step than a larger partnership.

The reason is as follows: a small, aggressive, growing partnership will rely heavily on its new partners to generate new work and keep growth at high levels. As far as the other partners are concerned, the high rate at which they give up new profits to new partners is more than outweighed by the profits the new partners themselves generate. The short gap between elevations acts as a strong encouragement to new partners. This may also be mixed with a relatively large gap between new partner and full equity points so that over the period of the time gap the new partner is taking a larger share of profits which he is responsible for generating.

This view can be contrasted with a much larger partnership. The firm itself relies very little on new partners for its growth, and because of the size of the firm, new partners can make little initial impact. The contradiction noted above leads to the conclusion that, as far as motivating the more junior partners by monetary means is concerned, a lock-step is more successful in a small firm than a large firm.

The largest firms tend to have the longest time gaps and points-gaps, and the smaller firms the shortest gaps. Additionally, firms with relatively high levels of profits can sustain wide points-gaps, whereas firms with lower levels cannot.

Although the mechanics of an individual firm's lock-step may reflect many aspects of its culture it is primarily a function of its size, its profit levels and its growth, both past and future. It may be, therefore, that a lock-step which is not working only requires a variation in, say, the points-gap, not a complete abandonment of the principle.

One of the criticisms of the rigid lock-step is that it is performance-blind. However, the above example of the small growing firm indicates that this may not always be the case. A steep lock-step can be successful because it reflects very much the culture of the firm and the way the partners wish to operate.

The issue of the lock-step being performance-blind is tackled first of all by reference to the senior partners. Despite having been a partner and therefore responsible in some measure for the success of the firm for a substantial period of time, there is a view that the older a partner is the less of a contribution he is making. This is obviously not always the case, and may reflect nothing but prejudice. However, some older partners do wish to take things easier in the years immediately before retirement, often so that retirement is not a complete break, and this should not be ignored. Some law firms take account of this by allowing partners past a certain age to drop equity points. In others the shedding of points is mandatory, often after 55, at which age a partner may be allowed to retire, or stay for a further five years, losing ten per cent of his points a year.

The issue of senior partners not performing is one of the greatest issues currently facing partnerships, not least because there are likely to be very different perceptions within a partnership regarding performance, and discussion can be far more acrimonious than a similar discussion concerning younger partners. Fixing profit share to a formula where points can be lost with age at least removes the potentially embarrassing situation of former junior partners commenting on the performance of their former principal.

Once one accepts that points can be lost, then the main feature of the rigid lock-step, the certainty of equality with seniority, is no longer present and some measure of performance related criteria is applied.

11.6 Lock-step meritocracy hyrids

As noted above, one of the main reasons the lock-step is under attack is because it fails to take account of performance, both under- and over-performance. The starting point is that monetary reward is both a carrot and a stick, and that over-performers can be motivated with more money, and under-performers encouraged by less. Although the money view is very simplistic, an important by-product of the process of assessing performance is that it is an operation of management which should, in the case of under-performance, identify the reasons for a lack of effort, and in the case of over-performance encourage effort and look at its future development. Therefore, firms which start to introduce meritocratic elements into their lock-step are increasing their appraisal of performance and, it might be thought, their overall management.

Firms have for some time varied rigid lock-steps, but the impetus for change has been particularly marked since the mid-1980s. First of all, when law firms were experiencing rapid growth, relatively junior partners perceived themselves to be responsible for that growth and wanted greater reward than was offered to them. In a large number of firms the growth was seen as the responsibility of individual departments, such as property and corporate finance, and some sort of reward over and above that given by the lock-step was claimed.

With the recession, and a fall in growth and profits, the issue of under-performance has come to the fore, first of all in respect of partners who were carried by the firm in the good years and, secondly, those partners who were elevated in the growth years on what are now seen to be very lax criteria. In these cases, the lock-step is seen to be over-rewarding.

Partnerships with rigid lock-steps usually say they take a hard line with under-performance (if, of course, it can be objectively recognised), and partners are asked to leave.

A much more common means of dealing with under-performance, and the only way of dealing with over-performance, is to vary the terms of the lock-step. This can be done as follows:

(a) allow the time gap to be extended or reduced;
(b) make the annual step up conditional each year on a certain level of performance;
(c) allow more points to be obtained after the 'maximum' number for a full equity partner;
(d) have a separate tranche of profits over and above a certain level which is divided among those partners seen as having made a special effort in earning those profits;
(e) have a 'phantom' full equity partner whose profit share is divided among those partners seen to have made a certain contribution, for example, bringing a large client in or taking part in the management of the firm; and
(f) having a system of points removal, or alternatively, increasing all points other than those of the under-performers.

It is possible to use these techniques to deal with over-performance, that is, increasing monetary reward, alone. However, it is only when an individual's profit share starts to fall because of a decision by management that a firm is wholly dealing with the meritocratic issues. Bonuses given to certain individuals in good years, when the overall profits of the firm are high and where nobody suffers a fall in actual profit share may do little if anything to change under-performance. But, the introduction to a partnership of the concept of using performance-related criteria will start a process which can be difficult to stop. Profit sharing arrangements which are based on contribution to the practice in only a partial sense can be difficult to sustain, and this will start to become apparent when profits are not sustainable.

11.7 Meritocracies

There are two types of meritocratic profit sharing system, the mainly quantitative and the mainly qualitative.

11.7.1 Quantitative

Mainly quantitative profit sharing seems to be primarily an American import, based on the rather alarming term 'eat what you kill.' A partner will receive his profit share annually in arrears based on a combination of his own billings, cash collections and 'profitability' and the billings generated by other partners on clients which the partner was responsible for generating.

A few points need to be made on this type of arrangement. First of all it needs a relatively sophisticated management information system which allows the measurement of partner or departmental profitability. The overheads will include costs incurred centrally over which one partner has no control, or which he feels do not benefit him. As much as possible, overheads need to be borne by partners on an individual basis, but this can be difficult to achieve, and can be cost-inefficient as far as the firm as a whole is concerned.

Next, it is vital that maximising profits is not achieved through short-term measures. Rapid growth may be uncontrolled and lead to, for example, large work-in-progress or bad debt write-offs due to poor working capital management. One bad debt can exceed a partner's profit for the year many times over, and the partnership as a whole may have to bear this expense.

Basing profit share on the billings of clients introduced can lead to a number of problems. The introductory link may be tenuous, and may be claimed by a number of partners. Where rewards are high (and sometimes where they are not so high) for introducing clients, spurious claims can hide the real source of an introduction, and cause problems between partners for years to come. For how long after introducing a client should a partner receive a percentage of billings on introductions? Only when he bills the amounts himself, or by diminishing amounts each year, or to retirement? Some American firms apparently pay a reduced percentage after retirement, and then to widows. Additionally why should a partner receive a percentage of billings if he no longer acts personally for that client, or never did in the first place? The main development of work may be by the partner who personally acts due to, for instance, the quality of his advice or his own relationship. The client may be much larger by virtue of a takeover which had nothing to do with anyone at the law firm.

Finally, a dependence on the top line may encourage new clients to be sought at whatever cost. That cost may be a high-risk client, or one brought in by virtue of a very low tender, the billings losses for which the introducing partner may avoid bearing, but still attain a client credit. Profit share arising from billings should lapse with time, where the partner no longer bills the work, and the profitability of clients should be taken into account.

New partners may find that such a system, if applied rigorously, would mean them initially taking a cut in earnings. Presumably it is not in the interests of the existing partners to give up a substantial amount of billings; some sort of cushion is required for 'young' partners from mainly quantitative systems. However, it can lead to more senior partners not receiving '. . . sufficient at the end of the year to pay for my mortgage . . . and all those other little luxuries, which I have incurred in the past year' (*Anatomy of a Successful Practice* Michael Simmons, 1987, p1). Such a system has been described as creating '. . . potentially catastrophic uncertainties . . .' (*ibid.*, p12)

The system provides little incentive to undertake management responsibility within the firm, and therefore part of the cake needs to be allocated for this type of activity. Finally, loyalty and long-service are not rewarded, and therefore it may be necessary to maintain a slice of profit share based on years of service, that is an element of lock-step.

As with any system of sharing profits, the irritations are overlooked if the firm is doing well and profits are rising. The problems outlined above can all be said to be a function of an over-concentration on the numbers, and not the story behind the numbers. This over-concentration is hopefully overcome using the mainly qualitative approach.

11.7.2 Qualitative

The qualitative approach to a meritocratic profit share is becoming more common in English firms, and is favoured over the quantitative approach.

The following profit sharing arrangements are common among firms of solicitors:

(a) *First tranche/second tranche.* The first tranche is generally a salary which increases each year by some pre-determined factor, for example the retail price index or the increase in the level of billings. The second tranche is allocated on the basis of merit. In some firms the first tranche can also be varied on the basis of merit, but not to the extent of the second tranche.

(b) *First tranche/second tranche/third tranche.* The first tranche is related to an assistant solicitor's salary, the second tranche is a reward for long-service, that is a form of lock-step compensation, and the third tranche the pure merit band.

(c) *Bonus tranche.* To each of the above there can be a discretionary amount of profit awarded for very special cases.

(d) *Bands system.* There are a number of bands of profit share, say three or four, and every partner is allocated to one of the bands. Band one may comprise the most recently appointed partners, and some obviously under-performing partners; band two comprises the majority of partners; and band three comprises the current high fliers and senior management. The number of bands can be extended, and given other fairly wide definitions.

(e) *Points system.* There are a pool of points which are divided up among all of the partners based solely on merit.

The assessment of merit and its communication are the most important factors in these systems. Before looking at the way in which these can be achieved, it is worth looking at how far the failures of the mainly qualitative meritocracy are a function of the failure to get these two considerations right.

11.7.3 Divisiveness

The most common criticism among solicitors is that the system is divisive (and this is also a criticism of the quantitative approach). It is true that to impose such a system on a culture which is fundamentally non-competitive, could be a disaster. Before a firm adopts such an approach, the partners have to be sure that they wish to give up equality for some semi-objective assessment of their worth to the partnership and each other to be measured in the very real form of money. However, the partners should also ask whether it is divisive or not for two individuals to be elevated to partnership at the same time, to put in greatly differing levels of effort, and reach equality at the same time having reaped the same rewards to date, with the prospect of similar rewards in the future. The system will also cause division if the parameters for assessing merit have been inadequately set, and this gives rise to the next major criticism, that the determination of merit takes time.

11.7.4 Management time required to implement

Given the statement at the beginning of this chapter, that profit share is closely linked to management, it is not surprising that a management tool that looks at performance and *ipso facto* tries to improve it, should take up a substantial amount of time. Indeed if it does not, then it has not been carried out properly, and problems will arise. Therefore, a pre-condition of a successful qualitative system must be a sophisticated management structure, appropriate to the size of firm, with partners willing to devote time to putting the procedures into practice. (This is not to say that a lock-step requires little management – see below.)

11.7.5 Acceptance of under-performance

The next criticism has two parts, but is to do primarily with the issue of under-performance, that is the very matter meritocracies are supposed to address. First of all, it is said that the mere fact of identifying the low-fliers and rewarding them accordingly is an admission by the partnership that under-performance is acceptable. In this view, all partners should pull together, and the correct method of dealing with a consistent under-performer is retirement. This is very much a cultural view, but it is one that a large number of firms hold. Someone who does not perform is not worthy to be a partner. This leads into the second part of the criticism which is that a meritocratic system for dealing with under-performance is avoiding the difficult issue of getting rid of, or demoting, such partners.

This is a particular problem for a large number of firms, mainly those which experienced rapid growth in the 1980s. It would seem that these firms viewed the offer of a partnership to an employee as a reward, similar to a bonus, but unlike a bonus, not one-off. One commentator has said the following:

> 'Contrast those essential characteristics (of partnerships, being the generation of work and letting other people do a lot of that work) with the type of person who is generally elevated to partnership in today's law firm. In essence he will probably be a competent lawyer who has been qualified for at least five years and who has spent, typically, at least three years with his present firm . . . In other words, any reasonably competent lawyer can expect to be offered a partnership if they stay at their firm long enough . . . the qualification criteria are too lax and elevation to equity partnership is now the norm.' (*The Traditional Partnership Model has Held Back Law-Firm Development*, John Pritchard, Legal Business Magazine, December 1991)

Such individuals should only have received a salaried partnership at the most, not equity, and calling them equity partners but giving them a low profit share misses the point. Having said this, it is part of the wider issue of practice management in the 1990s which many firms face. The problem of dealing with individuals who should never have been made partners in the first place is different from setting a meritocratic profit share scheme.

11.7.6 Use of money as a motivator

A final criticism is that any merit-based system uses primarily money, rather than the peer-pressure exercised by one's fellow partners. However, any competent system of appraisal which looks forward as well as looking back will achieve the peer motivation as well. It is now necessary to look at the features of competent systems of appraisal.

11.8 Appraising merit

There is no standard system; the rule often repeated in this chapter holds true, that the successful profit sharing system depends on the culture of the firm. The accountant should bear this in mind when advising on meritocratic profit share, as the following passage shows, taken from an article by a partner in a law firm discussing an attempt to implement a replacement for a lock-step:

> 'We had considerable experience in tinkering with an equity points system, but none in setting up a merit award system so we engaged management consultancy services. In conducting our beauty parade of candidates, it became obvious that their experience of the system we envisaged was non-existent; they had an overwhelming tendency to try to fit us into a pre-prepared mould which would clearly then have fitted in to one of their standard – and very expensive – sales packages. It was for this reason that we ultimately engaged the services of consultants . . . who showed a willingness to help us develop and implement a system tailored to our own specific needs.' (*Profit-sharing for the 1990s*, Stephen Finn, Law Society's *Gazette*, 9 October 1991)

The first requirement is that the practice itself has a method of assessing its performance as a whole and therefore it should have a series of objectives. Such objectives are normally the product of a strategy review and, although this may appear to be a rather grand term, it should include the fairly informal process of the partners sitting down together and chatting about the future of the firm. It does not always need a retreat or a full-blown consulting exercise.

Once the objectives have been clarified, they should receive the acceptance of the partnership as a whole, or be adjusted so that they are acceptable. At this stage there is consensus among the partners about where the firm wishes to be. The next stage is agreement over how the objectives are to be achieved. Within this overall strategy each partner will have a role. If the partnership is of a sufficient size individual strategies will be agreed for each department, and within each department for each partner. It is also important that the staff below partner-level are included within this strategy.

It is apparent that before a qualitative based system which makes use of appraisals can be implemented, the strategy has to be developed, and individual action plans for each partner within that action plan agreed.

The appraisal process is about both looking forward and looking back, and is therefore wholly reliant on performance against past plans, and plans for the future. The person initially responsible for this process is the partner himself, who will need to comment on his own past and future performance under a number of headings. These could include the following:

(a) billings;
(b) cash collections;

(c) work gained/lost;
(d) profits/losses on client work;
(e) work generated for other partners;
(f) management responsibilities taken on and success therein;
(g) degree of involvement in staff training;
(h) community or charitable responsibilities undertaken outside the firm;
(i) publications or external lecturing assignments;
(j) anticipated new work, collections etc. in forthcoming year.

The form, once completed, is then likely to go through a number of discussions. First of all the partner's departmental head may be required to discuss with the individual partner his answers and then provide comments of his own. Next, the form, with all of the other partners' forms, will be discussed at a senior level, possibly the compensation committee if there is one, or the 'management committee'. Following this, individual forms will once again be discussed with the relevant partner. Views arising from these meetings will be fed back to the management of the firm and the merit related profit share set for each partner. Depending on the size and structure of the firm, some arrangements may take place at a departmental level. It is vital that at each of the discussions, and in the final decision, the extent to which the firm's strategic objectives and any departmental objectives are being met are considered.

Two examples will illustrate this point. Firstly, one of the performance criteria noted above is charitable work. This type of activity can cost a partnership money to undertake, but it may be viewed as important for altruistic reasons. It would be wrong to penalise a partner for carrying out this work if the partnership as a whole believes that it is right to do it; in fact, if it is an objective then that partner, under the qualitative system, needs to be rewarded.

Secondly, there is the issue of less remunerative work, such as legally aided criminal cases or family law. To quote one partner in a firm with a qualitative profit share arrangement:

> 'If a practice is properly strategic and effectively managed then it will automatically establish certain goals. It may be agreed policy and in the practice's interests to maintain less remunerative areas.' (*Preaching the New Way*, Nigel Page quoting Peter Thompson, Legal Business Magazine, July/August 1990)

However, it is important at the strategic planning process to appreciate that there is no reason why, just because an individual has a particular skill or carries out work in a certain area, the practice of that area of the law becomes an objective in itself. The issue of less-remunerative work can cause extraordinary problems if not dealt with at this stage. The above quotation continues:

> 'Naturally, there are lawyers here who earn less than others because they chose to operate in the less profitable areas . . .', [but] 'their individual targets for the year, and against which they are assessed, will take into account the field in which they operate.' (*ibid*)

It is important that there is an appeals procedure which is seen to work in the case of manifest unfairness, and this includes those partners who find themselves over-rewarded as well as those not so fortunate. The appellate body should not be the remuneration committee, and should have the power to advise, rather than decide.

At this stage, the next requirements of a successful system, fairness and consistency, should have been satisfied. However, there are two other conditions, communication and involvement, which may have only been partially met. Communication needs to be in a way that is sensitive to individual feelings, but which fully explains how decisions have been reached. Partnership committees can be guaranteed to leak like sieves, but not always in a controlled manner, for example when the staff find out before the partners. The first part of the communication process should be at the appraisal meetings. For particular problems, some firms make full use of the senior partner to convey difficult news ('a word in your ear, old boy').

All of the partners need some input into the appraisal in a role other than as appraisee, that is there has to be an element of peer review; it is important to remember that this is a partnership, after all. The use of more junior partners on remuneration committees can assist and also dispel the belief that the meritocracy is really a lock-step in disguise or, even worse, a carve-up by the senior partners and a few of the firm's favourites. Other methods include every partner giving a merit rating to every other partner, and the results used to guide the final decision. As always, the choice will be determined by the culture and management style of the firm.

11.9 Meritocracy or lock-step

A great deal has been written in this chapter on the two principle means of profit share for medium and large firms of solicitors. Where the accountant is asked to advise on the need for a new system, or to modify an existing system, he needs to use his judgement based on a personal knowledge of the practice concerned, and discussions with the partners. There are no quick solutions to the problem, which is often why the accountant is asked to advise. The author does have strong views on the merits and de-merits of the two systems, but this tends to be a bias in favour of a means of sharing profit as regards individual firms rather than the systems themselves. For guidance, however, it is recommended that the accountant bears in mind the following comments on each.

Lock-step	Meritocracy
Divisive	Divisive
Not divisive	Not divisive
Basis of profit share clear	Basis of profit share can be unclear without proper communication
Money not seen as motivator	Money may be seen as the principle motivator
Peer pressure can be important	Peer pressure may be relatively unimportant
Does not require firm-wide strategic plan	Requires firm to have strategic plan
Requires little management input	Requires a lot of management input
Future problems may be stored up	A solution to many of those problems
Seen as old-fashioned	Seen as modern, American, slightly aggressive
Large firm	Medium firm
Favours teams	Favours individuals

It is interesting to note that some medium-sized firms view the lock-step as almost inevitible after a certain size, and accept that a meritocratic system could be abandoned when a critical mass has been reached.

11.9.1 A word about management

It is sometimes thought that because a firm has a lock-step, or because it does not have a meritocratic system of profit share there is little or no 'management' of the firm, or that what management there is is informal and unsophisticated. This is patently not the case, and there is no reason why the very large firms, simply because they have lock-step profit shares, should not have a fully rounded management structure. Indeed the large firms do have a comprehensive management process, strategy reviews, partner appraisals and all. Profit share is not the tail which wags the management dog.

Although a lock-step may require little management input, this is not the case for the firm as a whole and it is not a valid criticism to blame the inability of some law firms to develop solely on the lock-step.

As a final word on management under the two systems, it may be worth consider the following. Lawyers, by the nature of their work, and more so than accountants, tend to work first and foremost as individuals, rather than teams. Meritocracies, of whatever type, favour the individual performing to the best of his ability and out-performing his colleagues, and this militates against teamwork.

Lock-steps, on the other hand, do not favour individual performance so much as the performance of the firm as a whole; the development of a team-based ethos within a partnership may be best served by a lock-step. As a firm grows, and therefore the need for team-based work increases, the development of the practice is going to be better served by a lock-step than by a meritocracy. Rather than being a method of profit share destined for the bin, and quickly, the lock-step may have a long future as a tool of management.

11.10 Salaried or other classes of partner

Many firms have the position of salaried partner. Such a position is normally seen as probationary, with partners serving a fixed period of, say, two years before elevation to equity partner. It should be noted that for lock-steps, this has the effect of increasing the lock-step gap by the length of the probationary period.

There is a tremendous variation between law firms and their salaried partners and these variations do not reflect the size of the firm. First of all, some firms, including the very large, do not have salaried partners. Other variations are as follows:

(a) *Length of probationary period.* The most common is two years, but for some firms it is one year, in some it depends on performance and in others it is a permanent position.
(b) *Salaried partners as a percentage of total partners.* This can be as high as 45 per cent, and in general, the higher the percentage the more growth the firm is anticipating, or conversely the slower the firms's recent growth has been.
(c) *Method of remunerating salaried partners.* This can be at the level of an assistant solicitor, with a premium, fixed for the duration of the probationary period, increasing with merit through the period and with general pay increases in the firm, a percentage of first tranche profits either with or without a bonus.
(d) *Tax status.* Some firms have their salaried partners taxed under Schedule E, some under Schedule D. Some firms have two bands of salaried partner, the Schedule E and the Schedule D, each band representing progression up the firm.

The variation and lack of a common approach among firms begs the question whether such partners are really employees who are partners in waiting, with certain tangible and intangible benefits given to them while the partnership decides whether they really should be a partner. As an element in the overall profit sharing process, salaried partners can add further complication. In addition, once someone is called a partner, the move to equity partnership can be inexorable and probation becomes a misnomer. Further, the status of such partners can be uncertain. For many firms, appointing the first salaried partner is avoiding the issue of whether that person should be a partner. Thereafter, all partners go through the stage of salaried partner, regardless of how highly they are thought of. Where used, the position demands more consideration than it is normally given.

Some firms have more than one class of partner. These are often called As and Bs, or equity and associate, and the separation of the two classes is most obvious in the firm's profit share arrangements. For example, there may be equal numbers of each type of partner, but the As may receive 75 per cent of total profits, or of just the second tranche profits. What the differentiation should signify is an acceptance or understanding by the partnership that there is one group that runs the firm, through finding new work, to management, and another group providing support. What it sometimes indicates is a group of senior or founding partners who know that the firm cannot survive without new blood, but are unwilling to give up control in any circumstances. The latter is indefensible, but the former does have many merits.

Movement to the top class is possible but is by no means certain. Promotion only comes with seniority, management responsibility and proven client development and other skills over a number of years. Such firms are not partnerships in the normal understanding of the word, but they may provide a method of dealing with the conflict between partnership as ownership, and partnership as promotion.

Because of this rigorous approach to promotion at two different levels, the use of two distinct classes of partner may be the future route for many medium-sized partnerships.

11.11 Returns on capital and other forms of profit share

Partners normally have one or all of the following types of capital 'invested' in a firm:

(a) fixed capital in respect of the funding of the practice;
(b) fixed capital in respect of the funding of premises;
(c) current account;
(d) tax reserves; and
(e) premises.

As noted in Chapter 16 there is a distinction between the two types of fixed capital because some firms have two classes of partners: those who own a property, which is on the partnership balance sheet, the value of which is represented by capital accounts, and those who do not. Such arrangements are likely to arise after a merger. In addition, premises owned by certain partners may not appear on the balance sheet. The possible returns on these assets are considered below. On the other types of 'investment', the partnership generally has to decide first of all whether to pay, as a first charge on profits, notional interest and then on what.

11.11.1 Fixed capital

For firms where fixed capital between partners is in the same proportion as profit share, the issue need not arise. This will generally be the case with equalities and lock-steps; however, as can be seen in Chapter 14, in a number of meritocracies and hybrids this is not necessarily the case, for example where fixed capital is set in the proportion of only one tranche, say the meritocratic tranche of profit share, or the lock-step tranche; partners with higher amounts of fixed capital relative to their overall profit share may feel they are subsidising other partners. Further, a number of firms, including lock-steps, have generous rules regarding the capital contributions of junior partners, allowing a build up over a period of time. In this case there is a subsidy from the senior partners to the junior partners.

For these reasons a large number of firms pay interest on fixed capital. The interest rate used is often based on the rate paid on practice loans, allowing payments to cover the amounts paid by individual partners to the bank where they have funded their fixed capital through borrowing.

11.11.2 Current account

The current account will comprise non-fixed capital and undrawn profits. Some partners choose to leave large amounts of their own money within a firm, either when their fixed capital requirement has been reduced due to an increase in partners, or because they chose not to withdraw their profits. Why this is done is often a mystery, particularly if the firm does not need the money, and is making a lower return on the investment of excess cash than might be paid out in interest, and this can cause complaints. However, where a firm has a policy regarding its funding this should not arise.

It is invariably the case that the partner has a current account because the firm has a policy of making fixed monthly draws less than the monthly profits, and a condition that special draws of undistributed profits are only made when the firm has the cash to pay them or the firm has a long term rump of current account balance which should be considered as fixed capital.

Firms generally do not pay interest on undrawn profits. But, an effective subsidy between certain partners will exist because of the disparity between capital and profit share ratios; however, there will also be a mis-match on current accounts because the monthly draws may not be in proportion to profit or capital or both. This will be because of the partners' individual tax circumstances and the firm's drawings policies, for example with all partners receiving the same fixed monthly draw, or due to the treatment of motor expenses. Many firms will try to put current accounts back into profit sharing ratio on a regular basis, say when special draws are made. However, the situation needs constant monitoring because it can be a source of conflict.

Some firms will pay interest where profits remain undrawn for more than a certain period of time after a year end, say 12 months, or where current accounts are deemed to represent fixed capital.

11.11.3 Tax reserves

Tax reserves are not as important in the funding of partnerships as formerly and this trend will continue. However, some partners consider them to be personal property and, because they will never be in profit sharing or capital ratios for all of the reasons affecting current accounts and more, it is known for interest to be paid on them. The ownership of tax reserves is an interesting issue, but paying interest on them can be more trouble than it is worth, given the difficulty of calculating them accurately from one month to the next.

11.11.4 Non-distinguishable accounts

Some smaller practices do not distinguish between capital and current accounts and tax reserves. In these firms the issue of interest is not generally a problem. However, if it does become so an effort needs to be made to distinguish the accounts.

11.11.5 Expenses

Expenses can give rise to serious disagreements within firms. Firms often provide partners with fully expensed cars, payment of telephone bills and other domestic expenses, entertaining and travel allowances and various papers and publications. Whether all of these, and the amount spent on them, are considered by all partners to be fully justifiable expenses of the partnership is a moot point. The Inland Revenue often do not and will seek to come to an arrangement regarding the allowability of certain partners' expenses.

There are two points to be made here. First, such expenses are often little more than a profit share and should be netted off an individual's profits. This is increasingly the case with motor vehicles and motor expenses. Second, there needs to be personal responsibility if not central control over such payments to avoid the problems of individual partners deemed to be 'over-remunerating' themselves.

11.11.6 Premises

Many firms operate from premises owned by some of the partners, or all of the partners in different proportions. The reasons this can happen are considered in Chapter 16, which recommends that professional firms avoid the temptation of dabbling in property investment for a number of reasons. However, where this investment has taken place there can be a number of issues for profit sharing.

First of all, any rent paid should be notional only, and treated as an adjustment to profit share. Thus, the property is effectively rent-free. This is important for tax reasons. Second, there is the issue of how the notional rent is calculated. Market rent is a good place to start, but should a 25 year institutional lease with the normal conditions, a five year lease, or a licence be imposed? This becomes very important where market rents are experiencing sharp increases or falls. For example, say a partnership enters into a notional five year lease on a property owned by some of the partners at a market rent. Five years later, with the 'lease' up for renewal, market rents have plummeted. A market rent paid at this point may give the property investment partners personal difficulties. Or, say the partnership can obtain premises elsewhere with a large reverse premium. The property investment partners could be left with an unlet property.

Where the property is on the partnership balance sheet, but not owned by all of the partners, an alternative treatment may be to pay notional interest on the net book value of the property according to the accounts. In these circumstances, whatever payment is made, it is important that there is not also a payment of notional interest in respect of the element of the capital accounts which fund the property. If this were the case, the partnership would be suffering a double-charge, and certain partners benefitting from an extra share of profits.

11.12 Changes in profit levels

Steadily rising profits are easy to deal with. Problems occur when a firm experiences steeply rising then falling profits, 'losses' and static profits. Many of the issues raised here have implications for drawings policies, and they are all reconsidered in that context in Chapter 12.

11.12.1 Steadily rising profits

A gently rising trend of profits, at an annual rate above that of the growth of the firm and inflation should keep most partners happy. The senior partners are happy to give up profit share points, knowing that they will be more than replaced by increasing profit shares; the junior partners can see a steady rise in future earnings; and if the past provides any keys to the future, the rise would seem to be sustainable. There is also an implication that everyone is making the required contribution to the firm. (Presumably there are firms like this, but the author has not met any!)

11.12.2 Steeply rising then falling profits

The first problem arises from a combination of the fact that steeply rising profits are rarely sustainable, and a firm-wide blindness in appreciating this. The second problem arises when profits do start to fall and some of the profit-share arrangements of the good years start to come under scrutiny.

During very good years, especially those which are market-wide, many organisations believe that success is due to some particular characteristic of the business and firms of solicitors are no exception to this. Where a retail chain may put rapid growth down to the success of their particular products and increase the number of branches to meet the 'demand', professional practices will believe it is due to the quality of their advice, and so recruit more staff and promote more partners. Additionally, where profits are spiralling upwards, new partners may cost very little to the existing partners. Another trend, which only takes place where there is some element of merit rating in the profit share, is for certain individual partners to be identified with the growth, and to ask for, and then receive an increasing slice of a larger pie. These individuals may have certain skills, for example work in a particular field of law, such as property.

Another characteristic of firms is to increase expenditure on office refurbishment, motor vehicles and other items which do not directly cause an increase in business. Although margins may be reduced in percentage terms because there is always an increase in actual profits, the reduction in profitability is not considered serious.

If margins are falling, profits will start to dip as fees level out and the firm may be faced with a profit level equivalent to that of five years before, although it now has many more partners, some of whom have very large profit shares. At this point the firm will be calling in consultants to carry out a strategic review, one of the results of which will be a revised meritocratic profit share scheme.

All partnerships will have individuals who will be financially embarrassed by falling profits, due perhaps to taking on large mortgages in the good years.

To avoid a possible insolvency the matter should be dealt with by way of drawings or a reduction in capital rather than trying to maintain a level of profits for that individual at a manifestly unfairly high level.

11.12.3 'Losses'

There are two types of loss which a partnership can suffer. The first is the real loss where income exceeds expenditure before any appropriations by the partners. The second is where, in a meritocracy or hybrid, there is a profit before appropriations, but a loss before the final tranche of profit share is reached.

The only issue from a profit sharing perspective regarding the first type of loss is whether the partners should share the loss in the same proportions as they have previously shared the profits, or whether the loss should be shared equally. It is difficult to argue the latter successfully. There are a number of issues arising from the second loss.

If the firm has a two tranche system, and the first tranche profit exceeds the overall profit, is the first tranche shared in the normal way and then the 'loss' contributed to in the second tranche profit sharing ratios, or contributed to in another ratio, say equally? Alternatively, is the total profit shared in the first tranche profit sharing ratios?

If the first tranche effectively represents a salary, is there a stop on the individual profits of any one partner falling below this level, until profits are such that all partners are at this level, at which point all profit shares start to fall, say equally, or in first tranche, or second tranche ratios? Are the profit sharing arrangements scrapped and the distributions looked at on a hardship basis, or should this be dealt with through drawings?

Many firms are facing severe internal problems because of this issue. Although some ignore the problem and others investigate very complicated arrangements for dealing with it, there does seem to be general support for the idea of a minimum level of profit share per partner, equivalent to a salary.

11.12.4 Static profits

Static profits can create a problem for two principle reasons. First, they act as a deterrent to appointing new partners, because this would lead to an effective reduction in the existing partners' profit share, and the introduction of new blood may be the solution to the problem of static profits. Second, there will be some individual partners who consider that their contribution to the firm has been to make the practice grow, and therefore other partners must be helping in the firm's decline! Any profit sharing system is likely to be put under strain in these circumstances.

However, some practices are perfectly content with a position of no growth; these tend to be the small, say two partner firms, long established and sharing profits equally. By virtue of their culture, static profits are not a problem.

11.13 Exceptional profits and losses

Exceptional profits and losses, and how they are borne by individual partners can be the source of severe argument within a partnership. This arises because of the following reasons:

(a) the partners within a partnership can receive different profit shares from year to year;
(b) partners enter the partnership, and partners retire;
(c) partnership accounts may not and probably will not, comply with generally accepted accounting principles and many firms, for example, exclude certain assets from the balance sheet (see generally Chapter 9); and
(d) the nature of exceptional items is that they will not be recurring from year to year.

It would be most unusual for a law firm to have a formal mechanism for dealing with exceptional items; however, many firms take the robust attitude that profits and losses fall where they fall and that benefiting in or bearing an exceptional item is one of the facts of partnership life. Other firms recognise the difficulties that such an approach may cause, and will, in certain circumstances, try to apportion the exceptional item in a way which does not necessarily follow the profit share for the year when the item occurs. In general the former tend to be lock-steps and the latter meritocracies.

There are two types of exceptional item, capital and revenue.

11.13.1 Capital

Many law firms have over the past decade made substantial profits from the sale of their premises (normally a lease). At the current time, those firms fortunate enough to have leases coming to an end are benefitting from the inducements being offered to enter new premises, in some cases in the form of cash payments. Conversely, some firms have not been so lucky and are locked into paying rents, sometimes on unlet property, in excess of market rents.

When a company makes a substantial capital gain on the sale of a lease, it is normal for the partners to divide up the profit in the profit sharing ratios in the period when the gain falls. Law firms rarely, if ever, revalue their assets, and the lease may not even be on the balance sheet. The costs incurred in acquiring the lease and refurbishing the property may have been written off many years before and therefore the profit to be distributed may be the whole of the capital sum received.

Partnerships anticipating such a gain may, first of all, be disinclined to appoint new partners or to change profit sharing ratios in the years approaching the gain. Second, senior partners may delay their retirement until after the gain has been realised. Where the gain is not anticipated, senior partners who retire just before the sale will feel aggrieved, and the senior partners who stay may regret the introduction of new partners who benefit, by nothing more than luck, in the profits.

A mechanism is needed to take account of these problems, if there are likely to be difficulties and, as always, this will depend on the culture of the firm. However, it is as well for the firm, or its professional accountants, to keep in mind how the partners will react to the windfall, and plan in advance. It may be that no problems arise. However, it may also be necessary to make provision for a retiring partner so that he can benefit from the gain and not attempt to delay an impending retirement, or consider forcing a dissolution. With regard to potential partners, their profit share may need to specifically exclude the profits on sales in the year following appointment. Alternatively, the firm could adopt a very sophisticated arrangement, such as looking at the actual profits of the partners in all of the years that the lease was occupied, and using this as a basis to determine how the proceeds are to be split.

Losses on premises, whether actual, or due to, say, a large reverse premium or dilapidations provision, give rise to the problem in reverse. The biggest problem is likely to come from the junior partners who will object to paying for the firm not having made a dilapidations provision over the years.

The issue of inducements to enter new premises is currently exercising the collective partnership mind of many law firms. A firm is paid a substantial reverse premium, but at the same time has to incur substantial on-going costs on the new premises in fitting out and investing in new technology. The partners at the time of the move get the benefit of the premium, but the on-going partnership bears the new premises costs. An element of matching is important in this situation and, indeed, a number of law firms have preferred to take the inducement in the form of a contribution to moving and fitting out. There are no firm rules to dealing with inducements because the packages offered vary so much.

11.13.2 Revenue

The issues are broadly similar to those regarding exceptional capital items, but the instances are extremely varied. The cause is generally a failure to apply proper accounting policies, and in nearly all firms there is unlikely to be any adjustment to profit share. As an example, in a number of firms, there is no proper review of bad debts or work in progress undertaken at the year end. It is only when, for example, a client becomes insolvent that write offs are made in the account. This can obviously be unfair on new partners, although against that it may be argued that because new partners do not physically buy into partnerships any more there is little actual loss to them.

An issue which may face an increasing number of firms in the future is the professional indemnity claim. Firms may be exposed where they have a high excess (following the recent changes to the Solicitors Indemnity Fund's cover, see Chapter 2), where the claim exceeds their insured limit, where part of their cover falls out due to default, or where an insurance company states that the terms of the cover have been broken.

The loss on the claim will almost certainly arise in a period different from that in which the act giving rise to the claim occurred, in some cases many years later. Further, the loss may need to include the damages, the costs of any court action, and the internal costs of handling the claim. This last item, representing the loss in billable hours, may be substantial, and may build up over a number of years. In some instances this may be the only cost. One way in which firms can deal with this issue is by making provisions for such claims. However, law firms only rarely do this, and it is very uncommon to make a general provision for the costs of internal investigations arising out of each accounting period's work.

There are many other types of exceptional item, not all losses, including pension fund holidays and redundancy costs. Firms are unlikely to change profit sharing arrangements to deal with them in advance, but they may become an issue, and in the first instance firms should be advised to apply generally accepted accounting principles so that at least they are correctly treated in the accounts.

Chapter 12 – Drawings

12.1 Introduction

The issue of drawings is not as emotive or as potentially explosive as a firm's profit share. However, with many firms of solicitors facing the problems noted in Chapter 1 it is increasingly likely that the issue of drawings policy will be a regularly debated topic at partners' meetings. Although culture plays an important part in setting the drawings policy the financial viability of the firm is the key issue. There are two rules in drawings which must always be followed:

(1) the firm should never pay out in drawings to the partners as a whole what it has not got in the bank or in previously agreed facilities; and
(2) subject to the above, no individual partner should, because of his own financial circumstances, be personally financially embarrassed.

Rule (1) works on the basis that the firm has assessed what the levels of partners' capital and external borrowing should be, and therefore appreciates that some firms will have a relatively high level of borrowing and some firms no borrowing at all. What the rule means in effect is that a practice should never borrow money solely for the purpose of paying out to the partners profits not represented in the form of cash. If there is a problem with the capitalization of the firm, that is a different matter, but a partnership regularly borrowing for cash draws will be in financial trouble.

Rule (2) tries to avoid the situation of a partner becoming bankrupt or entering into a voluntary arrangement because of his own bad luck or financial mismanagement. Although partnership agreements may include provisions to exclude such individuals, presumably they were made partner for their qualities as a lawyer, which do not necessarily include financial prudence or good fortune. It may seem hard luck on the rest of the partners but if an individual is of worth to the firm, then the partnership as a whole is better off making him an advance of future profits rather than letting him suffer worry, stress and possibly worse, all of which will affect his performance. This is not to say that the debts of individuals who over-extend themselves due to business failure, gambling, or losses at Lloyds should be underwritten by the rest of the partnership. For any partner, no matter how successful within the firm, there will be an amount of liability which the rest of the partners will not support.

12.2 Small practices

Many small firms of solicitors will abide by rule (1) to the letter. Such firms will prepare all of their financial information on a cash basis, and therefore will not recognise a profit on work done until that work is billed, and the cash received. At the end of every month, or every ten days or every week, the partners will draw out surplus cash in profit sharing ratio.

The key is determining what is meant by surplus cash, and this of course depends on the overall capital and working capital requirements of the firm. Therefore, it would be expected that provision is being made for the expenses of the firm up until the next drawings day which will not be paid from further receipts, as well as ensuring that the firm will be able to pay the large regular cash outflows of VAT and rent. Therefore, even for the smallest practices it is necessary to prepare a future cash flow.

Some large firms will base their drawings policy on a variation of this basis. For example, it is possible to relate regular drawings to the amount of cash collected in the previous month, or the billings where there is a good history of discernable debtor days. Such practices will often have maximum and minimum levels of drawings where the basis is as described above, thereby having an element of a fixed amount in the monthly draw.

12.3 Fixed drawings

Most practices above three partners, and many below this number, have a policy of making monthly fixed payments of drawings to the partners. There are a number of reasons for this:

(a) individual partners should be entitled to expect a regular payment because it helps them budget for their own personal finances;
(b) by setting the fixed draw at an appropriate level, good months for cash will subsidise poor months and avoid the difficulty of some months when the firm is unable to make any drawings payments at all which is a problem for partners with fixed monthly outgoings;
(c) the monthly draw is treated as another cash outgoing of the firm, not the balancing figure on the cashflow, and encourages the partnership to take a more scientific look at its working capital requirements;
(d) for individuals who have risen from solicitor to partner, it avoids a potentially severe shock in their method of remuneration;
(e) by setting the overall fixed draw based on a certain level of performance, the distribution of undrawn profits becomes the indicator for the level of the performance of the firm.

There are two different methods of calculating the monthly fixed draw. The first is to make the same monthly payment to all partners regardless of profit share. This is quite a common procedure with lock-steps, especially in the larger partnerships. The monthly draw will be based on the monthly post tax earnings of an assistant solicitor, to which there maybe added a premium. The amount of the premium varies between the small, which reflects the difference in status between the employees and the partner, and the large to reflect the benefits and risks of ownership.

Such systems seem to work very well emphasising the aspects of equality in partnerships. They also act as a guarantee when profits are falling that a newly appointed partner will not receive a smaller monthly take than he received as an employee, so long as the fall is not too pronounced. One obvious issue that arises is that if the partners drawing the highest profit shares draw the same fixed monthly amounts as the junior partners, current accounts will not be in profit sharing ratio and there will be a subsidy from the senior to the junior partners. This can be resolved by paying interest on undrawn current accounts, but this is uncommon. However, some large partnerships do not see this as an issue, more a demonstration that for a practice to survive, the senior partners will be subsidising the junior partners in a number of ways. It therefore reflects the partnership ethos. Other firms are happy to accept the situation as long as the current accounts are put back into profit sharing ratio by means of special draws (see below).

The second method is to take the budgeted profit for the forthcoming year, calculate each individual's profit share, deduct a notional tax charge and a contingency, divide each amount by 12 and distribute this to each partner on a monthly basis. Thus, individual partners will receive their fixed drawings in profit sharing ratio and, tax considerations aside, current accounts will remain in profit sharing ratio as well.

There is a surprising variation between law firms as to the size of the contingency deduction, ranging from 15 to 60 per cent of budgeted profit. Some firms will also adjust the fixed monthly drawings as a result of any changes in the budget during the year, although this should only be adopted if profits start to fall below budget; increases in profits can be dealt with by way of special draws. This type of arrangement is used by both lock-steps and meritocracies.

A third method, which is only available to certain meritocracies, is to pay out the first tranche profit share as the fixed monthly drawing. In such practices current accounts may never be in overall profit sharing ratio, and therefore any imbalance between current accounts may not be apparent.

The interesting point about the second method is that it is based on budgeted profit rather than budgeted cash. This means that, where the contingency is not that large, the practice needs to make sure that its management of working capital is both efficient and successful. For firms where cash can be a problem, fixed monthly drawings should be based on cashflow, or the contingency deduction increased. However, this is not as reckless as those firms which used to increase their fixed drawings every year by some percentage, and did not bother to budget the profit; this practice, with the consequent dangers of overdrawing, is not as prevalent as in recent years. The first method can also suffer from the same problem, but being based on an overhead, i.e. salary, this is less likely depending on the amount of the premium.

All three of these methods can be subject to variations, for example an addition based on the amount of cash collections the previous month, thereby encouraging good work in progress and debtor management throughout the year, and not just in advance of the date of special draws. However, the most common variation is due to taxation.

12.4 Taxation and fixed monthly draws

One approach to taxing fixed monthly draws is to assume a flat rate for all partners of, say, 40 per cent. Additionally, a standard personal allowance can be taken into account. Depending on how sophisticated the firm wishes to be it can also include in the tax charge national insurance, pension payments (either the maximum required by the partnership deed, or the maximum possibly payable where relief is available) and actual allowances, for example interest relief on practice loans. It is also possible to take into account all of the personal taxation affairs of the partners such as losses in other trades, such as farming and Lloyds.

With the prior year basis of assessment sophistication can lead to a nonsense because one may be basing these deductions on, say, current allowances or rates which may not be applicable or on estimates or intentions which may not be appropriate when the profits are finally assessed. Taxation should therefore be kept as simple and as trouble-free as possible.

12.5 Changes in fixed monthly draws

A problem facing a large number of solicitors' practices is whether to cut the fixed monthly draw, either at the start of the year, as the budgeted profit is lower than the previous year or, because of an under-performance against budget, during the year.

A reduction in fixed drawings is thought to be a critical event in a partnership's affairs, similar to a company reducing or passing the dividend. It is a direct reflection of the health of the partnership and can only indicate further potential problems ahead. Another issue is that because so many partners treat the fixed monthly draw as a salary, their personal lives are geared to the receipt, until at least retirement, of at least that salary. Mortgages, maintenance payments and school fees may all have been based around the figure of the (most recent) monthly draw. In these circumstances everything will be done (delaying expenditure, increasing borrowings) to maintain the monthly draw at the same level.

There is an entirely contrary view, that is held by some senior partners, that the monthly draw should be cut every seven to ten years. This reflects economic cycles and reminds partners that they are proprietors and not employees. It is also true that where there is a general lack of performance by the firm, there should be no expectation of maintained drawings, and a cut may provide a strong incentive to try more or work harder. However, it is a curious fact that in partnerships that espouse reward for performance, profit share rather than advanced or delayed cash is the tool of motivation.

The problem of the drawings cut is more likely to be faced by those firms that have traditionally based their fixed drawings on the budgeted profit and maintained the same level of contingency deduction. Some firms during the 1980s recognised that the high levels of budgeted profit were unsustainable and therefore sought to restrict the amount of the fixed draws by increasing the contingency reduction. The primary effect is that partners do not expect, and therefore do not gear their personal lifestyles up to, the highest possible level of fixed draw. By distributing the excess profit in special draws, it emphasises the exceptional nature of these profits.

In some circumstances, no matter how prudent the firm has been in setting its drawings levels, a cut is inevitable due to sharply reduced profits. Here, the partnership should face reality and make the cut, but keep in mind the personal financial circumstances of the junior and less well-off partners in the practice.

12.6 Special draws

Undistributed profits represent part of the capital of the firm. They should not represent the core funding required by the firm, but inevitably they will fund a part of working capital. First of all they will fund that part of the profit of any one year, represented by the increase in debtors and work in progress, that has not been converted into cash; second, they will fund the future working capital needs of the firm due to expansion. It therefore follows that, as a firm grows, there will always be a requirement to retain a certain level of profits on current account, but as new profits accrue, previous profits can be distributed.

There is an extremely wide variation in the methods adopted by firms to make special draws. A majority of firms will base the draws on available cash, and will delay a draw if necessary, but others will have fixed dates for making distributions which are immovable. Some firms make special draws during the year on account of current year profits, based on properly prepared accounts at the quarter or half year stages. For most firms, determining the amount of special draws only starts after the year end, when the first draft accounts are available, when the accountants sign off the accounts, or when the accounts are approved by the partners at their annual meeting. For some firms these dates may be fixed in the calender and draws will always be made at this time. For others the special draw days will be the quarter days following the year end.

In all of these cases there may be no exact science to determining the timing or the amount of the special draw, other than a feeling that there is sufficient cash within the firm. It does however mean that a number of firms are under-drawing or are under-capitalised. Relating the dates of special draws to the firm's cash collection targets or to the expected periods of debtor and work in progress lock-up may be a better method, even though it may lead to the same result. First of all it relates drawings to cash collections, and secondly, it is easier to relate special draws to the overall financial management of the firm because cash is matched with cash.

When special draws are made, there is usually an attempt by the partnership to bring the individual partner's current accounts back into profit sharing ratio.

12.7 Tax draws

It was noted above that in attempting to set the tax charge for fixed monthly draws, all sorts of complications can arise. These complications are compounded when a practice attempts to release to partners those tax reserves no longer needed.

There are, however, two tax events which are, or should be, relatively straight forward to deal with, being the payment of pension contributions, and BES (or similar) payments. Both types of payment have the immediate effect of mitigating tax liabilities in respect of the tax year in which payment is made and certain prior years. Therefore, when a partner makes such a payment, to the extent that the firm maintains a tax reserve in respect of the tax liability reduced, the partner should be able to reclaim that tax from the partnership.

However, there is a problem with this because, depending on what assets the tax reserves fund, the partnership may not have the available cash. Additionally, because such payments are normally made at the same time of the year, that is towards the end of the tax year, the partnership may suffer some difficulty. The predictability of both the upper limit and the timing of these payments should make easy for the partnership to budget for their incidence and amount. In fact, in the case of pension contributions, some partnerships will pay up to the maximum amount on behalf of the partners, thereby avoiding the need to make a tax draw in respect of the amount paid.

There will of course always be problems if individual partners make payments at irregular times during the year, or make payments without telling the administration of the partnership. Such complications can be viewed in the overall context of the changing liability of individual partners to tax.

Throughout the year, the estimated liabilities in respect of taxation for previous years may be changed. Because a partnership may have investment as well as trading income, as new rates of tax or personal allowances become known, as the composition of the partnership changes, so the liability of the partnership, and individual partners will also change. Further, the partnership may provide tax on a cessation basis, and following the expiry of the time limit, yet again the liability will change. Each change will affect an individual's liability and thus the amount of tax reserved from his overall profit share. A change in an individual's own circumstances may also affect this liability. To the extent that tax reserves are no longer required they should be available for drawing (or at least released to current account).

The number of possible changes to an individual's liability, together with the sad fact that many partners are not as timely at providing financial information as they could be, means that one could spend every day of the year calculating the tax reserve releases for some large partnerships.

Some firms do require their accountants to produce on, say, a quarterly basis revised computations of tax liability by partner and by open year. At the very least the accountant should be expected to produce two computations a year, one on production of the accounts, and one prior to the end of the tax year to determine pension and other payments. Where tax is provided on a cessation basis, a calculation of the amount of the release on the expiry of the time limit should also be prepared. It is also reasonable to try and tie the production of revised computations to the dates of special draws, if there is not to be a special draw in respect of a tax reserve release. As individual drawings' levels fall or remain static, there is an increasing desire by partners to have their tax reserves revised and distributed on a regular basis.

12.8 The consequences of over-drawing and under-drawing

A number of firms of solicitors are currently experiencing the consequences of over-drawing. First of all, the working capital of the firm becomes depleted, and the firm finds itself consistently exceeding its optimal level of borrowing. Next, once the undrawn profits run out, the firm starts to draw on its fixed capital, which eventually, and perhaps quickly, becomes seriously depleted. The firm therefore finds itself without the capital to finance the business and has to resort increasingly to the bank for more and more borrowing. It is extremely difficult for firms to recover from this situation. At some time the increasingly hard decision of progressively severe drawings cuts needs to be taken. The level of debt finance may be making the firm unprofitable. Further, if a fall in business is the root cause of the firm's problems then it will not have the necessary working capital to deal with any expansion as business increases. If by this time the firm has not had a change in its fortunes, it will split, merge (that is, get taken over), or face some sort of arrangement with creditors.

As far as individual partners are concerned, over-drawing leads to an unreasonable expectation of future earnings, such expectation being translated into a need when personal commitments such as mortgages reflect a high level of earnings.

The problems of under-drawing may, given the above, be seen as a benefit. However, it may mean that the firm's resources are not being used in the most efficient manner. It also means that individual partners may be unnecessarily penalising themselves by keeping cash locked up in the practice. However, the most serious consequence is that, with a lot of undrawn profits, some of which may be represented by large amounts of surplus cash, the practice may become very inefficient at billing its time and collecting its debts. The partnership may fool itself into thinking that it is secure because of these assets. The problem in a recession is that clients go into insolvency or refuse to pay until the last possible moment sometimes because the firm has had a history of not chasing for its debts; the full recovery of time on late billing is also put in doubt. It would seem that if a practice wants to retain its profits and its cash, it should take the view that there is never enough of the latter.

For the individual partner, under-drawing can mean severe financial hardship or a lower standard of living. It is often the case that such circumstances have a direct effect on personal performance.

Chapter 13 – Methods of providing for taxation in solicitors accounts

13.1 Introduction

This chapter looks at the various methods for providing for taxation on the trading income of a solicitor's firm. This is primarily a consideration of the 'prior year' basis of assessment. By far the most important part of this chapter is an investigation into exactly what firms are trying to achieve with their provisioning policy, and the effect this has on the financial management of the practice. The first budget of 1993 contained details as to the way in which the basis of taxation of the self-employed will change from prior year to actual. This will continue the decline in the importance of tax reserves as a method of financing, as noted in Chapter 14.

13.2 Provisioning methods under the prior year basis

For an established partnership, the profits are currently assessed to tax on a prior year basis. This means that if the year end of the practice is between, say, 6 April 1990 and 31 December 1990, the profits arising in that year are assessed to tax as part of the 1991/1992 tax year, tax being payable on 1 January and 1 July 1992. If the year end is between 1 January 1990 and 5 April 1990, the tax year of assessment is 1990/1991. Therefore, by choice of the year end a firm gains a cash flow advantage in the date of payment of tax on its profits, and to maximise this advantage, most firms have a year end of 30 April, or even earlier than this, say 10 April. Some firms have a 30 June year end, and occasionally firms have a 30 September year end.

Because of the prior year basis, firms at any year end will have earned profits on which no tax may be payable for nearly two years. If the firm continues, profits at least remain static, and tax rates do not increase, then the firm may consider that it is being over-prudent in providing for tax so far in advance. In any case, the firm does not know what that tax bill will be because it will be affected by the tax regime and by the personal circumstances of individual partners in the future. The only certainty it has is the rate of tax, levels of personal allowances etc. in the current period. However, there is an understandable reluctance to assume that all future tax bills can be met out of future tax flow. Further, the composition of the firm may change and a partner who retires in respect of whom no amounts of tax on profits in his final years as a partner have been deducted, may leave the remaining partners with the liability for the tax on his profits, it being the joint liability of the firm as it is assessed on the firm and not the individual partners.

There are no statutory requirements for the ways in which a law firm provides for tax and consequently there are many methods:

(a) no provision;
(b) minimum provision;
(c) maximum provision;
(d) partial liability methods;
(e) providing for fiscal and financial year end gap; and
(f) discontinuance method.

13.2.1 No provision

This method involves no provision at all, and all profits capable of distribution are paid out to individual partners. Tax is paid out of cashflow, usually by a reduction of individual partners' drawings in the month when the tax is paid. This is a common approach for two and three partner firms, but occasionally a larger firm will use it. As a method of budgeting for tax it can be risky as the firm and each of the partners are gambling that future cash flow can generate sufficient funds for the tax payments and that each partner will be prudent enough to put some of his drawings aside if profits and cash flow start to dip. There is therefore a reliance on one's fellow partners which is not capable of control through any mechanism within the partnership. While not recommended in any economic climate, it is particularly dangerous with falling fees, high interest rates etc.

The remaining methods can be illustrated using the following tax profile:

Year end	*Assessment for*	*Estimated liability*
		£
30 April 1990	1991/92	500,000
30 April 1991	1992/93	600,000
30 April 1992	1993/94	700,000
30 April 1993	1994/95	800,000

13.2.2 Minimum provision

The minimum provision makes a provision for the next instalment of tax only. Therefore at 30 April 1993 the next instalment due is in respect of the 1992/93 tax year, that is half of the £600,000 liability due on 1 July 1993, the first instalment having been paid on 1 January 1993. The logic of this basis is that, if profits remain at least static, then by the time the first unprovided instalment is due, that is on 1 January 1994, the firm will have earned a further eight months of profits and collected a further eight months of billings, and will have sufficient funds to make that payment if, over that eight month period, it sets aside amounts to meet the next liability. Therefore, the firm is setting a policy of providing tax liabilities out of the cash flow arising in the period immediately prior to that liability becoming due.

Many firms feel comfortable with this method, because it ignores those liabilities to tax which, if the firm continues to show at leat some profit growth, will never fall due. It does of course require a semblance of a cash flow forecasting system, and drawings will require an adjustment if cash becomes tight.

13.2.3 Maximum provision

The maximum provision makes a full provision for all tax on profits up to the year end. Therefore, at 30 April 1993 the tax provision will be calculated as follows:

Year of assessment	*Estimated liability*
	£
1992/93 (year ended 30 April 1991)	600,000
1993/94 (year ended 30 April 1992)	700,000
1994/95 (year ended 30 April 1993)	800,000
Sub-total	2,100,000
Less 1st instalment 1992/93 paid 1 January 1993	300,000
Total provision at 30 April 1993	1,800,000

This is the most conservative basis to use and ensures that the partnership will always have sufficient reserves for any liability unless tax rates increase significantly or there is marked change in the composition of the partnership.

13.2.4 Partial liability methods

There is a marked difference between the actual amounts provided at 30 April under the two methods. A number of firms try to reach a compromise by calculating the maximum liability but only providing for, say, the next three instalments of tax. As at 30 April 1990 the future estimated instalments are as follows:

Instalment date	*Estimated liability*
	£
1 July 1993	300,000
1 January 1994	350,000
1 July 1994	350,000
1 January 1995	400,000
1 July 1995	400,000

Providing for the next three instalments would leave the whole of the 1994/95 liability unprovided. The rationale behind this method of provisioning is again based on the assumption that future profits and cash flow will be sufficient to generate the means of paying a liability that will not become due for nearly two years. Of course, it is also possible to provide for the next two or four instalments.

13.2.5 Providing for the fiscal year end and financial year end gap

As well as providing for some of the future instalments, some firms will make an attempt to provide for the tax liability for the period between the end of the fiscal year and the financial year. Therefore, for a practice with a 30 April year end, this would be on the liability for the period 6 April to 30 April, or more commonly, for one month of the next year's liability. The provisions could therefore be calculated for 30 April 1993 as shown at top of the next page.

If the year end is 30 June then the tax on the gap will be higher. In this circumstance the actual charge to taxation for the year ended 30 April 1993 will be eleven twelfths of the 1992/93 liability and one twelfth of the 1993/94 liability. This is not a charge on the profits for the period 6 April 1993 to 30 April 1993.

Year of assessment	*Minimum provision*
	£
1992/93	300,000
1993/94	not provided
1994/95	not provided
Tax for period 6 April 1993 to 30 April 1993, say $\frac{1}{12}$ of 1993/94 liability of £700,000	58,000
Total provision	358,000

13.2.6 Discontinuance method

This method provides tax on the basis that there is a discontinuation of the partnership at the balance sheet date, with the final years of the partnership being assessed on an actual basis.

In the above example, the provision at 30 April 1993, with a discontinuation at that date would be:

Year of assessment	*Profits assessed–actual basis*	*Tax liability–actual basis*
		£
1991/92	period 6 April 1991 to 30 April 1992, therefore $\frac{1}{12}$ of £600,000 plus $\frac{11}{12}$ of £700,000	642,000
1992/93	period 6 April 1992 to 30 April 1993, therefore $\frac{1}{12}$ of £700,000 plus $\frac{11}{12}$ of £800,000	791,000
1993/94	period 6 April 1993 to 30 April 1993, therefore $\frac{1}{12}$ of £800,000	67,000
Sub-total		1,550,000
Less tax paid 1 January as estimated on prior year basis	$\frac{1}{2}$ of tax for 1992/93 year on prior year basis	300,000
Total liability		1,250,000

13.2.7 Use of each of the methods

All of the above methods have their advocates, and the use of each is widespread among firms of solicitors. However, the two most popular appear to be the discontinuance and the next three instalments methods (partial liability method). What is surprising is the degree of confusion by some firms regarding the method employed, the reasons for that method, and what it is they are trying to achieve.

First of all, there are a number of different names for the above methods, and sometimes these names are interchangeable with, for example the next three instalments basis being known as a full continuation basis! Second, it is apparent that some firms do not know what method they adopt to provide tax, this being left to the accountants. This seems to be because of a widespread belief that tax provisioning is extremely complicated. This obviously has important implications for firms in what they are trying to achieve with their tax provisions.

It is important for the accountant to explain to his client not just what method is being used, but also the range of options. This theme is developed later on in this chapter.

13.2.8 Charge to the firm

The charge to the firm for tax for the year ended 30 April 1993 under each of the above methods will be as follows:

	Minimum	*Minimum plus one month*	*Next three instalments*	*Maximum*	*Discontinuance*
Provision at 30 April 1992	250,000	300,000	850,000	1,550,000	1,092,000
Paid in year to 30 April 1993	550,000	550,000	550,000	550,000	550,000
Provision at 30 April 1993	300,000	358,000	1,000,000	1,800,000	1,250,000
Actual tax charge for 30 April 1993	600,000	608,000	700,000	800,000	708,000

Therefore, the charge tax for the year ended 30 April 1993 is based on the following:

(a) *minimum provision* on profits for year ended 30 April 1991;
(b) *minimum provision plus one month* on profits for fiscal year 1992/93, less one month, plus one month of fiscal year 1993/94;
(c) *next three instalments* on profits for year ended 30 April 1992;
(d) *maximum provision* on profits for year ended 30 April 1993;
(e) *discontinuance* on profits for fiscal year 1993/94 less one month, plus one month of fiscal year 1994/95.

13.3 Charge to the partners and difficulties with the methods

Regardless of how the firm chooses to provide for tax, individual partners are assessed to tax in each fiscal year on the profits for that fiscal year on a preceding year basis, but according to the profit sharing ratio on a current year basis. Thus, for the year ended 1992/93, although the partnership will be assessed to profit based on its results to 30 April 1991, the assessment will be allocated among the partners on the basis of the profit sharing ratios over the fiscal year 1992/93.

13.3.1 New partners

This is the first area of difficulty; a partner is being assessed on profits which he may not necessarily have earned. Many firms of solicitors are now experiencing for the first time just how great this difficulty can be. With a falling profit profile, a new partner, or one who is increasing his profit share will be charged tax on profits, which will be higher than the profits he is currently earning. His tax bill will therefore be at a higher rate than his profit share would indicate. Where the profits fall by, say, half, then he may find that at the end of the year his current account is overdrawn to the extent that his fixed capital is substantially reduced, or that during the year is drawings are substantially reduced to build up a current account to meet the liability.

Whether this is a problem within a firm depends on whether the individual partners understand the implications of the prior year basis of assessment. Some firms have experienced this situation without individual partners who may have 'lost out' realising that there is a problem. Other firms do have a policy of explaining to new partners what the implications are, but make it clear that the problem is one of the many areas of partnership where an individual may feel that he has been unfairly prejudiced and that no allowance can be made. It could be argued that the partner benefits by not having to make any payment for the full worth of work in progress, or goodwill. However these arguments do not hold much water because the tax suffered is not meant to be a payment for work in progress or goodwill. Partners suffer the charge on an arbitrary basis and a partner coming in when profits are high and there is no tax problem is presumably benefitting from a higher level of work in progress and goodwill.

A number of firms are currently grappling with this issue because of its effect on new partners. Indeed there have been cases of salaried partners refusing to take equity because of a well-founded belief that their drawings will be reduced significantly below the level of their earnings as a salaried partner, or that any capital they introduce into the firm will be used to pay the tax liabilities on profits taken by more senior partners. Some firms which do not have a facilitating clause within their partnership agreement have found that new partners will refuse to sign a continuation election in an attempt to be fairly taxed.

This issue is likely to affect many firms and their are a number of possible solutions:

(a) tax indemnities within a partnership agreement can protect an incoming partner from suffering the effects of a continuation election compared with his tax charge under a cessation following his admittance as a partner;
(b) where there is no indemnity the continuing partners could agree to pay to the new partner or partners an amount to soften the blow of the tax charge. This might be a full tax indemnity, or an amount to ensure that their overall level of capital does not go below a certain level;
(c) an agreement whereby the required capital from a new partner is spread over a number of years;
(d) an agreement to maintain drawings at a certain level, regardless of the tax deductions required.

If there is to be any payment or allowance the partners in a firm with, say, a 30 June year end, should realise that a new partner will be getting an amount of tax rebate of PAYE as they move from Schedule E to Schedule D.

The first two solutions involve a payment from the continuing partners, whereas the second two effectively allow an amount of over-drawn current account until further profits reinstate the amount paid out in tax. Some partnerships are very much against the actual payment of money to individual partners because of the benefits which accrue to retiring partners on a continuation.

13.3.2 Retiring partners

Where a partner retires and there is a continuation some of his profits will escape taxation. Many partners have traditionally looked to this as a sort of large tax free golden handshake. One can imagine that many new partners, or those rapidly increasing their profit share, are non-too pleased with this arrangement, their benefit being many years into the future.

However, should there be a cessation on the retirement of the partner, this may be a decision in which he has played no part and which could result in him being assessed for more tax, thereby reducing the amount of capital he can ultimately withdraw from the firm. In these circumstances retiring partners regularly get a tax indemnity from the continuing partners should their retirement be prejudiced by a dissolution.

13.3.3 Other problems

A further area of conflict arises from the problems involved in trying to estimate future tax liabilities. At any one time many firms have a large number of years' accounts not agreed with the inspector; payments on account of the tax will certainly have been made, but the final liability not yet determined. On agreement of each year, if there is an amount of tax payable or repayable, then an adjustment will need to be made to the tax reserve of the firm and for each individual who was a partner for that fiscal year. Further, as each budget is announced, the rate of tax and personal allowances for a new fiscal year become known and an adjustment is made to the tax reserves for that year's tax reserve. Additionally, individual partners can affect the liability of the firm to tax by their payments into tax efficient schemes such as BES, or pension payments, and some of these payments can be made in one fiscal year but related back to earlier years. When one also remembers that if there has been a change of partners a firm has two years to decide whether there should be a continuation election then tax reserves could be the subject of continuous amendment.

The reason partners want to have updated tax reserves is to ensure that excess tax reserves are distributed to them.

13.4 What are tax reserves for?

There is inevitably a great deal of confusion within any partnership as to what it is which is being reserved, and what those reserves are supposed to represent. Many of the problems arise from partners being unable to separate the liability which the firm is providing for, and the way each individual is allocated his share of the tax charge on a yearly basis. The problem of understanding would disappear if the partnership provided tax on a maximum provision basis, but charged individual partners on an effective PAYE basis. To the extent that the amounts charged to partners were in excess of what was needed to meet liabilities, then this could be distributed to partners on an equitable basis. There would obviously be problems in determining what is equitable, but it would separate what is really a windfall from the method of providing for and charging tax. A number of firms, especially large ones, do charge individual partners on a PAYE basis and it would seem that few partners complain.

However the firm provides for tax it is essentially taking a view about the ability of the practice to provide tax liabilities out of future earnings and cash flow. Many firms that consider themselves to be prudent and conservative will always provide for the maximum amount of tax. Other firms will not, unless they foresee a significant dip in profits in which case they may increase the amount of provisions.

In either case a significant amount of tax reserve represents a significant amount of partners' capital which is financing some or all assets of the partnership. If one looks at a set of accounts of a partnership over the last 20 years the taxation reserves reduce markedly with time. Up to the early 1980s they may still have been greater than the overall fixed capital and current accounts and as such provided a significant amount of the finance of many firms. The fall has arisen for two main reasons. First of all, it is only comparatively recently that the self-employed have been able to put more than a minimal amount of money into a pension scheme that would attract tax relief. With the introduction of retirement annuity premiums partners found a way of reducing the tax bills on their Schedule D income. There have always been tax saving schemes, such as the use of farm losses, but not all would invest in these. Pensions provided a safe way of investing money, and some firms required their partners to make provision for their pensions within their partnership agreement. Secondly, since the late 1970s there has been a fall in the higher rates of income tax, from 83 per cent to 40 per cent on earned income.

Tax reserves are still important for financing some firms, obviously those which make full provision. However, for those which make small provisions tax may play little effective part in financing a firm, and tax has been replaced by, say, external borrowings and, again over the last 10 to 15 years, the accounts of some partnerships show increasing levels of overdraft as the tax reserves decrease.

This very much emphasises the point that the method of tax reserving chosen by any one firm should not be looked at in isolation from the capital structure of the firm and therefore the culture. Accountants may disagree on the niceties of different methods of reserving, but it may be an academic exercise in all senses, and it is important that firms are told the full range of options.

It is sometimes the case that the partners in a firm do not know what the tax reserves represent. Firms can be cash rich, and delude themselves into thinking that high levels of cash mean a successful firm. A firm in this position may become complacent in its working capital management; many firms in this position have experienced the double bind of falling performance, and therefore insufficient profits to replace tax reserves which become payable, and a poor system of system of debtor and work in progress control inherited from the days of higher profits and cash on the balance sheet. Additionally, firms which rely on tax reserves to fund working capital will have to find new sources of finance when the tax reserves come payable and profits have reduced.

It is for this reason that firms traditionally invested some or all of their tax reserves in a separate asset not used for the firm's trade; very few law firms now do this. However those that do will take the view that the tax will always eventually be payable and that the working capital of the firm should be separately and clearly financed from elsewhere. That part of the tax reserve which is separately invested is considered inviolable. Common forms of investment include or have included gilts or local authority bonds with a maturity date just prior to the instalment dates, certificates of tax deposit or high interest bank deposits. These are all risk-free investments and the choice will be determined by which generates the most income.

13.5 Deferred tax

It is rather strange although many firms of solicitors take great pains to calculate tax reserves and allocations of tax charges among their partners, most will not take any aspect of deferred tax into account, let alone to provide for it. Many solicitors do not understand the concept of deferred tax and those that do will have had it confirmed to them that bringing deferred tax into the tax equation will make matters even more complicated and a source of further fees for the accountants as they struggle to update the allocation of deferred tax by partner.

For many partnerships, because of the way they account for certain items, such as expenditure on fixed assets, there is a policy of writing off to profit and loss account as much as possible, or leases. That is, they are all treated as operating leases regardless of the terms, deferred tax is not an issue. However, there are some circumstances where it can become very much an issue, and the accountant should be prepared to deal with this eventuality.

As far as reserving for tax is concerned, deferred tax plays no part; its only role is to deal with the inequities which can arise between partners where there are changes in the composition of a partnership or profit sharing ratios due to short-term timing differences.

A deferred tax liability will arise where the firm gets tax relief on items within the computation of Schedule DII profits, but there is a lesser charge within the accounts for the same item. The most obvious situation where this will occur will be where the firm gets capital allowances on fixed assets in excess of the depreciation charged on them. Many firms have recently been incurring heavy amounts of capital expenditure on new offices, and may be depreciating these assets over a long period of time, say 15 years. A rarer situation would be a firm accounting for its work in progress at full value including profit, but agreeing with the inspector that for taxation purposes, the work in progress should be reduced by the profit element.

More likely is that there will be the possibility of accounting for a deferred tax asset because a charge in the accounts does not get immediate tax relief. These will include general provisions for bad debts, although this will not normally be material from one accounting period to another. Far more important will be where the firm writes of all of its capital expenditure in the profit and loss account but does not get full relief in the tax computations, such expenditure qualifying for capital allowances. Again, many firms who have heavily invested in new offices recently are in this position.

Some firms do not account for work in progress in their accounts, but nevertheless the inspector has sought to tax a deemed increase in work in progress by reference to, say, the increase in professional salaries from one accounting period to the next. The partners are taxed on a deemed profit which they have not received.

A problem which inevitably some firms will face in the future will arise from professional indemnity claims. A firm may provide for elements of such a claim which are uninsured due to, for example, the failure of the insurer of one band of cover, but not get relief in the tax computation until the claim is paid. The nature of indemnity claims may mean that this is many years after the original provision is made. Partners who are facing retirement and have been charged for the provision in their profit share will not be pleased with the prospect of the tax relief being given after their retirement.

In most cases the deferred tax effects of short period timing differences are likely to be small given the size of the overall tax charge and the number of partners, and should therefore be ignored. However, where there is the possibility it should be calculated and an equitable adjustment proposed to the partners (although this begs the question raised repeatedly in this section, what is equitable?).

Chapter 14 – Financing firms of solicitors

14.1 Introduction

Giving advice on financing a firm of solicitors is, like advising on profit sharing arrangements, an area fraught with difficulty for the accountant. Many lawyers, who can be expected to have some knowledge of the alternatives for profit sharing, will treat finance as a completely separate issue, the responsibility of bankers and accountants. However, it is as much subject to the firm's culture as profit share and an accountant asked to advise a law firm must bear this in mind before he starts his work.

Having established the cultural attitude of the firm to the source of finance, the accountant should then be able to discuss with his client the relative merits and demerits of internal and external finance. However, the boundary between the two types of finance is not, or at least should not be considered to be, clear cut. Further, the accountant must be aware of recent and proposed changes in the tax regime and their effect on the financing of professional practices generally. Finally, the issue of financing cannot be separated from the issue of working capital management, and any advice the accountant gives on finance may need to be accompanied by recommendations on this aspect of practice management.

14.2 Culture

The first question the accountant must ask, when asked to advise on financing any practice is,

> 'Are you as a firm prepared to borrow to finance the firm?'

If the answer to this question is no, the accountant must then ask,

> 'Are you as a firm prepared to allow any individual partner to borrow to finance the firm?'

It may be curious that despite the tax and financing advantages of borrowing, the view that firms should not borrow at all is fairly common.

The reason given is prudence, and that reason is valid as much in an economic boom as in a recession.

Although it may be understandable that a firm does not want to borrow externally on the grounds of prudence, how can that apply to practice loans taken out individually by partners? The answer is still prudence; the individual partners are guarding against the possibility of an insolvency of one of the partners, and the call on the firm's finances when the bank calls in the practice loan. Indeed, the author is aware of firms of solicitors where the practice as a whole will attempt to restrict severely the borrowings of individual partners such as mortgages. A number of firms may wish they had adopted this policy five or six years ago.

Attempting to change the culture of a firm so that it accepts the concept of borrowing can be a very difficult and dangerous move, and the accountant should only do it with extreme caution.

14.3 Internal finance

Internal finance is comprised of three sources:

(a) fixed capital;
(b) undrawn profits; and
(c) tax reserves.

In many firms there may be no distinction between the various categories, but they should be considered in isolation.

14.3.1 Fixed capital

Fixed capital is traditionally the amount, fixed by the partnership agreement, which a partner puts into the firm on admission to equity and which is left in the firm until retirement. From this it follows that as a new partner joins the firm the fixed capital of the firm will increase and as a partner retires from the firm the fixed capital will reduce. It is an obvious point to make, but the question needs to be asked whether the admission or retirement of an individual is an event within the life of a partnership requiring an increase or decrease in capital.

Fixed capital is normally contributed by partners in proportion to their profit sharing ratios, either in total, or according to the ratio of one slice of their profit where there is a meritocracy, say the merit slice. It therefore also follows that the fixed capital of the firm may increase as a result of partners moving up, say, the lock-step. Of course, the level of capital may stay the same, and in any firm with changing profit shares this would mean that some partners would be returned fixed capital as others put more in. In lock-steps this is not normally the case, and it does not always occur in meritocracies. Therefore, with time, the fixed capital of the firm increases, and again, the question has to be asked, is the annual change in profit shares an event justifying of itself an increase in capital. The point is illustrated below.

Partner	*Equity at 30.6.93*	*Equity at 1.7.93*	*Capital at 20.6.93*	*Injected (repaid)*	*Capital at 1.7.93*
1	25%	24%	£250K	(£10K)	£240K
2	22%	21%	£220K	(£10K)	£210K
3	21%	21%	£210K	nil	£210K
4	18%	19%	£180K	£10K	£190K
5	14%	15%	£140K	£10K	£150K
Total			£1000K	nil	£1000K

The overall capital of the firm remains unchanged and therefore Partners 4 and 5, in increasing their profit share percentage, repay some of Partner 1 and 2's capital, whose percentages reduce. However, it is more common for there to be a net increase in capital, such as in the following example.

Partner	*Equity at 30.6.93*	*Equity at 1.7.93*	*Capital at 30.6.93*	*Injected*	*Capital at 1.7.93*
1	25%	24%	£250K	£1K	£251K
2	22%	21%	£220K	nil	£220K
3	21%	21%	£210K	£10K	£220K
4	18%	19%	£180K	£19K	£199K
5	14%	15%	£140K	£17K	£157K
Total			£1000K	£47K	£1047K

To avoid a repayment of capital to any one partner, the capital of the partner whose share has fallen the most is chosen as the new base for working out the new capital contributions. In a number of firms the capital contribution is calculated on a value per equity point. The number of equity points in issue may increase as partners are brought into the practice, or advance up the lock-step, and again on each change in profit sharing, the fixed capital of the firm will increase because new points are issued. Alternatively, the fixed capital would remain the same if equity points were effectively bought and sold.

New partners may be faced with a very large 'bill' for their capital contribution. Although many firms will come to an arrangement with a bank regarding the provision and subsequent financing of a practice loan, the overall burden of such a loan is often considered too great for a new partner. Other partnerships will restrict the amount of capital that can be financed by a practice loan, resulting in the prospect of the new partner financing a large amount of fixed capital out of his own immediate resources. To get around these problems, many firms, especially the larger firms, will provide a maximum period of time within which the full amount of capital has to be contributed, for example, within six months. A number of the larger lock-steps recognise that there will be a continuing demand for capital contributions as an individual partner moves up the lock-step, and therefore provide a period of years over which full capital has to be provided, for example as set out in the following table:

Years in lock-step	*Number of equity points*	*Capital contribution at £1000K per point*	*% of capital actually required*	*Capital actually required*
0	50	50000	70	35000
1	55	55000	80	44000
2	60	60000	85	51000
3	65	65000	90	58500
4	70	70000	95	66500
5	75	75000	100	75000
6	80	80000	100	80000
7	85	85000	100	85000
8	90	9000	100	90000
9	95	95000	100	95000
10	100	100000	100	100000

The new partner is allowed to build up his capital, perhaps by a mixture of practice loan and undrawn profit. It can be seen from the above that for a number of firms the overall level of capital changes in only a very arbitrary fashion compared to the changing commercial requirements of the practice, and one wonders whether the concept of fixed capital is more an issue of investing in the business and becoming a proprietor, than providing the firm with a source of finance.

Some firms will try to take a scientific view of increases in their fixed capital, and will increase it each year in line with an index. For example, an increase in fixed capital in line with the retail price index, will assume that any growth in the firm is financed from another source, but that to stand still, the overall requirements of the firm are still increasing. An alternative to the RPI would be an index on solicitors' salaries. Alternatively, the practice will increase its requirements in line with the increase in its fees rendered, attempting to measure the growth of the firm. If the firm makes an accurate estimate of its annual cash requirements, and only makes special draws in accordance with these forecasts, then perhaps a more accurate method of increasing the fixed capital is by capitalising profits which remain undrawn after a certain period of time.

14.3.2 Undrawn profits

Undrawn profits fluctuate throughout the year, as new profits are earned, and as old profits are drawn. The methods of calculating drawings, and particularly special draws, are considered in Chapter 12.

A number of firms, especially smaller firms, do not have fixed capital; all of the partners' direct capital is provided through undrawn profits. Effectively, as the practice has grown, and the partnership has recognised the need for more cash, it has provided some or all of that cash by not paying out to partners all of the profits to which they are entitled. There need not necessarily be a decision to build up capital through the use of undrawn profits; it is more likely to arise from a conscious decision not to fund special draws wholly or partly out of borrowings. This decision will have given the practice its cultural attitude to the use of borrowings. The firm will have come to realise that an amount of profits will never be available for withdrawal, unless the firm is prepared to borrow.

Larger practices will use undrawn profits to increase the capital of the firm in one of two ways. They will either restrict the amount that junior partners are allowed to draw so that they can build up an amount of capital; or, because of the cash requirements of the business, there will be a realisation that the overall capital requirements of the business have increased. In both of these instances, these amounts of undrawn profits should be capitalised. Alternatively, the cash requirements of the business may have increased because working capital management has deteriorated. Unless this deterioration is permanent, this should not be converted to fixed capital.

It therefore follows that the amount of undrawn profits within a firm should be linked to the collection of net working capital which represents those profits. Therefore, if a partnership bills and collects its work in progress within at least 12 months, then it should aim to have either distributed the cash in respect of those profits within 12 months of them being earned, or alternatively converted the profits into capital within that time. If one assumes that profits are earned evenly throughout the year (note that the billings profile tends to be weighted towards the latter six months), then the decision over the special draw/capitalisation should take place, in the above example, six months after the year end.

14.3.3 Tax reserves

To complicate matters, many firms are substantially financed out of tax reserves. The various methods of reserving for partnership tax are considered in Chapter 13, where it can be seen that there is an extremely large range of possible provisions that a firm can make. However, in the past, when marginal rates of tax on earned income were at 83 per cent, the non-distribution of profits to provide for future tax payments was a significant aspect in the capital of firms. There are a number of problems in using tax reserves to finance a firm. First of all, as tax reserves are used to pay tax liabilities, to continue the funding of the firm they need to be replaced by reserves of at least the same amount. With falling tax rates this is not the case, and therefore the amount of fixed capital should increase. This has not been a major issue, as long as it has been realised, because the reduction in tax has resulted in increased drawable profits, which would be available for conversion into capital without a consequent fall in a partner's drawings.

More importantly, as profits have started to fall, the tax reserves have started to fall, and therefore the capital requirements have had to be met from another source. Consequently, this has provided many firms with a cash squeeze. Those firms which have refused to borrow in the past have been forced to go to a bank, and firms which already borrow have had to increase such facilities. This would not be a problem for firms which take a critical look at what their tax reserves represent and treat them, unlike undrawn profits and fixed capital, as a potentially short term loan. Unfortunately a number of firms did not take this approach, and in the years of high profits their balance sheets misled them as regards their financial well-being, one reason possibly being that tax reserves appear on the capital side of the balance sheet.

For a few firms the presence of tax reserves has never misled them as to the strength of their balance sheet because some or all of the reserves have financed separate assets. Thus, some firms will invest part or all of their tax reserves in liquid assets such as short dated gilts, high interest deposit accounts or certificates of tax deposit, the maximum return being obtained from the investment itself, not through any self investment back into the partnership. The most prudent of these firms, even if they are prepared to borrow to fund working capital, will consider tax reserve investments as inviolable.

For all firms, the time at which the tax is payable can be subject to great uncertainty. For example, the final amount payable in respect of any one year will depend on agreement with the inspector, something which can be difficult to budget for with any certainty. Additionally, some partners will mitigate their liabilities by the use of Business Expansion Scheme (BES) and pension contributions and on payment, will expect the tax rebate to be provided to them immediately by the firm. Although some firms seek to control this, as noted in Chapter 12 on drawings, the effect of half of the partners in a less well organised firm demanding payment of part of their tax reserves can cause a cash crisis.

Tax reserves will inevitably become less important with the change from the prior year to the current year basis of assessment and firms should seek to remove these as a source before the change takes place. Firms should also consider what it is that their reserves are financing and be aware of the shorter term nature of this as a source.

14.3.4 Internal funding

The internal funding of a practice should comprise fixed capital and undrawn profits, with fixed capital providing the bedrock of the partnership's fixed asset and working capital finance, and undrawn profits the swings in short term working capital requirements. Where undrawn profits are undistributed after the normal time when they would be expected to be converted into cash, then they should be capitalised, being indicative of a change in the firm's business due to, say, growth, or a new market where profits are converted into cash later; or the firm should look at its working capital management to see why it has slipped. Conversely, the ability to distribute profits earlier than anticipated may indicate the need for a capital repayment. In either case the firm should be aware of the reasons giving rise to the requirement for a change.

Increases in fixed capital are rarely required by the business as profit shares increase, or as new partners are admitted; in particular, new partners are demonstrating an investment in the business, not providing desperately required cash. If a firm has got its level of fixed capital right, then increases in the fixed capital of some partners can be accompanied by a repayment of capital to others or, alternatively, at the time that special draws of undistributed profits are made. This will have the additional advantage of not having senior partners with an extremely large capital account which is difficult to replace on retirement in the form of new fixed capital. This will ensure that capital increases are made in as scientific a manner as possible.

Tax reserves should no longer form a significant part of the funding of the practice, and as the change to a current year basis of assessment approaches, firms should be advised to start matching more of their reserves with liquid assets.

In the context of these considerations on what internal capital is, one can start to consider how external capital can be brought into the equation.

14.4 External funding

The common forms of external capital are as follows:

(a) bank overdraft;
(b) bank debt;
(c) practice loans; and
(d) lease finance.

14.4.1 Bank overdraft

Bank overdrafts are used first of all to finance drawings to partners in respect of profits not available in the form of cash. When a partnership starts up the initial overheads and any drawings will normally be provided out of the initial fixed capital. Therefore, any practice that borrows on overdraft is to a certain extent prepared to finance drawings from the bank. A reluctance to borrow from the bank on overdraft to pay what is in effect a salary to the partners probably explains the reluctance many firms have to borrow at all.

Despite this reluctance for a number of firms to borrow, banks are very willing to lend on overdraft to firms of solicitors, and firms are able first of all to pay out to partners the majority of undrawn profits and secondly, can even start to repay fixed capital. There are some firms which have overdraft facilities in excess of four times their fixed capital. Given what has been said above about the relationship between fixed capital and undrawn profits, such practices must have repaid a significant amount of fixed capital from overdraft. Like undrawn profits, the level of the overdraft as a source of finance will fluctuate through the year, as profits, draws and payments such as tax and VAT are made.

14.4.2 Bank debt

Bank debt, in the form of a medium- or long-term loan is a much less common method of finance for firms. Some banks will only consider making such a loan if it used to finance a particular asset which has a life linked to the term of the loan. Therefore, 10 year loans to finance the refurbishment of a building will be granted; however, it is less common to find banks willing to consider long-term loans to finance, say, the hard core element of an overdraft and some will even consider that the need to replace the hard core to be indicative of financial problems. Given what has been said above about the role of fixed capital, undrawn profits and overdraft in funding the practice, such a need may well be indicative of an under-capitalised firm.

Medium- and long-term loans are available from lending institutions for non-property lending in the form of specific loans of a duration of anything up to 25 years; they are commonly of a duration of 10 to 15 years. The time element is important because the loan is effectively providing finance at anything up to the period of the working life of many partners. With the availability of financial products, such as capital holidays and interest caps, such loans can effectively replace a substantial amount of the fixed capital of a number of partners.

The importance of being able to replace fixed capital in this way obviously has implications for the repayment of capital on retirement, and reinforces the view expressed elsewhere in this book that firms of solicitors are becoming more important in terms of income generation through the working lives of partners, than for capital appreciation realisable on retirement.

14.4.3 Practice loans

Practice loans are included within external funding to demonstrate that there is a wide grey area between the borrowing and the non-borrowing partnership. A firm can only really consider itself a non-borrower if it does not allow its partners to borrow to fund practice loans on which interest is to be paid out of profit share, whether designated for that purpose or not.

All banks offer practice loans for solicitors, normally at favourable rates compared to, say, overdraft. It is often the case that the bank which provides finance to the practice will also provide finance to the individual partners. Indeed, many banks offer a streamlined service to their solicitor clients whereby the requirements of any partner to put up fixed capital due on admission to equity or an increase in profit share are given to the bank on the first day of the accounting period, and the bank organises the necessary finance, requiring little more than a signature from each partner on a piece of paper. The payment of interest on the loans is similarly organised so that the individual partners do little more than sign a form arranging a direct debit of an amount transferred into their bank account on a six monthly basis by the practice. The only remarkable thing about such seemingly informal arrangements is that some firms who receive the benefit of such borrowings, but have no actual borrowings on their own balance sheet, consider themselves to be ungeared.

Even medium-term loans can effectively be redesignated by the lender from the practice to the individual partners, and some practices, for tax reasons alone, may consider that all borrowings should be switched to individual partners.

An appreciation of the grey area between internal and external borrowings is important when considering the overall gearing of a practice, which is discussed in detail below.

14.4.4 Lease finance

Many firms of solicitors lease finance all of their office equipment, from the computers to chairs. Lease finance makes sense from a financial perspective in that it matches the term of finance to the life of the asset. Finance leases are preferred over operating leases, and true finance leases, where the capital allowances remain with the lessor, are more attractive than hire purchase arrangements, where the capital allowances go to the lessee, because of the prior year basis of assessment.

As noted in Chapter 9, many firms of solicitors will treat all of their leases as operating leases, not finance leases, with the result that neither the asset nor the liability appear on the balance sheet. This obviously makes a mockery of attempting to look at the true financing of certain partnerships.

14.5 Gearing

Gearing, when applied to a partnership, is a measure of the ratio of partners' capital to borrowings, or in the definitions used above, the ratio of internal finance to external finance. However, from even this basic approach to gearing there are difficulties; internal finance may include tax reserves, and external finance may include the loans for practice borrowings. There is no agreed method of determining gearing of professional practices. Having said that, the majority of firms of solicitors will not attempt to calculate their gearing and therefore not consider it an issue. It is, of course, if only because a possible lender will try to make an assessment of gearing. In addition, depending on the cultural attitude of the practice to borrowing there is an optimal level of gearing for each practice which, if assessed, is important in terms of the financial cost of all capital and in how the firm approaches its financial practice management.

The first point to make on gearing concerns the inclusion of tax reserves in internal capital. The amount of tax reserved is arbitrary, as is whether firms include it on the asset or the capital side of the balance sheet. As tax reserves become of less importance they should not form part of the consideration of the firm's capital and therefore should be excluded from calculations of gearing. Internal capital, therefore, should only include fixed capital and undrawn profits. However, because of the timing and amount of special draws, and the 'lumpy manner' in which some solicitors earn profits, the balance on the undrawn profits account can be subject to wide, often artificial, variation. Where this is the case, and where, for example, there is a realisation that the year end balance of undrawn profits is unrealistic then an averaging of undrawn profits throughout the year may afford a better measure for a gearing calculation.

In terms of external capital, the first consideration is whether one looks at the actual borrowings or, say, the facility. A bank looking at a firm's accounts to determine its risk will consider the facility, because the bank is ultimately concerned with the worst scenario situation of full exposure. However, the firm should be looking at actual borrowings and, for those solicitors that do attempt to measure gearing, this is what is used. However, if one looks solely at year end borrowing, the view portrayed will certainly be misleading. For a firm with a year end of 30 June, on 1 July the second instalment of the tax is due, there is a quarterly VAT bill soon to be paid (assuming the firm is not a large VAT payer making on account payments), and the last month of the year will have seen a particularly heavy bout of feeing and an even heavier bout of cash collection. In addition, the firm may have held back paying its suppliers until early in the new year. The result is that the 30 June balance will show one of the healthiest cash positions in the year (and the 31 July balance one of the worst). Therefore, the firm must look at its average balance on a monthly if not a weekly basis.

An adjustment also has to be made if the firm does not apply SSAP21 and treats all finance leases as operating leases. To determine this aspect of the firm's overall borrowing, a calculation should be done to restate the finance lease creditor. The next adjustment concerns practice loans, and starts to approach the most difficult and contentious area of practice management: looking through the partners to ascertain their personal borrowings.

If non-practice borrowings are initially excluded, one can see from the table overleaf that although each partnership's balance sheet is the same, if the practice borrowings are considered, the gearing of each practice is different. Only Practices B and D will have the same interest burden per year because

Partnership	*A*	*B*	*C*	*D*
	£	£	£	£
Net assets	1,000,000	1,000,000	1,000,000	1,000,000
Partners' capital				
1	250,000	250,000	250,000	250,000
2	250,000	250,000	250,000	250,000
3	250,000	250,000	250,000	250,000
4	250,000	250,000	250,000	250,000
Total	1,000,000	1,000,000	1,000,000	1,000,000
Partners' practice borrowings				
1	0	125,000	250,000	250,000
2	0	125,000	250,000	250,000
3	0	125,000	250,000	0
4	0	125,000	250,000	0
Partners' mortgages				
1	0	125,000	0	250,000
2	0	500,000	0	0
3	0	125,000	0	0
4	500,000	125,000	0	500,000

the overall level of debt is £500,000 as far as the partners are concerned. This is because the partners have to finance out of their profit shares interest on their own practice loans. Practice A has no debt to finance and Practice C £1,000,000. Of course, the partners in the highly geared firms may have removed all of their capital, replaced it with practice loans, and invested the released capital in eurobonds; there again they may not have done. The contentious question is how far one has to consider the individual capital statements of the partners to assess gearing.

One might now say that Practice C is healthier than Practice B. The reason that the C partners have such high practice borrowings is that they have repaid their mortgages using the release of their capital. The partners' borrowings in Practice B are higher than those of Practice C, mainly due to the very high mortgage of one partner. However, what if that mortgage is mainly funded by the partner's spouse whose earnings are greater than his. The assessment of what is borrowing in respect of the practice and what is in respect of mortgages is by no means easy, especially as partners may have the choice in the way they wish to be borrowed. The situation is even more complicated if one takes into account other borrowings.

At a minimum, to make a realistic assessment of gearing one must include each of the individual partner's practice loans. One should also consider bringing into the calculation other borrowings. One point which comes out of the consideration of non-practice loan borrowings is that of the partner who becomes over-exposed personally. It was noted above that some firms of solicitors try to restrain the amount which individual partners can borrow, but most do not. The risk each partner faces is that due to bad luck or bad judgement, an individual partner cannot pay his debts and has to be bailed out by the other partners who wish to keep him as a partner within the firm. Even worse is the situation where there is a claim on the firm which cannot be met by the firm and therefore the individual partners have to meet it out of their own resources. In the case of Practice D, above, Partner 3 has no borrowings at all, but Partner 4 has a half million pound mortgage. If the firm was faced with a large claim, Partner 3, the non-borrowed partner, may find himself paying on behalf of everyone else.

It is therefore recommended that, at the risk of causing problems between the partners, a record is kept of personal assets and liabilities to be monitored by, say, the senior partner, so that some degree of control can be kept on individual partners causing a problem to the firm as a whole.

Having determined what the various components of the gearing calculation are, one then has a measure of the overall exposure of the firm to its bankers. For those firms which do measure gearing, the ratio is used as a financial management tool to provide a base level of borrowing which should not be breached. For example, the firms will have a policy of ensuring that there is a ratio of capital to borrowing of one to two at the worst point in the year, or that on average gearing should not exceed one to one. One to one is by far the commonest target quoted by firms of solicitors, although there appears to be little understanding why it is used and what it means. The one to one ratio traditionally came from the lending policy of banks to all types of business where one pound of the bank's money had to be matched by one pound of the proprietor's. It is still common for banks to allow a firm of solicitors to be geared to the extent of one to one.

There are strong commercial reasons why it is unwise for a partnership to attempt to become highly geared, and good reasons why it should keep its borrowings as low as possible. For most commercial organisations, borrowing money from a bank provides a source of capital which, it is hoped, will aid or even drive the expansion of that organisation, generate a return in excess of that which is paid in interest and, in turn, provide funds from which to repay the original borrowing. A successful manufacturing company invests in more machinery to make more products, or a chain of retail outlets invests in more shops to generate more turnover. The investment opportunities for firms of solicitors are limited. The structure of the solicitors industry in England and Wales is generally locally based, and firms have not, in the main, tried to set up chains of offices trading under a common name. The nature of the solicitor's product is such that one cannot specialise to the exclusion of all competition, or generate revenue from one 'product' following substantial investment. Unlike many businesses it is not possible to generate further profits in a solicitors' practice just by raising a large amount of cash.

Where firms have tried to expand is by increasing the quantity of the advice they provide by increasing staff and partner numbers and therefore their premises costs. However, it is not possible to expand in this manner for any sustained period of time, and certainly the opportunity for increasing profits at an exponential rate does not exist. Some solicitors make a lot of money; however, there is a ceiling on their earnings that does not exist for an organisation which is based on other than professionals selling their time and that of their staff.

There is a limit to what a firm of solicitors can do with borrowed money, other than provide for modest expansion and then repay the partners own money invested in the firm. There is therefore a restriction on how geared a firm of solicitors need be. In looking at the repayment of partners' capital the question then becomes, where is it most efficient to have the borrowing, in the practice or in the partners?

14.6 Tax and interest efficient gearing

There is an argument, which is often ignored, that the partnership is run for the benefit of the partners. Therefore, considering the partners collectively, if there is an efficient way of carrying out a transaction which benefits them, then it should be carried out, even if it is not beneficial to the partnership. Obviously, it is in the best interest of the partners that the partnership continues trading. In addition, one must have regard for those not yet partners; this is seen most clearly in the ownership of property (see Chapter 16). However, with borrowing, it is possible that the most efficient structure is one which minimises the overall financial costs to the individual partners (after including their profit share) notwithstanding that the practice has a greater financial cost.

The first consideration is the matching of interest. It makes little commercial sense if a partnership has surplus cash throughout the year on which it earns deposit interest if all of the partners have borrowings on which they are paying a higher rate of interest. Each of the partners would benefit from a capital distribution or special draw which would allow them to repay their borrowings. If the practice has borrowings, it may be more efficient to swap the higher rates of interest paid on overdrafts for the lower rates of interest achievable on practice loans taken out by the individual partners.

There is a tax advantage in paying practice loan rather than overdraft interest. A firm will get tax relief on any interest it pays on overdraft. At the same time it is taxed on income received in the same period as the interest is paid, that is, under the prior year basis of assessment around 18 months to two years after it has actually been paid. Therefore, if the accounts are drawn up to 30 April, interest paid on 31 March 1992 will be allowable against profits, the tax on which will be paid on 1 January 1994 and 1 July 1994. The interest on a practice loan is tax deductible in the year it is paid by the individual partner. Therefore, interest paid on 31 March 1992 is paid in the fiscal year 1991/92 and will be offset against profits earned in, say, the year ended 30 April 1990, that is in respect of profits earned two years earlier.

While all interest paid on a practice loan is tax deductible, the individual partner may have other borrowings which do not qualify for full or any tax relief. If the partner has fixed capital or a rump of undrawn profits in these circumstances, the partner should seek to re-arrange his personal borrowings by taking out a practice loan in respect of his fixed capital and undrawn profits, up to the limit of his mortgage for instance, so that any personal loans are in respect of the practice, the interest thereon thereby qualifying for full relief.

Although interest rates on overdraft may be higher than rates on practice loans, in some circumstances firms will achieve a very low rate of interest on their overdrafts due to the interaction with clients' money held on deposit. Some banks have traditionally offered the facility to consider the level of borrowing by the practice against the level of client money held on general deposit, and to the extent that there is a matching of the two, only charge a minimal rate of interest on the overdraft. Of course the firm still has an obligation to pay interest on client money under Part III of the SAR91.

However, this can readily be seen to provide a significant advantage in terms of the financing of an overdraft compared to a practice loan.

14.7 Working capital management

The above considerations apply to all firms; however, only firms which are able to reach an understanding of how the practice is financed are those which can determine what their financial requirements are, and can to a large extent control the flows of money in and out of the practice. To reach the former demands a process of budgeting, and to control the latter means managing the working capital. These are considered in the next chapter.

14.8 A bank's approach to a firm of solicitors

Given what has been said above, borrowing may be appropriate for many firms of solicitors. Where it is proposed to take out, or increase borrowings, the accountant may be asked by his solicitor client to advise on which bank should be approached or the information to be presented to the banker. The accountant should therefore be aware of how the bank will view the solicitor and the financial information likely to be presented, principally the accounts, both in support of the loan, and as the bank monitors the performance of its customer.

First of all, all banks, even those which specialise in lending to solicitors, will look at the borrower in the same way they assess any lending proposition. They will therefore examine cashflow, the quality of management, the quality of management information, the history of the previous banking relationships of the firm and so on. Therefore, lending managers will have a series of checklists which they will attempt to fill out in respect of the firm. Additionally, in monitoring the firm's performance, the bank will look at the sort of management information it would ask of a limited company.

The immediate hurdle which a banker will have to cross concerns the quality of the accounts. Many firms provide such poor quality accounts, some of which have an accountant's certificate on them, that the bank is immediately given a negative impression of the firm. Unfortunately this often continues after an overdraft has been agreed.

Chapter 9 dealt with the type of accounts which can be presented, but many sets of accounts are little more than a balance sheet and an income and expenditure account with no further information. The first thing many banks will do is look at the tax charge, and if it appears to be less than a full provision, will recalculate it to determine what the full provision should be. This will occur even if the full provision is not appropriate. The next area of difficulty concerns the value of work in progress. Banks will be aware of the wide range of possible treatments for this item, but will only make adjustments if it considers that profit has been included. This will be the case even if there are perfectly good reasons to include profit, as noted in Chapter 9.

Having scrutinized these two areas, the banker will look at all of the other opportunities the solicitor has for constructing the accounts in ways which do not show a true and fair view. It is obvious that one of the principle problems that bankers have with solicitors' accounts is the lack of any accounting policies. Further, because of the lack of reliability of many accounts, little attention is paid to any accountant's certificate. Indeed, it is said by some bankers that the quality of the annual accounts can be so bad that any firm of accountants putting their name to the accounts may be doing their client a disservice.

The quality of other management information produced, such as profit forecasts or cash flow projections is also poor, and in many cases non-existent. Indeed, it is said that many firms provide information which would not be acceptable for a limited company. However, despite the poor quality of information, banks do lend to solicitors, although the rates offered may not always be as keen as they might be if the financial information produced was better. The reason why solicitors are able to borrow is down to a realisation that firms rarely become insolvent, and therefore the bank's risk is very low.

Banks have a number of financial ratios which they will apply to firms, and these should be considered in the light of the discussion on gearing above:

Debtors and work in progress. Where this is monitored, the bank will look to lend against a discounted value of debtors and work in progress, say 50 per cent of each;

Capital Banks will not include tax reserves in the computation of partners' capital;

Extent of personal borrowings. Banks will look to individual statements of partners' assets and liabilities for partnerships up to a certain size, generally less than 20. Above this size there is a realisation that the information is difficult to obtain and keep updated, and also an expectation that firms above this size will not fail;

Gearing. As noted above, banks will ignore the actual borrowings, but will look instead at the facilities in order that they can assess their exposure if there is a failure;

Profitability. Banks, if looking at a profit based financial ratio, will tend to adjust the profit to take account of a reasonable level of 'salary' which a partner in a firm of solicitors should take. This would need to take account of tax and pensions;

Fees. Because the profitability of some firms will be distorted by their policy of accounting for work in progress, some banks will place more emphasis on the level of fees and try to keep borrowing within a certain percentage of gross fees;

Interest cover. If the profitability measure above is used, some banks will make a further adjustment to take account of notional interest on partners' capital. Interest cover ratios tend to be fixed at two- or three-times interest. This is in line with the interest cover covenants of many corporate loans. A problem for some banks to interpret is the significantly low rate of interest some firms achieve because of the interaction with client account money. However, many banks would appear to assume that this is not a problem, either because there will always be a high level of client deposits, or because of a belief that the Law Society will not attempt to tighten this area still further (see generally Chapter 4).

14.9 Conclusion

Financing legal practices is an issue which many accountants will avoid, especially when faced with the question, 'What should my gearing ratio be?' It is, without doubt, a complicated area on which to advise, but so much of the ability to advise well depends on an understanding of the firm's culture and its business. Perhaps the best approach for the accountant when faced with such a question is to turn it back on the firm:

> 'Why do you want to be geared in the first place?'

Chapter 15 – Working capital management

15.1 Introduction

This chapter examines various methods of working capital management, an area of practice management which has become more important to firms of solicitors over recent years, and especially in the current recession. However, working capital management is not only concerned with the billing of work in progress and the collection of debtors; those aspects can only be carried out successfully if they are done in the overall context of the financing and cash requirements of the firm. The financing of the firm, while dependent on the firm's cultural attitude, is influenced by the operational factors affecting the firm's business of selling time. Finally both the cultural and operational aspects should be reflected in the firm's strategic and operational plans, as evidenced by its budgets and forecasts.

15.2 Strategic planning, budgeting and forecasting

Many of the books published over the last few years which deal with practice management for solicitors devote considerable space to planning, budgeting and forecasting, processes with which accountants will be very familiar, but with which, it would appear, many lawyers are not.

The accountant should advise any of his solicitor clients not budgeting for future performance to do so; for small practices he may well be asked to assist in the production of the budgets. Although it is likely that the accountant will get involved in setting up a budgeting and forecasting process, and in the actual production of the forecast documents, it is important that the budgets are those of the firm of solicitors, not the firm of accountants. The solicitor needs to have a thorough understanding of what is in the budget as well as an acceptance of the assumptions.

It is also vital that forecasts are based on both the short and medium term objectives of any strategic plan, and that the budgets take account of any spending decisions which are included in the plan, but which may not be part of recurring annual expenditure. For these reasons, the budgetary and strategy processes are part of the overall process of managing the firm and each should complement and confirm the other.

'Strategy' and 'strategic planning' may sound grand terms to many solicitors, and indeed to many firms of accountants; however, at their simplest they need be no more than a formalisation of the approach which all businesses will adopt when looking to their future, that is, recording the results of any agreed plans, and then monitoring actual performance against planned performance. Thus, a two partner firm of solicitors specialising in conveyancing and criminal legal aid work may intend to stay the same size carrying out broadly the same work over the foreseeable future. Therefore its strategic objective is to remain the same firm. Having agreed on that objective, at the very least it will need to consider how changes to the system of Legal Aid will affect its plan to remain the same, and to consider how it will deal with future changes in the level of residential property sales.

Having considered the influences on its sources of income, the firm will need to look at its own resources, for example its staff and its premises, and consider how these may change, and then calculate the costs of these resources. By now the firm will have been able to draw up an initial forecast of profits and cash, and can start to determine whether the objective will be achievable in a financial sense, that is on the basis of the assumptions underlying the overall objective. The firm will need to revise its assumptions if, for example, the forecasts show a sharply decreasing level of profits, or the need for an overdraft arises which is yet to be arranged.

Making matters slightly more complicated, the two partner firm may decide that its overall strategy is to maintain its conveyancing and legal aid work, while at the same time it wishes to build up an expertise in family law and open a branch in a particular location. It may have identified, for instance, that one of the solicitors employed by the firm has been successful in attracting family law work and that a sole practitioner in a nearby town is nearing retirement. The development of each of these strategies will require resources, for example, the appointment of the solicitor specialising in family law as a partner, the provision of a full time secretary and recruitment of an articled clerk to assist the new partner. The provision of these may themselves require further resources in the form of office space, equipment and training. These costs, and the associated expected income, will be reflected in the initial forecast used to determine the overall feasibility of the business objectives and underlying assumptions.

The result of the above process is to produce a set of objectives and underlying assumptions which set out what the firm wishes to achieve in the future, and the resources which will be required to achieve the stated goals.

From this it will be possible to draw up a budgeted profit and loss account, balance sheet and cash flow for at least the next 12 months.

15.3 Profit and loss account

The profit and loss account will consist of two principal parts, income and overheads. The production of the income budget will be based on the production of individual budgets by each fee earner in the firm. These will be based on levels of chargeability which will reflect historical chargeability and any planned changes as a result of the strategic plan, for example, expected increases in chargeable time and increases in charge out rate. The starting point for each individual should be the available working hours in the year, that is, say, 40 hours a week, less annual leave and public holidays. From this will be deducted any time required for continuing professional education, or training and administrative responsibilities.

The basis of calculation of charge out rates for solicitors is set out in a booklet published by the Law Society entitled *The Expense of Time* (5th ed., 1992). The approach adopted is as follows:

(a) determine the annual expenses of the firm, based on previous year's accounts, but after taking account of projected inflation, and notional rent on premises, notional interest on partners' balances and notional salaries for partners;
(b) determine the chargeable hours incurred by each fee earner as a percentage of normal working hours;
(c) deduct from the annual expenses of the firm a proportion of each fee earner's salary based on the proportion of their time which is chargeable;
(d) calculate the hourly expense of each fee earner as follows:

(i)	relevant salary (annual salary multiplied by percentage of time which is chargeable)	x
(ii)	plus a proportion of half of the annual expenses of the firm based on that fee earner's chargeable hours compared to total chargeable hours	x
(iii)	plus a proportion of the other half of the annual expenses of the firm based on that fee earner's relevant salary compared to total relevant salaries	x
		x
(iv)	divided by that fee earner's chargeable hours	x
(v)	equals hourly expense.	x

To this is added the mark up for profit, and from this is calculated the total chargeable output for the year.

Having produced the budgeted chargeability, it will be convenient to group these by partner for whom the fee earner works, or categories of law, or department within the firm. Depending on the size and structure of the firm there will be a number of levels of grouping, accompanied at each stage by a review for reasonableness. However, the final result will be a budget for production for the forthcoming year. Depending on how the firm accounts for billings, this will need to be converted into cash received in respect of chargeable time. For the firm which accounts for transactions on a cash basis, the conversion will take place for the purposes of the profit and loss account which will equate to the cash forecast.

The production of the expense budget will normally use as a base the previous year's level of expenditure. Many items, such as rent, will be fixed and therefore predictable. Others, such as the amount of professional salaries, will depend on market forces about which the firm will need to make a prediction, and the requirements of the strategic plan. In the first instance individuals within the firm should prepare budgets in respect of expenditure over which they have direct control. Again, there will be a nesting of expenditure depending on the firm's structure, with reviews at each level. In the same way that the budgeted profit and loss account has been produced at a number of different levels, expenditure should be stated at the same levels to enable a comparison with actual as the year progresses.

15.4 Balance sheet and cash forecast

The firm's budgeted balance sheet will flow from the profit and loss account, as adjusted for any capital items, appropriations or introductions by partners, and the firm's estimate of the time to bill its work in progress and collect monies due. At the same time a cash forecast will be produced, again taking account of these items.

The identification of capital items should be a relatively straightforward matter. Appropriations and introductions by partners will be less easy, and some elements of these may be the 'balancing figures' in the cash flow. For example, the firm will be able to predict the payment of tax and may have based its fixed monthly draws to partners on budgeted profit. However, any special draws of profits may be left out of the cash flow altogether, or only introduced at a certain level of cash collections. Introductions of capital as a result of admitting new partners will be certain, but a repayment of capital or the need for a cash call may not.

The quantification of work in progress and debtor days will reflect both the firm's historical performance and the targets set, either to bring down the number of those days, or to encourage collections to enable the firm to make special draws, or both. A term used by accountants in the measure of work in progress and debtors which is starting to be used by solicitors is 'lock-up' and this aspect of practice management is dealt with next.

15.5 Control of lock-up

15.5.1 Calculation of lock-up

Lock-up is a measure of how much of a firm's financial resources are 'locked up' in debtors and work in progress and its use provides a firm with a method of determining how efficient it is at billing work in progress and then collecting the cash on those bills.

A typical lock-up calculation for a firm as a whole could be as follows:

• work in progress	x
• less provisions	(x)
• debtors (including VAT)	x
• less provisions	(x)
• gross lock-up	x
• divided by x months time costs and disbursements ('input')	x
• lock-up percentage	x%

The number of months' input to be applied to gross lock-up is based on the firm's target for the months it should take to convert time costs into cash. Therefore, if the target for months is four, then for a calculation of lock-up at 30 June, the firm will calculate the lock-up percentage using the input for the months of March, April, May and June.

Using the above calculation, and a target of four months

	£'000
• work in progress	100
• less provisions	(10)
• debtors (including VAT)	180
• less provisions	(20)
• gross lock-up	250

If four months input is £250,000, then the target has been met, lock-up is 100 per cent and input is being billed and paid within a period of four months, that is the value of work in progress and debtors at 30 June is equivalent to the input for the four months to 30 June.

If four months' input is £125,000, then lock-up will be 200 per cent and therefore, on the assumption that input is accruing evenly, the value of work in progress and debtors is equivalent to the last eight months input. If four months input is £500,000, then lock up is 50 per cent and input is being billed and collected within two months.

Given what has been said in Chapters 12 and 14 concerning the need to estimate the length of time taken to convert input into cash for the purposes of making special draws and the firm's level of gearing, the target which is set for lock-up and then the extent to which it is achieved become critical in practice management.

15.5.2 Work in progress and fees ledger control

In order to be able to make the calculation of lock-up, and then to control it, it is necessary to have a time and disbursements recording system and a fees ledger. Although all firms will have the latter, some firms will not maintain the former. However, in all but the smallest firms, this is becoming less common, and even if a firm does not account for work in progress on its balance sheet, it may have a system of recording time and costs on a client matter basis.

In order to control work in progress, a monthly or even weekly reporting procedure is necessary which will give fee earners details of the work in progress on client matters for which they are responsible. These will be the primary source of information allowing a fee note to be issued. In addition, exception reports should be produced giving details of client matters over a certain value, where the input is over a certain number of months old and where there has been no input in recent months indicating the matter is closed and is capable of being billed.

As well as receiving reports to prompt the billing of work in progress, billing by fee earners can also be encouraged by comparison with their targets of fees to be rendered in the budget as discussed above.

A similar system of reporting will be adopted for the control of the fees ledger, with fee earners receiving reports on outstanding debts, and exception reports based on size of debt and age of debt. Debt collection can also be encouraged by setting cash collection targets, based first of all on the budgeted cash forecast, and secondly on the levels of work in progress which, according to the lock-up target, will be billed and collected within a set number of months.

This last point is particularly important, but often overlooked, by firms experiencing growth above the budgeted level. If the firm is basing its cash collection targets on its forecast, then it may be achieving these easily. However, what it should be looking at, if the forecast has not been updated, are the levels of input and unbilled work in progress. Therefore, using the above example, with the lock-up target of four months, if the work in progress at 28 February is £500,000 then cash collections in the four month period to 30 June should be £587,500, being the value of work in progress plus VAT.

As well as controlling work in progress and fees on an individual fee earner basis, control will also take place at the other levels in the budget, being partner, department, type of work and firm.

The final matter which needs to be discussed is the extent to which a firm should employ individuals such as credit controllers to ensure work in progress is billed and fees collected, rather than leave it in the hands of fee earners or partners. Some firms will only allow assistant solicitors and partners to raise bills and collect cash, believing that the relationship between the professional and the client is paramount and should in no way be interrupted by non-professional staff, or staff with no knowledge of the client. Other firms employ departments of controllers whose sole function is to get partners to bill work and then collect cash, believing that the partner/client relationship can get in the way of efficient management of the firm's lock-up.

Much of this depends on the culture at the firm; however, in the survey carried out by the author many firms expressed the view that the control of lock-up by firms of solicitors generally had been poor, and that most had only started to take measures to improve control over the last two years, as the recession had deepened. Firms were experimenting with a number of techniques, including the use of credit controllers, and these firms reported a great deal of success. Some finance partners are of the view that poor control is the fault of certain aspects of the partnership system, including the identification of client responsibility with client 'ownership', resulting in the firm as a whole being able to do little about the poor record of a complacent partner. There is no doubt a balancing act to be performed in this, but it should be apparent that the control of these matters by the firm must be an integral part of the appraisal system where the firm operates a meritocratic profit share.

15.5.3 Understanding lock-up

At its most basic, lock-up will provide a measure of how long it takes to bill input and then collect the resulting fee. The author's research indicates that, in general, firms aim to bill input within four months of it being incurred, and collect the debt 60 days later, an overall lock up target of six months. However, a number of firms do not achieve these targets and work in progress in particular appears to be the difficult area.

Although the firm's lock-up is important to its financial management, analysing the lock-up first of all by department or partner, and secondly by looking at trends in lock-up by department and partner is extremely instructive. First of all, the analysis by partner or department, if it is accompanied by details of the calculation, will provide an insight into how various areas of the firm are 'responsible' for the firm's lock-up. The next stage from here is to determine why some departments or partners have low lock-up, and why some high. The reasons may be particular to the type of law being practised, but it may also be as a result of different practices by different partners. The partners with poor lock-up can then be encouraged to adopt the techniques of the better partners.

The trend of lock-up over many months will provide other useful information for management, such as growing problems within one partner's portfolio, or another partner improving his practice management. Additionally, lock-up reports on individual clients, where a lot of work is carried out over a period of time can be useful.

Finally, lock-up should not be looked at in isolation from the other financial aspects of the firm's, or an individual partner's, financial performance. Because of the ability to agree a fee note by taking a loss on the recovery of work in progress, or to speed the collection of a fee by offering a discount, losses on jobs and credit notes issued must be considered at the same time.

15.6 Conclusion

Most of what has been discussed in this chapter is linked with arguments developed in the other chapters in this section. Therefore, the firm's efficient use of internal and external finance is dependent on the accurate forecasting of cash levels, which is dependent on setting targets for, say, lock-up; individual partner forecasts and financial performance as measured by billings targets, and lock-up also form part of the system of appraisal, which itself forms part of the strategic planning process. The practices noted in this chapter are likely to be most successful as part of an overall structured approach to the financial running of the practice by the management, as indeed is the case with all of the issues raised in this section.

Chapter 16 – Ownership of property

16.1 Introduction

This chapter is concerned with the way in which firms of solicitors own their offices and the problems which can arise. The issues for profit sharing, where there is ownership by less than the full partnership, are dealt with in Chapter 11.

16.2 Property investment clubs

'It is the view of the writer that, generally speaking, professional partnerships are well advised not to acquire appreciating property' (Nigel Davey in *Successful Mergers – Planning, Strategy and Execution*, Michael Simmons et al, 1988, Waterlow). The writer might have added 'or depreciating property as well!' That view still makes for very good advice for any partnership which is likely to experience a change in its composition in the near future, and it is primarily the issues arising from changes in the partners which cause the problems that give rise to such a strong view. The writer quoted above described the partial change of a partnership into a property investment club. So why should solicitors wish to join such a 'club'?

For many solicitors, the biggest cost in their accounts after salaries is the rent, and it always appears attractive to remove such a large overhead to improve profitability. Additionally, rents are notoriously difficult to predict if a rent review is approaching or if the property is let on a licence. Further, once a firm is committed to an institutional lease with the rents fixed for five or seven years, the profits towards the end of the rent review period may be significantly distorted where there have been large increases in market rents since the last rent review; and the firm may not be prepared for the rent hike approaching. For example, if charge out rates do not reflect the true costs of the business, that is including a contemplated market rent, there may need to be a significant increase in these rates, or there will be a decline in profitability. Profits will also be distorted where rents are falling, although firms locked into an institutional lease will not be able to take advantage of this even at the next rent review because of upward only rent review clauses.

Next, there is a belief by some firms that part of the value of the building and the rent which is paid attaches to the name and quality of the firm, and that someone else is benefitting from the firm's 'goodwill.'

Many firms, especially at the peak of an economic cycle, will look at the increases in property prices over recent years, and see the possibility of real capital appreciation. If there is the opportunity to borrow, this does provide the prospect of gearing up to create wealth, with the firm having to do little more than pay the interest on the loan. This is probably the principle reason for many firms buying their freeholds or long leaseholds. The problems facing some of these firms, and one of the main causes of solicitors seeking some sort of arrangement with creditors, is where interest rates rise, profits fall, and the value of the purchased premises does not exceed the loan financing the purchase. However, the problem dealt with here is not falling property prices and the recession *per se*, but what happens when the composition of the partnership changes.

16.3 Incoming partners

If the firm owns its own premises, purchased some time ago, say, and with little extant borrowing, the possibility of an incoming partner creates a number of problems. It raises the question of whether the property should be revalued. In the balance sheet it may be included at its original cost, which could be significantly less than the current market value. If a revaluation takes place, does the partnership insist on a vacant possession valuation, or one which takes account of the tenant? If the latter, this may be equivalent to placing a value on goodwill.

Second, the new partner, having been presented with the partnership accounts as adjusted for the increase in value, may find that he is expected to put up a large amount of capital, capital which the firm might not need, or which the existing partners use to repay part of their own capital accounts in respect of an unrealised profit. This will also be a deemed partial disposal for capital gains tax purposes. One can imagine the arguments which would ensue if a new partner had put up significant capital, much of it in respect of a property which then starts to fall in value.

However, the new partner may decline to join the club, or the existing members may decline to have him as a member, allowing him to share in the profits of the firm but not its premises (and this somewhat unreal approach to 'partnership' does occur). In this case problems will arise with the fair charge (or notional charge taken as first share of profits) to the firm by the club members for the use of the premises. Non-property owning partners will wish to ensure they pay a fair rent based on market rents, whereas the club may wish an institutional type arrangement. If rents go up or down, whatever the arrangement, one side will complain, and this splitting of the firm into sides, where club members look to their interests as landlords rather than partners will inevitably lead to a partnership split. Further, where some partners do own a property against which there is heavy borrowing and interest rates rise steeply, the rent may fall far short of the interest cost. The non-property owning partners may not be prepared to subsidise any of the shortfall.

Any borrowings in respect of a property only partially owned should be taken off-balance sheet and designated as personal borrowings; if this does not happen, non-property owning partners may be paying interest on the loan as well as rent, and they will also be liable for the borrowing, it being a partnership loan. It is also essential that any interest on capital excludes capital in respect of the property, otherwise again there will be a double charge on the non-property owning partners.

16.4 Changes in profit share

Some of the problems outlined above will also occur if there is a change in profit share which is accompanied by a change in equity. Partners experiencing increases in profit share may balk at having to put up even more capital for the office block. It also means that the premises need to be revalued whenever there is a change in profit share, and the cost of this, and sorting out the tax implications, can be excessive.

16.5 Retiring partners

The problems caused by retiring partners are slightly different. For many partners in firms owning the premises, the increasing value is seen as part of the provision for a pension. The big problem facing both partner and firm is how to pay the retiring partner, or what could be much worse, two or three partners, their share. The firm or individual partners may have severe difficulties raising sufficient money to buy the retiring partners out. Additionally, the issue of the valuation is raised, and further there is the obvious problem of paying out an unrealised profit. One solution may be that the retiring partner stays on in some capacity as a property owning partner only, something often not seen as a solution at all.

If the property market is in a slump, but with the prospect of an upturn, a partner may decide to delay his retirement until the upturn arises and the value of the premises goes up; however, the prospect of a partner staying on merely to benefit from the capital value of the property is for many too dreadful to contemplate under any circumstances. It may be that although the firm owns property, there is no general sharing in the appreciation of capital growth, and if there happens to be a disposal, the lucky partners share in the profit in the accounting period in which they fall. This possibility was noted in Chapter 11. The retiring partner will feel particularly aggrieved if a property in which he has had his office is sold for a handsome profit just after he has retired. Again a partner may decide to delay his retirement in anticipation of a future sale of the office block.

16.6 Means of ownership

The ownership contemplated above is either by the partnership as a whole, or having separate partnerships, one owning the property which has a limited number of partners, or having different classes of partners, the property owning and the non-property owning partners. Where a firm has grown through mergers and has a number of offices, then a number of different partnerships or classes of partner could be formed.

Another way of owning the property could be using a pension fund, set up for the property owning partners. There are still the problems noted above, but at least the property owning partners are further away from direct ownership of the property. This does suffer from the problem of having a significant investment of the pension fund monies in one asset.

Another route could be for the partners to form a Friendly Society and transfer the property to that, although Friendly Societies, unlike pension funds, cannot borrow, and therefore the whole of the purchase would have to be financed by contributions.

Finally, the firm could arrange for the premises to be owned by the staff pension fund, thus removing the partners altogether from ownership.

Chapter 17 – Financial aspects of admission and retirement

17.1 Introduction

This chapter sets out some of the financial considerations which a firm should address in the period prior to the admission of a new partner or the retirement of an existing partner. For many firms, a change in the composition of the partnership can be a critical event, and some firms heighten the potential problems that will arise by not planning for the change. The most serious issues will tend to arise in smaller firms on the retirement of a 'key' partner, or more than one partner. It should be possible to reduce the impact of these issues by planning for all of the change and the accountant can be expected to be asked to advise in these areas.

17.2 Admission

The most important aspect of admission is one on which the accountant will be unlikely to be consulted, that is whether an individual should be asked to join the partnership in the first place. Whatever selection criteria firms use will probably not be discussed with their accountants. Having said that, to the extent that an accountant becomes involved in strategic planning for the firm, his client, he may well have advised on the inclusion within the firm's objectives of the need to guarantee a succession, and how a policy of continuing admission of new partners achieves the firm's other strategic objectives such as a target for growth. Similarly, in any forecasts or projections on which the accountant advises, the impact of planned new partners will have been considered by him.

The immediate financial matters on which the accountant will be asked to advise will concern the introduction of capital, profit share, drawings, taxation and pensions, and assets owned or occupied by the partnership.

17.2.1 Capital

It has already been stated that the admission of a new partner is not an event which of itself will require an increase in the capital requirements of the firm. There may be such an increase if, for example, a partner is retiring on the same day and immediately receiving repayment of his capital account;

however, that is an increase due to retirement, not admission. Injection of capital is more important in the way it changes the status of the individual from employee to proprietor. It also becomes important when it is required that partners receiving equal profit shares have contributed equal amounts of capital to the practice. The partnership should therefore time its injection of capital from new partners to coincide with other events which will give rise to a requirement to increase the capital of the firm, such as a special draw of undrawn profits or repayment of loan facilities.

The partnership should also give the facility to allow new partners to build up their capital over time, rather than immediately. This is very important for most individuals who would not have the ability to raise a large amount of unencumbered cash to join a partnership. The reasons individuals are asked to join firms of solicitors as partners do not normally include the ability to invest a large capital sum. The firm therefore must have the flexibility to allow less than a fully paid up capital account at the outset. The inequality between individual partners regarding their amount of paid up capital can be dealt with by the crediting of notional interest or a restriction on the amount of drawings.

Where it is intended to allow the new partner the borrow some or all of his required capital, it is important to ensure that there is a source of finance available and that both the firm and the individual will have access to that source at the necessary time. For all firms this will mean letting the proposed source have financial information on the firm and for smaller firms the information will need to include financial information on each of the partners.

In summary, the partnership should consider the issue of how much capital contribution is actually required as part of the overall consideration of the practice. The firm should then look at the ability of the partner to pay up capital (or borrow to pay up capital) and then consider whether it is realistic to expect the full required contribution to be met immediately. Any issues concerning perceived inequalities between partners because of, say, differences in the level of capital contribution should be dealt after these stages.

17.2.2 Profit share and drawings

Where a firm has an established profit share system, the proportion of profit which the new partner will receive need not, of itself, be an issue. The amount will be determined by, for example, the lock-step. The matter which will become an issue will be that of drawings which, because they are determined by profit share may make profit share an issue.

A new partner will have an expectation that his drawings will be received regularly and will not be less than his net pay as an employee. What the partnership will effectively be asked to provide is a regular monthly amount of drawings at least equal to his monthly net pay. An issue may be raised by the existing partners to the extent that the drawings so calculated are a greater percentage of account profits than is normally distributed on a monthly basis. It would be wrong to take account of this by an increase in profit share; the firm may have to come to an arrangement with the new partner for a gradual reduction in the rate of fixed monthly draw. However, where it can be seen to be a potential problem, it should be addressed early between the firm and the new partner.

Another aspect of profit share which will be an issue will be where there is an exceptional profit or loss, either anticipated, or realised just prior to the new partner's admission. Chapter 11 identifies a number of these exceptional items and how firms deal with them. It should be borne in mind that a new partner will feel greatly aggrieved if he is asked to bear a loss which arose from incidents prior to his admission, such as a lack of a dilapidations reserve. The existing partners may also feel aggrieved if a new partner immediately shares in the profit on the disposal of premises. It may not make sense to delay admission to partnership for the sole reason of removing a new partner from the impact of an exceptional item; if planned for, it can be resolved in the period immediately leading up to admission by, for example, coming to an arrangement with the potential partner concerning his entitlement to share in the gain on any disposals of premises already owned.

17.2.3 Taxation and pensions

For a new partner who was previously an employee, the move to partner will involve a change from the Schedule E basis of assessment to Schedule D, that is from actual to prior year. It may also mean having to make provision for his own pension.

One issue which a number of newly appointed partners have experienced has arisen where their firms have experienced a declining profit trend, and where, under the prior year basis of assessment, they have been taxed in their first year on a level of profits greatly in excess of current profits. The way in which the firm actually accounts for tax will determine how much of the charge they will actually suffer, but it can happen that any paid up capital is immediately removed by the size of an over-drawn current account due to the level of the tax charge. Some new partners, if they are aware of tax legislation, and if their firm does not have provision within its partnership agreement for compelling new partners to sign a continuation election, will be able to avoid this problem by forcing a dissolution for tax purposes on their admission. It is obviously unsatisfactory for the firm to be put at risk in this way, and there should be such a provision within the partnership agreement. However, new partners should not be exposed to a liability which arises out of benefitting the rest of the partners and therefore an indemnity or some other form of compensation should be discussed in the period prior to admission.

Depending on when the new partner is appointed in the tax year, there will be a repayment to him of some of the Schedule E tax paid under PAYE. This amount can therefore be taken into account when determining the amount of any indemnity payable by the partnership because of the signing of a continuation election.

Where the partnership does not have an established method of providing partners with the facilities to obtain advice on pensions, it should bear in mind the need to ensure that new partners make adequate provision for their own pensions. It may consider doing this by including a clause to this effect in the partnership agreement. Solicitors' practices no longer represent vehicles for the appreciation of capital for a partner's retirement; additionally, methods of providing a pension such as annuities and consultancy arrangements are becoming less common than previously. It is therefore vital that individual partners ensure they themselves adequately plan for retirement.

17.2.4 Assets of the partnership

Chapters 11 and 16 deal with some of the issues which can arise in respect of property owned by partners. Of particular concern to a new partner will be the value attributable to any property owned by the partnership to which he is expected to contribute, and any rent paid by the partnership to some or all of the existing partners in respect of a property occupied by the partnership.

In each instance there will be an expectation by a potential partner that the value or the rent is fair. It is therefore recommended that in discussions with the potential partner the basis of calculation of either is raised as soon as possible, and if necessary an agreement to use independent advice made. It should never be the case that a new partner discovers that the landlords to the firm's offices are some of his existing partners only after he has been appointed and signed the partnership agreement.

It would be unusual to expect a new partner to make a specific contribution in respect of any other tangible asset of the partnership. However, it is still the case that some firms will recognise goodwill, either on the balance sheet, or on a change in the composition of the partnership. Where goodwill is carried on the balance sheet, prior to the admission of any new partner, the firm should consider whether any value is represented by the goodwill. Some firms will continue to carry goodwill which has arisen, say, from a merger, but without any amortisation since it was brought into the accounts. The capital accounts of existing partners can be represented by a substantial amount of goodwill, leading to a large imbalance between capital accounts on admission of a new partner who is required to invest only a moderate amount of fixed capital. It may prove expensive for the new partner to bring his capital account into line with the remaining partners in future, and in any case he may doubt whether there is anything of value in his effective purchase of goodwill.

Where the firm accounts for goodwill only on a change in the composition of the firm, there will be a valuation of goodwill prior to the new partner being admitted. He will then be admitted and be required to purchase a certain proportion of the goodwill owned by other partners, and goodwill will then be written off. This can be an unsatisfactory arrangement with the requirement to fund the purchase of an asset which is not represented on the balance sheet of the firm. In any case, many new partners will consider that they have contributed to the goodwill of the firm during their time as employees. It is, however, becoming increasingly common for firms to ignore goodwill altogether.

Finally, it is recommended that firms discuss with their new partners their accounts and the nature of any claims against the firm. It is often suggested that potential partners speak with the firm's accountants regarding the financial aspects of the firm. Given the variation in techniques of accounting for transactions undertaken by firms of solicitors, this must be good advice.

17.3 Retirement

For many firms the retirement of a partner raises serious issues in the continuation of the partnership. Even without the financial issues, the removal of someone of long standing, closely involved in the management of the firm, the firm's culture and with a loyal portfolio will give the firm problems in management, its identity and the continuing relationship with clients. Many firms do not plan adequately for these aspects of retirement, with the perception that a key individual is being lost. The aim should be to ensure that, for the partnership as a whole, the retirement of any one individual takes place smoothly and therefore the process of retirement happens over an extended period of time. The financial aspects of retirement need to be planned for similar reasons.

17.3.1 Capital

There is no reason why the retirement of a partner, of itself, should give rise to a repayment of capital. However, many partners will expect, not unreasonably from their own point of view, to have not just their capital, but also their current account repaid to them the day they retire. This can create a severe strain on the firm's finances; it is almost inevitable that retiring partners will be the longest serving partners, with the largest capital accounts. The preparation for retirement therefore takes place many years before by ensuring that no individual can build up such a large capital account, or balance of undrawn profit or that the firm cannot easily repay the monies owed to him.

It is also important that partnership agreements are drafted to include provision for the repayment of capital which is certain, but ultimately at the firm's convenience. A means of doing this may be to continue to pay the retiring partner monthly drawings, thereby gradually bring down the level of his capital. Alternatively, capital could be repaid in tranches at the time of special draws, and in preference to the payment of undrawn profits to existing partners. During this time it is important that any notional interest continues to be paid on capital account.

As part of its normal planning process, a firm should consider the timing of retirements of individual partners. Notwithstanding the management issues, retirements at regular intervals are less of a strain on the firm's finances.

17.3.2 Annuities, consultancy and pension payments

As noted above, although goodwill continues to be accounted for, it has become of less importance in solicitors' accounts. Therefore, for many partners facing retirement there is a perception that, on the repayment of their capital accounts, they will be receiving less than their portion of what the practice is worth. This is particularly true for partners in firms which prepare their accounts on a cash basis, or which do not account for work in progress. Some firms have provisions for making a notional repayment of work in progress to a retiring partner in the form of an annuity for a period after retirement. Such an annuity will be calculated by reference to the billings to clients in respect of clients of the retiring partner in, say, the 12 month period following retirement. Alternatively, where the firm does not account for work in progress, but does maintain a time recording system, then it will be calculated by reference to the uncleared time on clients of that partner at the date of retirement.

Annuities paid to retiring partners are also a common feature of many practices seeking to make a payment for goodwill, or to take account of the legislation which existed in the 1970s which restricted the ability of the self-employed to make provision for retirement. Firms of solicitors, recognising that the purchase of goodwill by incoming partners could represent a heavy financial burden wrote into partnership agreements clauses setting out annuities to be paid to partners on retirement. Sometimes the beneficiaries of such annuities were restricted to a select core of partners, and these have come to be known as founding partners' annuities. In essence, new partners are mortgaging their future income to gain a stake in the business; however, some annuity provisions were drawn up to set the annuity at an amount based on profit share, say the average of the best three years out of the last five before retirement, thereafter increasing by inflation. In this way it has become possible for the annuities paid out to many retired partners to exceed the highest profit share of any existing partners, when profits have started to fall. Some annuities devolve onto widows or other dependents after the death of a retired partner.

There are a number of good reasons to set up an annuity, for example the ability, under certain circumstances to have the payment tax deductible as a charge. However, to create such a potential liability which the firm may find itself unable to fund is not such a good idea. Commitments of this sort may deter new partners from joining the firm. For these reasons, arrangements to pay such heavy amounts are unlikely to be contemplated presently. There will almost certainly be restrictions on the amount payable, the amount by which the annuity can increase, and the length of time over which it is payable. Some firms will take the view that there is no reason why any amount payable to former partners should not be funded out of assets separate from those of the continuing partnership.

Additionally, some firms are reported to have come to arrangements with existing senior partners to scrap annuity arrangements because of pressure from younger partners who fail to see why their earning capacity should be treated as a fund for the pensions of retired partners.

Some firms enter into arrangements with their retired partners to pay them a consultancy fee after retirement. Such payments may not be as tax efficient as annuities, for example to be allowable for tax they have to pass the wholly and exclusively rule, and the recipient consultant may be required to charge VAT on the sum received. However, they may be more controllable by the partnership where the receipt of the consultancy services is at the option of the firm, and thus should not saddle the firm with an ongoing liability.

It is clear that firms are best advised to ensure that partners take advantage of the pensions legislation and proper provision for their retirement and, as noted above, many firms will require their partners to do just that by a clause in the partnership agreement. This will avoid the problem of a partner being unwilling to retire because of a lack of provision for the future.

However, there is one piece of pensions legislation which may see a change in the way partners currently provide for their retirement. The 1989 Budget introduced a limit on the net relevant earnings for the calculation of tax relief on personal pension payments. That limit was set at £60,000 and increases with inflation. Given that professional earnings outstrip inflation, and the high earnings capacity of partners in some solicitors' firms, the ability of partners to make tax allowable pension contributions to fund pensions of the size of their profit shares will be restricted. As the disparity between the inflated net relevant earnings limit and earnings increases, new ways of providing for pensions may be developed, and some old methods resurrected.

17.3.3 Exceptional and unrealised profit shares

As noted in Chapter 9, the methods of accounting adopted by solicitors can lead to items not being accounted for in the correct year. Large profits or losses, which have arisen for exceptional reasons, can fall in an arbitrary manner, and as with new partners, problems can arise on the way these are borne or shared. Retiring partners will wish to share in the proceeds of any large capital gains on the disposal of properties which have been owned by the partnership during their period as a partner. They may, therefore, delay their retirement to ensure that they retire in the period of sale. Sale may be delayed, and therefore they may defer their retirement for a further period. Arrangements need to be made to account for this, and Chapter 11 considers ways in which such exceptional profits can be distributed.

In the case of losses, the remaining partners will feel aggrieved if a partner retires in the year prior to a large loss on, for example, a defaulting client or a professional indemnity claim. In these circumstances the partnership does have the advantage of being able to leave its accounts open for some substantial period of time while the settlement of such matters is discussed. This does of course mean that a retiring partner can be uncertain as to the amount finally payable; however, this need not preclude the payment on account of his capital and current account, and indeed, the phased payment of these is suggested in any case.

Finally, where property is owned, there is the difficult problem of valuing the asset and coming to an arrangement with the retiring partner concerning his share of an unrealised profit, or what may currently be an unrealised loss. Again, partners may delay their retirement to ensure they maximise the profit arising on a valuation. Given that some partnerships will always wish to invest in property, these issues can only be resolved by facing them in advance and planning for their eventuality by negotiations among the partners.

APPENDICES

List of appendices

Appendix 1 – Definitions used in the Solicitors Accounts Rules 1991 and the Accountants Report Rules 1991

Extract from the Solicitors' Accounts Rules 1991:

'In these Rules, unless the context otherwise requires:

the expressions *accounts*, *books*, *ledgers* and *records* shall be deemed to include loose-leaf books and such cards or other permanent documents or records as are necessary for the operation of any system of book-keeping, computerised, mechanical or otherwise and where a computerised system is operated, the information recorded on it must be capable of being reproduced in hard printed form within a reasonable time;

bank shall mean the branch, situated in England or Wales, of a bank as defined by section 87(1) of the Solicitors Act 1974, as amended by paragraph 5 of Schedule 6 to the Banking Act 1987;

building society shall mean the branch, situated in England or Wales, of a building society as defined by paragraph 11(5) of Schedule 18 to the Building Societies Act 1986.

client save in Part III of these Rules, shall mean any person on whose account a solicitor holds or receives client's money;

client account shall mean a current or deposit account at a bank or deposit account with a building society in the name of the solicitor or his or her firm in the title of which account the word *client* appears;

client's money shall mean money held or received by a solicitor on account of a person for whom he or she is acting in relation to the holding or receipt of such money either as a solicitor, or, in connection with his or her practice as a solicitor, or, as agent, bailee, stakeholder or in any other capacity; provided that the expression *client's money* shall not include:

(a) money held or received on account of the trustees of a trust of which the solicitor is a controlled trustee; or

(b) money to which the only person entitled is the solicitor himself or herself or, in the case of a firm of solicitors, one or more of the partners in the firm;

controlled trust in relation to a solicitor shall mean a trust of which he or she is a controlled trustee;

controlled trust account shall mean a current or deposit account kept at a bank or deposit account kept with a building society in the title of which the word *trustee* or *executor* appears, or which is otherwise clearly designated as a controlled trust account, and kept solely for money subject to a particular trust of which the solicitor is a controlled trustee;

controlled trustee shall mean a solicitor who is a sole trustee or co-trustee only with one or more of his or her partners or employees and any reference to a controlled trustee shall be construed as including:

(a) a recognised body which is the sole trustee or co-trustee only with one or more of its officers, partners or employees; and
(b) a solicitor or a recognised body who or which is an officer or employee of a recognised body and who or which is a sole trustee or co-trustee only with one or more other officers or employees of that recognised body or the body itself;

costs include fees, charges, disbursements, expenses and remuneration and, for the purpose of rules 7(a)(iv) and 9(2)(c)(i), shall include costs (including VAT) in respect of which a solicitor has incurred a liability but shall exclude the fees of counsel or other lawyer, or of a professional or other agent, or of an expert instructed by the solicitor;

local authority shall have the same meaning as is given to this expression by the Local Government Act 1972;

private loan shall mean a loan other than one provided by an institution which provides loans in the normal course of its activities;

public officer shall mean an officer whose remuneration is defrayed out of moneys provided by Parliament, the revenues of the Duchy of Cornwall or the Duchy of Lancaster, the general fund of the Church Commissioners, the Forestry Fund or the Development Fund;

recognised body shall have the meaning assigned to it by the Solicitors' Incorporated Practice Rules 1988 as may be amended, re-enacted from time to time;

separate designated account shall mean a deposit account at a bank or building society in the name of the solicitor or his or her firm in the title of which account the word *client* appears and which is designated by reference to the identity of the client or matter concerned;

solicitor shall mean a solicitor of the Supreme Court and shall include a firm of solicitors or a recognised body;

statutory undertakers shall mean any person authorised by or under an Act of Parliament, to construct, work, or carry on any railway, canal, inland navigation, dock, harbour, tramway, gas, electricity, water or other public undertaking;

trust money shall mean money held or received by a solicitor which is not client's money and which is subject to a trust of which the solicitor is trustee whether or not he or she is a controlled trustee of such trust;

words in the singular include the plural, words in the plural include the singular and words importing the masculine or feminine shall include the neuter; and

Other expressions in these Rules shall except where otherwise stated have the meanings assigned to them by the Solicitors Act 1974.'

Appendix 2 – Extract from the Accountants Report Rules 1991 – Accountants Report

THE SCHEDULE

ACCOUNTANT'S REPORT

Section 34 of the Solicitors Act 1974,
Section 9 of the Administration of Justice Act 1985
and Schedule 15, paragraph to the Financial Services Act 1986

Accountant's Report Rules 1991

NOTE – this Form may be used for a Report in respect of:

1 a solicitor;
1a a registered foreign lawyer (RFL);
2 a firm of solicitors, provided the names of all the partners in the firm appear in Section A1 below;
2a a multi-national partnership, provided the names of all the partners appear in Section A1 below;
3 a recognised body.

SECTION A – Do not complete if Report is submitted on behalf of a recognised body

Please indicate whether this report covers all the partners within the firm who have held clients' monies (or money subject to a controlled trust) during the period under review or whether individual reports are being submitted

* Tick box as appropriate	* covers all partners/ sole principal	* individual reports submitted
	☐	☐

Note – Please complete in block capitals; the letters "(RFL)" must be entered against the surname of any RFL.

1. *Full Name of Solicitor(s) and/or RFL(s)*

FORENAMES SURNAME

....

....

(continue on a separate sheet if necessary)

Note – All addresses at which the solicitor(s) RFL(s) practice(s) must be covered by an Accountant's Report(s). If an address is not so covered the reason must be stated.

(In the case of an RFL, this Report only refers to his or her practice(s) as partner of a solicitor(s) or as director of a recognised body.)

2. *Firm(s) Name(s) and Address(es)*

....

....

....

....

....

....

....

....

....

(continue on a separate sheet if necessary)

Note – The period must comply with Section 34(3) of the Solicitors Act 1974, and the Accountant's Report Rules 1991.

3. *Accounting Period*

Beginning.. Ending Section

Note – Delete (a) or (b) as appropriate.

4(a) I/we confirm that a copy of this Report has been sent to each of the solicitors and/or RFLs to whom this Report relates.

or

(b) I/we confirm that one copy of this Report has been sent to the following partner of the firm, on behalf of all the partners of the firm:

....

SECTION B – To be completed only if Report is submitted on behalf of a recognised body

Note – This name must comply with Rule 22 of the Solicitors' Incorporated Practice Rules 1988.

1. *Name of Recognised Body*

....

....

....

Note – The registered office must comply with Rule 8 of the Solicitors' Incorporated Practice Rules 1988.

2. *Registered Office*

....

....

....

3. *Principal Office, if different from Registered Office*

....

....

4. *Place of Business other than those specified in 2. and 3.*

....

....

Note – Please complete in block capitals; the letters "(RFL)" must be entered against the surname of any RFL.

5. *Name of Officers of Recognised Body*

SURNAME	FORENAMES	OFFICE HELD
....	....	....
....	....	....
....	....	....

(Continue on a separate sheet as necessary)

Note – The period must comply with Section 34(3) of the Solicitors Act 1974, and the Accountant's Report Rules 1991.

6. *Accounting Period*

Beginning .... Ending ....

Note – Delete (a) or (b) as appropriate.

7(a) I/we confirm that a copy of this Report has been sent to each of the directors of the recognised body to which this Report relates.

or

(b) I/we confirm that one copy of this Report has been sent to the following officer of the recognised body, on behalf of the recognised body;

....

SECTION C

1. In compliance with section 34 of the Solicitors Act 1974, and the Accountant's Report Rules 1991 made thereunder and under section 9 of the Administration of Justice Act 1985 and Schedule 15, paragraph 6 to the Financial Services Act 1986, I/we have examined to the extent required by Rule 4 of the said Rules the books, accounts and documents produced to me/us in respect of the above practice(s) of the above-named solicitor(s)/RFL(s) named in section A1/the recognised body named in section B1.
2. In so far as an opinion can be based on this limited examination I am/we are satisfied that during the above-mentioned period he/she/it has/they have complied with the provisions of Parts 1 and II of the Solicitors' Account Rules 1991 and where he/she/it is/they are authorised in the conduct of investment business by the Law Society, Rule 13 of the Solicitors' Investment Business Rules 1990 except so far as concerns:

    (a) certain trivial breaches due to clerical errors or mistakes in book-keeping, all of which were rectified on discovery and none of which, I am/we are satisfied, resulted in any loss to any client;
    (b) the matters set out in Section E, in respect of which I/we have not been able to satisfy myself/ourselves for the reasons therein stated;

(c) the matters set out in Section F, in respect of which it appears to me/us that the solicitor(s)/RFL(s) recognised body has/have not complied with the provisions of Parts I and II of the solicitors' Accounts Rules 1991 and, where he/she/it is/they are authorised in the conduct of investment business by the Law Society, Rule 13 of the Solicitors' Investment Business Rules 1990.

3. The results of the comparison required under Rule 4(1)(A)(f) of the Accountant's Report Rules 1991, at the dates selected by me/us were as follows:

(i)	at	£
(a)	Liabilities to clients as shown by clients' ledger accounts	....
(b)	Cash held in client account and client's money held elsewhere than in a client account after allowances for outstanding cheques and lodgments cleared after date	....
(c)	Difference between 3(i)(a) and 3(i)(b)(if any)	£
(ii)	at	
(a)	Liabilities to clients as shown by clients' ledger accounts	....
(b)	Cash held in client account and clients' money held elsewhere than in a client account after allowances for outstanding cheques and lodgements cleared after date	....
(c)	Difference between 3(i)(a) and 3(i)(b)(if any)	£

Note: The figure to be shown in 3(i)(a) and 3(ii)(a) above is the total of credit balances, without adjustment for debit balances (unless capable of proper set off, i.e., being in respect of the same client) or receipts and payments not capable of allocation to individual ledger accounts.

SECTION D – do not complete if Report is submitted on behalf of a recognised body

1. The following solicitor(s) [RFL(s)] having retired from active practice as solicitor(s) [practice in partnership with solicitor(s) or as director(s) of a recognised body] ceased to hold clients' money (or money subject to a controlled trust) on the date indicated and in respect of this solicitor/these solicitors [this RFL/these RFLs] the Report covers the period up to the date of cessation:

FULL NAME   DATE CEASED TO HOLD CLIENTS' MONEY (OR MONEY SUBJECT TO A CONTROLLED TRUST)

....

....

2. The following solicitor(s) [RFL(s)] having left the firm and ceased to practise under this style, ceased to hold clients' money under this style (or money subject to a controlled trust in connection with this practice) on the date indicated and in respect of this solicitor/these solicitors [this RFL/these RFLs] the Report covers the period up to the date of cessation.

FULL NAME   DATE CEASED TO HOLD CLIENTS' MONEY UNDER THIS STYLE (OR MONEY SUBJECT TO A CONTROLLED TRUST IN CONNECTION WITH THIS PRACTICE)

....

....

3. The following solicitor(s) [RFL(s)] has/have joined the firm during the period under review on the date indicated and in respect of this solicitor/these solicitors [this RFL/these RFL(s)] the Report covers the period from the date on which clients' money was held under this style (or money subject to a controlled trust was held in connection with this practice):

FULL NAME   DATE FROM WHICH CLIENTS' MONEY HELD UNDER THIS STYLE (OR MONEY SUBJECT TO A CONTROLLED TRUST HELD IN CONNECTION WITH THIS PRACTICE)

....

SECTION E

Matters in respect of which the accountant has been unable to satisfy himself or herself and the reasons for that inability:

....

....

....

SECTION F

Matter (other than trivial breaches) in respect of which it appears to the accountant that the solicitor(s)/RFL(s)/recognised body has/have not complied with the provisions of Parts I and II of the Solicitors' Accounts Rules 1991 and, where he/she/it is/they are authorised in the conduct of investment business, Rule 13 of the Solicitors' Investment Business Rules 1990:

....

....

....

SECTION G

Particulars of the Accountant:

Note: Please complete in block capitals.	Full Name ....
	Qualifications ....
	Firm Name ....
	Address ....
	....
	Date ....
This Report may be signed in the name of the firm of accountants of which the accountant is a partner or employee provided that the particulars of the accountant signing the Report are also specified.	Signature ....

To: The Law Society
Accountants' Reports
Ipsley Court
Redditch
Worcs. B98 0TD

(Dx: 19114 Redditch)

Appendix 3 – Extract of form from the Solicitors Investment Business Rules 1990

The following is the format of paragraph 2 of Form FSA2 and paragraph 1 of Form FSA4.

These forms are used by solicitors for the annual application to the Law Society for authorisation to conduct investment business.

Information regarding Investment Business
The amounts received by the firm during its last financial year were as follows:

(1) (i) aggregate gross commissions attributable to investment business received from authorised and exempted persons less amount thereof paid or credited to clients;
(ii) gross fee income (excluding commissions) in respect of the following in so far as constituting discrete investment business (except where the activity is incidental or is as referred to in Rule 3(2)(c)(ii):
(a) arranging or advising on life policies (as defined in the Rules)
(b) discretionary portfolio management
(c) any other discrete investment business________________

£ ____________________________

(2) Total gross income of the firm (investment *and* non-investment business)..

£ ____________________________

Therefore percentage of firm's total income attributable to (1) above .... %

Appendix 4 – Suggested format of a letter of engagement to be sent to a firm of solicitors

Dear

We refer to our appointment as Accountants and Tax Advisors to your partnership. We set out below our understanding of the basis on which we are to act.

Responsibilities under the Solicitors' Account Rules 1991 and the Accountant's Report Rules 1991
As partners you are responsible for maintaining adequate book-keeping and recording systems as required by the Solicitors' Accounts Rules 1991. You are also required to submit to the Law Society once every practice year a report by a duly qualified accountant.

As reporting accountants to your firm, the work which we are required to carry out in order to enable us to complete a report suitable for submission to the Law Society is set out in the Accountant's Report Rules 1991. Within this requirement it is our aim to carry out our work in as efficient a manner as is possible. To ensure this, we shall use staff who are suitably experienced in carrying out audits under the Accountant's Report Rules 1991.

Accounts
By Clause xx of your partnership agreement, the partnership is required to prepare or have prepared on an annual basis accounts for the year ended 30 June from the accounting records of the partnership.

Option 1 – preparation of accounts. We will prepare the annual accounts for the partnership from the accounting records and from information and explanations to be supplied by you. We will not carry out any audit or other verification work on the accounts.

Option 2 – certification that accounts are in accordance with accounting policies. We will prepare the annual accounts for the partnership from the accounting records and from information and explanations to be supplied by you. We will not carry out any audit or other verification work on the accounts. However, we will ensure that the accounts are prepared in accordance with the stated accounting policies of the firm regarding the following:

- recognition of income;
- valuation of work in progress;
- valuation of debtors;
- method of providing for future taxation; and
- capitalization and depreciation of fixed assets.

We will not express any opinion on the appropriateness of the accounting policies used. The annual accounts of the firm should not therefore be taken as showing a true and fair view of the financial position of the firm at each year end, or of its result for each year.

Option 3 – certification that accounting policies are appropriate. We will prepare the annual accounts for the partnership from the accounting records and from information and explanations to be supplied by you. We will not carry out any audit or other verification work on the accounts. However, we will ensure that the accounts are prepared in accordance with the stated accounting policies of the firm regarding the following:

- recognition of income;
- valuation of work in progress;
- valuation of debtors;
- method of providing for future taxation; and
- capitalization and depreciation of fixed assets.

We will confirm whether or not the stated accounting policies of the firm are (*Option 3A*) – appropriate for a firm of solicitors (or) (*Option 3B*) – in accordance with generally accepted accounting principles. The annual accounts of the firm should not therefore be taken as showing a true and fair view of the financial position of the firm at each year end, or of its result for each year.

Option 4 – audit certificate. We will prepare the annual accounts for the partnership from the accounting records and from information and explanations to be supplied by you. We will carry out an audit on the accounts of the partnership in order that we can report to the partners on whether, in our opinion, the accounts show a true and fair view of the result of the partnership for each year and of its state of affairs at each year end.

Option 5 – confirmation of allocation of profit share. We will calculate the profits attributable to each partner for each year, in accordance with Clause xx of your partnership agreement and report on this to the partners. Based on our calculation of the firm's liability to taxation for each financial year, we shall allocate the tax liability by partner. We will provide schedules to the accounts setting out details for each partner of:

- the allocation of profit and taxation;
- the movement on capital and current accounts; and
- the breakdown of the taxation reserve by tax year.

Management Letter
At the end of our work each year, we will report to you of any significant weaknesses in, or observations on, the partnership's systems which come to our notice and which we think should be brought to your attention. We will draw attention to improvements in internal controls, reporting procedures and accounting systems which can lead to savings in operating costs and audit time or improvements in control.

Partnership Taxation Services
For each accounting period, we shall prepare a computation of profits adjusted in accordance with the Taxes Acts, and submit it to the Inspector of Taxes. We shall deal with all assessments in respect of accounting periods ending on or after 30 June 1992.

We shall lodge formal notice of appeal against excessive or incorrect assessments to tax where notice of such assessments is received by us. Where appropriate, we shall also apply to delay the payment of tax in dispute. We will tell you of the appropriate payments on account to make.

We understand that your previous accountants will deal with assessments relating to earlier years.

We will deal with all other correspondence with the Inspector of Taxes including queries arising on computations in respect of accounting periods ending on or after 30 June 1992. We understand that queries in respect of earlier years will be dealt with by your previous accountants.

Personal Taxation Services
For each of the partners set out in the Appendix to this letter we will prepare returns of income and, subject to their approval and signature, submit them to the Inland Revenue. We will also act on their behalf in the agreement of all

assessments to income tax and capital gains tax raised by the Inland Revenue and in advising of the due dates of payments.

The first returns of income tax that we will be dealing with on behalf of the partners will be those relating to income and gains of the year ended 5 April 1994 together with the relevant assessments arising thereon. We understand that your previous advisers will be dealing with outstanding returns and other matters relating to earlier years.

We also deal with the preparation of any return or account which may be required for inheritance tax purposes. The reporting requirements of transactions within the scope of inheritance tax are quite distinct from the completion of returns of income for income tax and capital gains tax purposes and we would therefore ask that you advise us as early as possible of any such transactions completed or contemplated.

Every February, we will advise each partner whose affairs are dealt with by us of his entitlement to make RAP or PPP payments, including payments which can be related back to prior years, subject to us being provided with the relevant information by your previous tax advisers.

We are authorised to give investment advice to clients of the firm in accordance with the Financial Services Act 1986. If such advice is provided a separate engagement letter for any work carried out on your behalf will be issued.

Fees
Our fees are based on the time spent on your affairs. They reflect the level of skill and responsibility involved. Unless otherwise agreed, we will charge separately for each of the main classes of work described above.

Work will be billed as it progresses.

Bills are due for payment on presentation.

Files and Records
Would you please note that in the absence of other instructions from our clients, it is our normal practice to destroy correspondence and other papers which are more than 12 years old.

Agreement of Terms
In the event of any dispute arising in respect of or relating to the services to be provided in accordance with this letter or any additional services to be provided by us such dispute shall be determined by the exclusive jurisdiction of the English Courts.

We shall be grateful if you will confirm in writing your agreement to the terms of this letter. Once it has been agreed, the letter will remain effective until it is replaced.

Yours faithfully

____

Signed on behalf of the Partnership

____

Date

Appendix 5 – Permanent file update programme

CLIENT______________________________

ACCOUNTS TO_________________________

PERMANENT FILE UPDATE
PROGRAMME___________________________

Prepared by	
Date started	
Date finished	
Reviewed by	
Date	

Sch No.

1. Have the Professional Standards Bulletins for the period since last audit been reviewed for changes to SAR91 or the ARR91? Have the guidance notes thereon been reviewed?	
2. Have copies of Bulletins been placed in permanent file?	
3. Have the audit programmes been adjusted for any changes?	
4. Has the list of partners been updated for changes and have dates of changes been noted?	
5. Has the list of specimen signatures of all partners and employees authorised to sign cheques or other withdrawals from client account been updated?	
6. Have any branches opened or closed since the last audit?	
7. Has the list of banks and building societies where any money is held been updated for changes in the year? Place copies of mandates for new banks or building societies on the permanent file.	
8. Has the organisation chart been updated?	
9. Has the systems documentation been updated?	
10. Is there an up to date engagement letter on file?	

Appendix 6 – Audit programmes

CLIENT ______________________________

ACCOUNTS ______________________________

OBJECTIVE: To ensure that client bank accounts have been properly maintained under the SAR91

Ref. to Rules	*Rule*	*Test*
ARR91-4(1)	The accountant shall ascertain from the solicitor particulars of all bank accounts and building society accounts kept, maintained or operated in connection with his practice at any time during the period to which the report relates (including controlled trusts and other accounts which are not client accounts).	1. Obtain a list of bank accounts kept during the period under review. 2. Ensure it agrees with bank accounts at the beginning of the year plus accounts opened or closed during the year.
SAR91-2(1)	All bank and building society accounts in the name of the firm which are used to hold client money have the word 'client' in their title and are only maintained at banks and building societies as defined.	3. Ensure that all bank accounts which purport to be client accounts have the word 'client' in their title. 4. Ensure all client accounts are held at a bank or building society as defined in the SAR91.

Prepared by	
Date started	
Date finished	
Reviewed by	
Date	

Sch. No.

/1

Result	*Sch. Ref.**	*Error Noted*

* Letters appearing in this column are references to Appendix 7 where the appropriate Test Sheet can be found.

CLIENT____

ACCOUNTS______________________________________

OBJECTIVE: To ensure that client money has not been incorrectly paid into office or other non-client bank accounts

Ref. to Rules	*Rule*	*Test*
SAR91-3 ARR91-4(1)A(i)	Where a solicitor holds or receives client money he shall pay such money into a client account other than as allowed by Rule 9. Rule 9(1) allows client money not to be paid into a client account when: • it is received in cash and is paid without delay to the client or a third party on the client's behalf; • it is received by cheque or draft and endorsed over to the client or a third party on the clients behalf; • it is paid into a separate account opened in name of the client. Rule 9(2) forbids client money being paid into a client account where the client requests the money to be withheld from the client account, or where it relates to fees or bills of cost (subject to Rule 5A which allows settlement for fees to remain in the client account for up to seven days). Certain types of payment from the Legal Aid Board can remain in an office account for up to 14 days (Legal Aid Temporary Provisions). The accountant shall check such office ledger and cash accounts and bank and building society statements as the solicitor maintains with a view to ascertaining whether any client money has not been paid into a client account.	1. Review a sample of lodgements on the office bank or building society statement to ensure cash and cheques which include client money are not paid into an office bank account in accordance with Rule 3 but subject to the exceptions in Rule 9 and the Legal Aid Temporary Provisions. 2. Compare office cash book with office bank statements and enquire as to nature of any amounts in cash book but not on bank statement.
ARR91-4(1)A(j)	The accountant shall check the books of accounts which contain details of client money which, with the client's consent, is not held in a client account, to ascertain what transactions have been effected in respect of such an account.	3. For a sample of entries in the books of accounts containing client money not held in a client account, ensure movements are in accordance with client's written instructions.

Prepared by	
Date started	
Date finished	
Reviewed by	
Date	

Sch. No.

/2

Result	*Sch. Ref.*	*Error Noted*
	/A	

CLIENT____

ACCOUNTS______________________________________

OBJECTIVE: <u>To ensure that client money has been correctly paid into client bank account</u>

Ref. to Rules	*Rule*	*Test*
SAR91-3	Client money shall without delay be paid into a client account other than certain payments from the Legal Aid Board. These must be bulk payments from the Legal Aid Board in respect of costs, all or part of which relate to unpaid professional disbursements, providing that within 14 days any part of payment relating to fees still unpaid is transferred to client accounts.	1. Observe post-opening procedures to ensure that money is paid into client accounts without delay. 2. For a sample of receipts in client accounts, by reference to documentation in the client file, ensure money has been banked promptly. 3. For a sample of Legal Aid Payments, check the disbursement of the money to ensure the rules are being complied with.
ARR91-4(1)A(c)	The accountant shall compare a sample of lodgements into . . . the client account as shown in bank and building society statements with solicitor's records of receipts . . . of client money.	4. Select a sample of lodgements from the client account bank statements and trace back to the corresponding entries in the clients cash book and ledger.
ARR91-4(1)A(b)	The accountant shall make test checks of postings to clients' ledger accounts from records of receipts and payments of client money and make test checks of the casts of such accounts and records.	5. For the sample chosen above vouch from entries in the clients' cash book and check postings to clients' ledger accounts. 6. Check a sample of casts and clients' cash book and ledgers.
SAR91-6	No money other than money which a solicitor is required or permitted to pay into a client bank account under SAR91-4, 5 and 5A, shall be paid into such an account. Rule 4 allows the following to be paid into a client account: • trust money; • solicitor's money necessary to open or maintain the account; • money to correct withdrawals made in error. Rule 5 allows a solicitor to pay money which includes client or trust money into client accounts without splitting it. Rule 5A allows a solicitor to pay money received in settlement of bills into client accounts for up to seven days.	7. Ensure that these amounts are only money which is permitted or allowed to be paid into client account. (*NB.* if to correct withdrawal made in error, note error.)

Prepared by	
Date started	
Date finished	
Reviewed by	
Date	

Sch. No.

/3

Result	*Sch. Ref.*	*Error Noted*
	/B /A & /B	
	/B	
	/B & /C	
	/B	

CLIENT____

ACCOUNTS____

OBJECTIVE: To ensure that any withdrawals of client money are in accordance with the Rules

Ref. to Rules	*Rule*	*Test*
ARR91-4(1)A(c)	The accountant shall compare a sample of . . . payments from the client account as shown in bank and building society statements with the solicitor's records of . . . payments of client money.	1. Select a sample of payments at random from the client account bank and building society statements and trace back to the corresponding entries in the client's cash book.
ARR91-4(1)A(b)	The accountant shall make test checks of postings to clients' ledger accounts from records of receipts and payments of client money and make test checks of the casts of such accounts and records.	2. For the sample chosen above vouch from entries in the clients' cash book and check postings to clients' ledger accounts. 3. Check a sample of casts and clients' cash book and ledgers.
SAR91-7(a)	In the case of client money, no monies may be drawn from a client account except:	4. From the above sample of payments and transfers from client account check to: • clients file; • office accounts with copy bills; • third parties; and verify that such payments and transactions are either:
	• money properly required for payment to or on behalf of a client;	• paid to or on behalf of clients; or
	• money properly required in full or partial reimbursement of money expended by the solicitor on behalf of the client;	• reimbursing in full or in part money expended by the solicitor on behalf of the client (having regard to the definition of 'costs'), or
	• money drawn on the client's authority;	• drawn on the client's authority;
	• money properly required for or towards payment of the solicitor's costs where there has been delivered to the client a bill of costs or other written information and it is clear to the client that money held for him is being applied towards or in satisfaction of such costs;	• paying in full or in part the solicitor's costs where the required bill or written intimation has been rendered to the client; or
	• money which is transferred into another client account.	• transferred into another client account; or

Prepared by	
Date started	
Date finished	
Reviewed by	
Date	

Sch. No.

/4

Result	*Sch. Ref.*	*Error Noted*
	/C	
	/C	

CLIENT________________________________

ACCOUNTS________________________________

OBJECTIVE: To ensure that any withdrawals of client money are in accordance with the Rules (*Continued*)

Ref. to Rules	*Rule*	*Test*
SAR91-7(b)	In the case of trust money no monies may be drawn from a client account except: • money properly required for a payment in the execution of the particular trust; or • money to be transferred to a separate bank or building society account kept solely for the money of the particular trust.	• in accordance with the execution of the trust; or • paid into a bank or building society account kept solely for the money or the trust; or
SAR91-7(c)	In the case of other monies, no monies may be drawn except: • money, previously paid in by the solicitor to open or maintain the account under Rule 4(b); or • money including client and other money paid in under Rule 5(b); or • money in full or partial settlement of the solicitor's costs paid in under Rule 5A.	• is the repayment of money to open or maintain the account; or • is the splitting out of client and other money; or • is the payment out of money received in respect of costs within seven days.
SAR91-7(d)	Money paid in contravention of the rules.	Is the repayment of money paid in contravention of the rules. (*NB*. note original error.)
SAR91-8	Money transferred from client account to pay the solicitor to reimburse him or to settle his costs or under Rule 7(c) and (d) shall be by cheque in favour of the solicitor or by transfer to a (non-client) bank account in name of solicitor.	5. In the above sample ensure cheques are properly drawn or transfers paid to a non-client bank account.
ARR91-4(1)A(h)	The accountant shall make a test examination of the clients' ledger accounts in order to ascertain whether payments from the client account have been made on any individual account in excess of money held on behalf of that client.	6. For the sample chosen in 1 above, ensure no payment results in an overdrawn client ledger account.

Prepared by	
Date started	
Date finished	
Reviewed by	
Date	

Sch. No.

/5

Result	*Sch. Ref.*	*Error Noted*
	/C	
	/C	

CLIENT______________________________________

ACCOUNTS____________________________________

OBJECTIVE: To ensure that any withdrawals of client money are in accordance with the Rules (*Continued*)

Ref. to Rules	*Rule*	*Test*
SAR91-11(6)	A withdrawal from a bank account, being or forming part of a client account, may only be made where specific authority in respect of that has been received, by one of the following (either alone or in conjunction with other persons) namely: (a) a solicitor who holds a current practising certificate; or (b) an employee of such a solicitor being either a solicitor or a Fellow of the Institute of Legal Executives who is confirmed by the Institute as being a good standing and who shall have been admitted a Fellow for not less than three years; or (c) in the case of an office dealing solely with conveyancing, an employee of such a solicitor being a licensed conveyancer.	7. Review client's ledger accounts to ensure that none are in debit during the year. (Rule 7 of the SAR91 which provides that money drawn shall not exceed the money held on each client account). 8. Obtain list of duly authorised persons and their signatures. 9. From the sample chosen in 1 above examine returned cheques, withdrawal slips or written authorities for authorised signatures.

Prepared by	
Date started	
Date finished	
Reviewed by	
Date	

Sch. No.

/6

Result	*Sch. Ref.*	*Error Noted*

Appendix 6

CLIENT____

ACCOUNTS____

OBJECTIVE: To ensure that the client account reconciliations have been correctly carried out and maintained

Ref. to Rules	*Rule*	*Test*
ARR91-4(1)A(g)	The accountant must satisfy himself that the reconciliation statements have been kept in accordance with Rule 11(5).	1. Ensure that a bank reconciliation and a reconciliation with client's ledger balances has been prepared not less than once every five weeks and that these are kept.
SAR91-11(5)	Every solicitor shall at least once every five weeks: (a) compare the total of the balances shown by the client's ledger accounts of the liabilities to the clients, including those for whom trust money is held in the client account, with the cash account balance; and (b) prepare a reconciliation statement showing the cause of the difference, if any, shown by the above comparison; and (c) reconcile that cash account balance with the client account bank and building society passbooks or statements and money held elsewhere and shall preserve the records of all such reconciliations.	
ARR91-4(1)A(f)	The accountant must extract (or check extractions of) balances on the client's ledger accounts during the accounting period under review at not fewer than two dates selected by the accountant (one of which may be the last day of the accounting period), and at each such date: (a) compare the total as shown by such ledger accounts of the liabilities to the clients, including those for whom trust money is held in the client account, with the cash account balance; and (b) reconcile cash balance with the balances held in client account and elsewhere as confirmed direct to the accountant by the relevant banks and building societies or other institutions (subject to the dispensation regarding non-manual systems under Rule 4(3) of the ARR91).	2. At each of the two dates: • check the extractions of all balances in the list of balances on client account to the underlying client's ledgers (the dispensation regarding non-normal systems allows the accountant to carry out a test check of the extraction against the individuals records at no fewer than two dates); • obtain bank and building society certificates for all client accounts and agree balances on such certificates to bank reconciliations; • ensure that all lodgements and unpaid cheques forming part of the reconciliation clear without delay; • check cast of reconciliation; • investigate any reconciliating items; • ensure there are no debit balances.

Prepared by	
Date started	
Date finished	
Reviewed by	
Date	

Sch. No.

/7

Result	*Sch. Ref.*	*Error Noted*

CLIENT____

ACCOUNTS______________________________________

OBJECTIVE: To ensure that there is an adequate system for recording costs

Ref. to Rules	*Rule*	*Test*
SAR91-11(4)	The solicitor is required to keep a record of all bills of costs (distinguishing between profit costs and disbursements) and all written intimations the record of which shall be contained in a bills delivered book or file of copies of bills and intimations.	1. Ensure solicitor keeps such records.
ARR91-4(1)A(d)	The accountant shall enquire into and test check the system of recording costs and of making transfers in respect of costs from the client account.	2. Ascertain and record the system of recording costs having regard to definition of 'costs'. 3. Select a sample of entries in the bills delivered book or file of copies, vouch if applicable to copy bills and intimations. 4. Ensure distinction between profit costs and disbursements. 5. For each copy bill trace costs/ disbursements to supporting information. 6. For each bill agree transfer or payment by cheque from client account.

Prepared by	
Date started	
Date finished	
Reviewed by	
Date	

Sch. No.

/8

Result	*Sch. Ref.*	*Error Noted*
	/D /D /D /D	

CLIENT______________________________

ACCOUNTS______________________________

OBJECTIVE: To ensure that the Rule 11(3) has been complied with

Ref. to Rules	*Rule*	*Test*
ARR91-4(1)A(k)	The accountant shall make a test examination of the client ledger accounts in order to ascertain whether Rule 11(3) of the SAR91 has been complied with, *i.e.* where the solicitor acts for both borrower and ledger in conveyancing transactions.	For a sample of transactions where only one account has been opened, ensure that funds belonging to each client are clearly identifiable and that the lender is an institutional lender providing mortgages in the normal course of business.

Prepared by	
Date started	
Date finished	
Reviewed by	
Date	

Sch. No.

/9

Result	*Sch. Ref.*	*Error Noted*

CLIENT____

ACCOUNTS______________________________________

OBJECTIVE: To ensure that interest on client's money is correctly accounted for under the SAR91

<table>
<tr><th>Ref. to Rules</th><th>Rule</th><th>Test</th></tr>
<tr><td>SAR91-20(1)(i)</td><td>For client money held on deposit in a separate designated account, the solicitor shall account to the client for interest earned on that money.</td><td>1. For a sample of separate designated accounts, ensure that interest credited to the account is accounted for to the client by, e.g. a transfer to the client ledger.</td></tr>
<tr><td colspan="3">N.B. The following tests need not be carried out for the purposes of the ARR Report.</td></tr>
<tr><td>SAR91-20(1)(ii)</td><td>For client money not held on deposit in a separate designated account, the solicitor shall account to the client for interest which would have accrued if the money had been held on deposit, but in accordance with the provisions of Rules 21, 22 and 23 of the SAR91.</td><td>2. For a sample of interest payments made to clients arising on money held in non-designated accounts, ensure that such amounts have been correctly calculated in accordance with Rules 21, 22 and 23 of the SAR91.
3. For a sample of entries in the non-designated accounts, enquire whether any interest has been credited to the client and if not, confirm that this is correct.</td></tr>
<tr><td>SAR91-24</td><td>Interest arising on stakeholder monies shall be paid to the person to whom the stake is paid.</td><td>4. Carry out above tests with regard to stakeholder money and ensure any interest is paid to the correct person.</td></tr>
</table>

Prepared by	
Date started	
Date finished	
Reviewed by	
Date	

Sch. No.

/10

Result	*Sch. Ref.*	*Error Noted*

CLIENT ____________________

ACCOUNTS ____________________

OBJECTIVE: To ensure that solicitor's book-keeping system complies with the SAR91

Ref. to Rules	*Rule*	*Test*
ARR91-4(1)A(a)	The accountant shall examine the bookkeeping system in every office of the solicitor as to enable the accountant to verify that such system complies with Rule 11 of the SAR91.	1. Take notes or make other records of the accounting systems in place. 2. Ensure that the systems are adequate to ensure compliance with Rule 11 and in particular ensure that: • the solicitor maintains a client ledger account for each client. • the ledger accounts show, other than in the case of Rule 11(3), particulars of all money received, held or paid on account of that client, and the current balance of each client's ledger; • that money received, held or paid out on behalf of a client is recorded in a client's cash account or client's ledger or client's columns of a ledger; • that practice monies are dealt with in the appropriate office cash book and office ledger; • that records are kept of all written intimations regarding bills of costs made to the client; • that the five-weekly client account reconciliations are carried out and records of the reconciliations kept; • that all records and bank statements, other than returned cheques, are retained for at least six years by the solicitors, and that all returned cheques for at least two years by the solicitor or the bank where a written authority exists.

Prepared by	
Date started	
Date finished	
Reviewed by	
Date	

Sch. No.

/11

Result	*Sch. Ref.*	*Error Noted*

CLIENT____

ACCOUNTS______________________________________

OBJECTIVE: To ensure the solicitor's bookkeeping system complies with Rule 13 of the SIBR90

Ref. to Rules	*Rule*	*Test*
ARR91-4(1)A(a)	For those solicitors authorised in the conduct of investment business by the Law Society, the accountant shall examine the bookkeeping systems in every office of the solicitors as to enable the accountant to verify that such system complies with Rule 13 of the SIBR90 and: (a) the system is so designed that an appropriate ledger account is kept for each client; (b) the system is designed such that the ledger accounts show separately from other information particulars of all client money received, held or paid on account of each client; (c) the system is designed such that money and other money dealt with through a client account are recorded in the books so as to distinguish such transactions from transactions relating to any other money received, held or paid by the solicitor.	1. Review system to ensure that information regarding investment business is recorded separately on bills of cost and that such bills are maintained separately and that the information for the annual returns is properly kept. 2. Review system to ensure that an appropriate ledger account is kept for each client. 3. Review ledger account to ensure that they show separately from other information particulars of all client money held or paid on account of each client. 4. Review records to ensure that transactions relating to client money and any other money dealt with through a client account are recorded in the books as to distinguish such transactions from transactions relating to other money received, held or paid by the solicitor.
SIBR90-13(a)	All bills of cost shall record the amount attributable to discrete investment business separately from the amount of costs attributable to other work.	5. Ascertain the system for identifying investment clients, and ensure that all bills for such clients are separately maintained. 6. Review a sample of such bills and ensure amounts attributable to investment business are separately identified.
SIBR90-13(b)	All bills of costs containing an amount related to discrete investment business are to be kept from other bills of cost.	7. Review a sample of other bills of cost to ensure these do not refer to investment business. 8. Ensure records for the production of information for the two annual applications is sufficient.

Prepared by	
Date started	
Date finished	
Reviewed by	
Date	

Sch. No.

/12

Result	*Sch. Ref.*	*Error Noted*
	/E	
	/D	

CLIENT ____

ACCOUNTS ____

OBJECTIVE: To ensure that controlled trust accounts have been maintained in accordance with the SAR91

Ref. to Rules	*Rule*	*Test*
SAR91-19	Where controlled trust money is not treated as client money *i.e.* under Part I of the Rules, solicitors who are controlled trustees are required to keep accounts to: • show separately in respect of each controlled trust all dealings with money; • distinguish from money regarding other accounts; • keep records for at least six years; • keep these records either centrally or maintain a central register of controlled trusts.	
ARR91-4(I)B(a)	The accountant shall ascertain details of the record keeping system relating to controlled trusts.	1. Take notes or make other records of the systems in place and ensure these are sufficient to: • show separately, in respect of each controlled trust, all dealings with money; • distinguish from money regarding other accounts; • keep records for at least six years; • keep these records either centrally or maintain a central register of controlled trusts.
ARR91-4(I)B(b)(i)	For a limited number of controlled trusts: • the accountant shall make test checks of postings to the accounts kept pursuant to Rule 19 from records of receipts and payments of money and test checks of casts of such accounts and records.	2. For a limited sample of controlled trust files carry out such postings and cast tests.
ARR91-4(1)B(b)(ii)	• request documents from the solicitor to ensure that transactions evidenced by the document are in accordance with Part II of the Rules.	3. For each controlled trust selected: • ensure money paid into controlled trust account is subject to that trust; or belongs to trustee to open or maintain the account; or is to replace money withdrawn in contravention of the SAR91 (Rule 13); • ensure money drawn from a controlled trust account is properly required for payment in execution of the trust; or is to be transferred to client account; or is trustees' money used to open or maintain the account; or is to withdraw money paid in contravention of the SAR91 (Rule 16).
ARR91-4(I)B(b)(iii)	Enquire into and test check the system of recording costs and making transfers in respect of such costs.	4. Take notes or make other records of the systems in place.

Prepared by	
Date started	
Date finished	
Reviewed by	
Date	

Sch. No.

/13

Result	*Sch. Ref.*	*Error Noted*
	/F & /G	
	/F & /G	

CLIENT____

ACCOUNTS______________________________________

OBJECTIVE: To ensure that controlled trust accounts have been maintained in accordance with the SAR91 (*Continued*)

Ref. to Rules	*Rule*	*Test*
ARR91-4(I)B(b)(iv)	Compare the balance on the last day of the accounting period as shown by the records kept under Rule 19 with balance confirmed by bank.	5. At that date carry out the comparison and investigate any discrepancies.

Prepared by	
Date started	
Date finished	
Reviewed by	
Date	

Sch. No.

/14

Result	*Sch. Ref.*	*Error Noted*

CLIENT____

ACCOUNTS______________________________________

OBJECTIVE: To ensure that Branch Records are properly maintained and proper returns are made to Head Office

Ref. to Rules	*Rule*	*Test*
ARR91-4(1)	The work in previous sections should be carried out on the accounting records maintained for each branch.	
	In addition, the recording of transfers between branches needs to be checked. Special care is needed when client's accounts are maintained at more than one office, to ensure no breaches of the rules occur such as paying out the same amount from two offices.	Select a sample of transfers of client and office money to and from branches and: • trace the corresponding entries in the head office account, checking that the dates correspond; • verify with supporting documentation that the transfer has been properly reflected in the books; • in respect of the two dates selected for reconciliations, list all outstanding transfers and: • check entries in the cash books of the transferee branches; • verify that money has been correctly recorded in both sets of books, checking the supporting documentation; • agree cheque transfers to bank reconciliation statements for each office; • check transfers are valid and do not represent breaches or correction of breaches of the rules.
		For a sample of entries from the branch return of receipts and payments and:
	When branches pay and receive money, but do not keep client records, work should be directed to checking that branch returns are accurate.	• ensure client money is separately identified; • check entries in main cash book; • check to bank statements; • check to supporting documentation.
		Review the branch cheque book and ensure all cheques issued have been included on the return.

Prepared by	
Date started	
Date finished	
Reviewed by	
Date	

Sch. No.

/15

Result	*Sch. Ref.*	*Error Noted*

Appendix 7 – Test sheet for audit programme

CLIENT____

ACCOUNTS____

OBJECTIVE: Test sheet to ensure CLIENT MONEY or CONTROLLED TRUST MONIES (per office bank statement) NOT paid into office bank account (Test No. 1 on /2)

Date of Receipt	*Receipt Reference*	*Amount* £	*Trace to Office Cash Book?*	*What is Receipt For?*

Prepared by	
Date started	
Date finished	
Reviewed by	
Date	

Sch. No.

/A

Is This Client or Controlled Trust Money?	*Exception Under Rule 9?*	*If Legal Aid, Treated Correctly? [Also Test No.3 on /3]**	*Any Errors?*

* Tests appearing in this column are references to the appropriate tests contained in Appendix 6.

Appendix 7

CLIENT____________________________________

ACCOUNTS____________________________________

OBJECTIVE: Test sheet for CLIENT MONEY IN per client bank statement

Account Name	*Date of Receipt*	*Receipt Reference*	*Amount* £	*Trace to Client Bank Account? [Test No.4 of 13]*	*Trace to Client Ledger Account [Test No.4 of 13]*	*By Reference to Client File, is this Client Money? [Test No.7 of 13]*

Prepared by	
Date started	
Date finished	
Reviewed by	
Date	

Sch. No.

/B

If No, is it an Exception under Rule 4, Excluding Adjustment of Error? [Test No.7 of /3]	*By Reference to Client File, Correct Client?*	*If Payment in, Refer to Client File – was Money Paid in Promptly? [Test No.2 of /3]*	*If Legal Aid Money Treated Correctly? [Test No.3 of /3]*	*If Transfer, do Dates Agree?*	*If any No's Errors?*

Appendix 7

CLIENT ____

ACCOUNTS ____

OBJECTIVE: <u>Test sheet for CLIENT MONEY OUT per client bank statement</u>

Amount Name Account	*Date of Payment*	*Payment Reference*	*Amount £*	*Trace to Client Cash Book [Test No.1 of /4]*	*Trace to Client Ledger [Test No.2 of /4]*	*What is Payment For?*	*Does it Come Under Rule 7 Other than Error Adjustment? [Test No.4/4 & /5]*

Prepared by	
Date started	
Date finished	
Reviewed by	
Date	

Sch. No.

/C

If Written Intimation or Bill for Costs, has it been Delivered? [Test No.2 of /4 and /5]	*Check Signatures – Correct Authority? [Test No.9 of /6]*	*If Under Rule 7 does it Have Clients Authority? [Test No.4 of /4 & /5]*	*If Transfer, do Dates Agree? [Test No.4 of /4 & /5]*	*If re Solicitor's Costs is Payment Made by Cheque to Solicitor or Transfer to Office A/C? [Test No. 5 of /5]*	*Does the Transaction Lead to Overdrawn Client A/C? [Test No. 6 of /5]*	*Error?*

Appendix 7

CLIENT____

ACCOUNTS ____

OBJECTIVE: <u>Test sheet for BILLS DELIVERED BOOK (non-investment business)</u>

Date of Bill	*Account Name*	*Trace to Copy Bill* *[Test No.3 of /9]*	*Profit Costs* *Distinguished From* *Disbursements* *[Test No.4 of /8]*	*Trace to Supporting* *Documentation per* *Client File?* *[Test No.5 of /8]*

Prepared by	
Date started	
Date finished	
Reviewed by	
Date	

Sch. No.

/D

Agree to Transfer From Client A/C or Cheque Direct to Solicitor? [Test No.6 of /8]	*Refer Investment Business? [Test 7 on /12]*	*Error?*

Appendix 7

CLIENT____

ACCOUNTS______________________________________

OBJECTIVE: Test sheet for BILLS DELIVERED BOOK (investment business) [Test No. 6 of /12]

Date of Bill	*Account Name*	*Profit Costs* £	*Disbursements* £	*VAT* £

Prepared by	
Date started	
Date finished	
Reviewed by	
Date	

Sch. No.

/E

Trace to Supporting Documents per Client File?	*Agree to Transfer From Client A/C or Cheque Direct to Solicitor?*	*Refers to Investment Business?*	*Amount Attributable to Investment Business Separately Identified?*	*Error?*

Appendix 7

CLIENT ____

ACCOUNTS ____

OBJECTIVE: Test sheet for CONTROLLED TRUST MONEY IN per controlled trust bank statements

Account Name	*Date of Receipt*	*Receipt Reference*	*Amount* £	*Trace to Controlled Trust Bank Account?*	*Trace to Controlled Trust Account?*

Prepared by	
Date started	
Date finished	
Reviewed by	
Date	

Sch. No.

/F

By Reference to Controlled Trust, is This Controlled Money?	*If No, is it an Exception Under Rule 13, Excluding Adjustment of Error?*	*By Reference to Controlled Trust File, Correct Trust?*	*If Payment in, Refer to Trust File – was Money Paid in Promptly? [Test No.2 of /3]*	*If Transfer, do Dates Agree?*	*If Any No's Errors?*

Appendix 7

CLIENT____

ACCOUNTS____

OBJECTIVE: Test sheet for CONTROLLED TRUST MONEY OUT per controlled trust bank statements

Account Name	*Date of Payment*	*Receipt Reference*	*Amount* £	*Trace to Controlled Trust Cash Book?*	*Trace to Controlled Trust Ledger?*

Prepared by	
Date started	
Date finished	
Reviewed by	
Date	

Sch. No.

/G

What is Payment For?	*Does it Come Under Rule 13 Other Than Error Adjustment?*	*Properly Required for Payment in Execution of Trust?*	*Check Signatures – Correct Authority?*	*If Transfer, do Dates Agree?*	*Does the Transaction Lead to Overdrawn Controlled Trust A/C?*	*Error?*

Appendix 8 – Test sheet for error evaluation

CLIENT ____

ACCOUNTS ____

OBJECTIVE: Test sheet for evaluation of errors

Schedule Ref.	*Description of Error*	*Amount £*	*Date of Error*	*Discovered by?*	*Date of Discovery*	*Date of Rectification*

Prepared by	
Date started	
Date finished	
Reviewed by	
Date	

Sch. No.

Any Loss to Client?	*Reason for Error*	*Results of Further Testing if Necessary*	*Is Amount Trivial?*	*Is There a Weakness in the System?*	*Conclusions*

Appendix 9 – Model set of accounts for a firm of solicitors

MACKENZIE, MACDONALD AND MCINTOSH

ACCOUNTS

Year Ended
30 June 1993

Mackenzie, MacDonald and McIntosh

Accounts for the year ended 30 June 1993

Contents

Mackenzie, MacDonald and McIntosh

Approval of accounts for the year ended 30 June 1993

D Mackenzie ....

A MacDonald ....

I McIntosh ....

J McMurdo ....

J McAndrew ....

S McCallister ....

F MacBean ....

G MacAskill ....

J Campbell ....

R Campbell ....

Date ....

Mackenzie, MacDonald and McIntosh

Income and expenditure account for the year ended 30 June 1993

	Note	*1993* £		*1992* £	
Fees Receivable – time costs			x		x
– disbursements			x		x
			—		—
Increase in work progress			x		x
Interest receivable	2		x		x
Commissions receivable			x		x
			—		—
			x		x
Expenses					
Staff costs	3	x		x	
Accommodation costs	4	x		x	
Office expenses	5	x		x	
Equipment charges	6	x		x	
Professional charges	7	x		x	
Financial charges	8	x		x	
		—		—	
			x		x
			—		—
Profit available for distribution			x		x
			═		═

Mackenzie, MacDonald and McIntosh

Balance sheet at 30 June 1993

	Note	*1993* £	£	*1992* £	£
Goodwill	9		x		x
Fixed assets	10		x		x
Investments	11		x		x
			—		—
			x		x
Current assets					
Work in progress	12	x		x	
Debtors and prepayments	13	x		x	
Client ledger bank accounts		x		x	
Client ledger balances		(x)		(x)	
Cash in hand		x		x	
		—		—	
		x		x	
		—		—	
Current liabilities					
Creditors & accrued exps	14	x		x	
Provision for taxation	15				
Office bank account		x		x	
		—		—	
		x	x	x	x
		—	—	—	—
			x		x
Long term liabilities					
Future tax reserve	16	x		x	
Less investments	16	(x)		(x)	
Medium term loan	17	x	(x)	x	(x)
		—		—	
Deferred tax	18		(x)		(x)
			—		—
			x		x
			═		═
Represented by:					
Partners' accounts			x		x
			═		═

Mackenzie, MacDonald and McIntosh

Notes to the accounts for the year ended 30 June 1993

1. *Accounting Policies*

BASIS OF PREPARATION – OPTION 1 These accounts have been prepared under the historical cost convention using the following accounting policies consistently applied.

BASIS OF PREPARATION – OPTION 2 These accounts have been prepared on a cash basis.

FEES RECEIVABLE – OPTION 1 Fees receivable comprises work billed to clients in respect of completed matters up to 30 June each year, exclusive of Value Added Tax.

FEES RECEIVABLE – OPTION 2 Fees receivable comprises work billed to clients in respect of completed matters together with interim bills up to 30 June each year, exclusive of Value Added Tax

FEES RECEIVABLE – OPTION 3 Fees receivable comprises work billed to clients, up to 30 June each year, exclusive of Value Added Tax.

FEES RECEIVABLE – OPTION 4 Fees receivable comprises work billed to clients, up to 30 June each year, exclusive of Value Added Tax and work billed after 30 June each year in respect of matters completed at 30 June.

NOTIONAL EXPENSES Charge is made in the profit and loss account for the following notional expenses:

- partner charge, representing for each partner a charge based on the salary and normal benefits, including the provision of a pension, of an assistant solicitor;
- notional interest, being a charge for interest on each partner's capital account, at average bank base rate for the year; and
- notional rent, being a charge for the market rent on the (freehold premises at High Street)/(short leasehold premises at High Street, the actual rent on which is below market levels).

All notional expenses are reversed prior to the appropriation of profit by the partners.

FOREIGN CURRENCY Foreign currency transactions of the firm are translated at the rate ruling on the date on which they occurred. Foreign currency monetary assets and liabilities, including assets denominated in a foreign currency and loans taken out specifically to finance that asset in that currency, are translated at the rate ruling at the balance sheet date. All differences are taken to the profit and loss account.

Mackenzie, MacDonald and McIntosh

Notes to the accounts for the year ended 30 June 1993

GOODWILL – OPTION 1 No account is taken of goodwill in these acounts.

GOODWILL – OPTION 2 Goodwill is carried in the accounts at a value of £x, which was the value placed on goodwill by the partners as at 1.7.X1. Goodwill is not written off.

GOODWILL – OPTION 3 Goodwill is carried in the accounts based on the agreed value of the goodwill at 30.6.X1 of the individual firms of Mackenzie and MacDonald & Co, and McIntosh & Co, prior to their merger on 1.7.X1. Goodwill is being written off in equal instalments over ten years, that being the partners' estimate of its economic life.

CONSOLIDATED ACCOUNTS AND INVESTMENTS IN RELATED ENTITIES These accounts consolidate the individual accounts of the head office at Carlisle, and its branch offices at x,x and x to 30 June 1993. The accounts do not consolidate the results of MMM Limited, the service company, which are attached to these accounts. The investment of the partnership in MMM Limited includes amounts loaned to that company. MMM Brussels is a separate partnership, to which the firm has advanced certain assets, included within debtors.

VALUATION OF FIXED ASSET INVESTMENTS Fixed asset investments comprise life assurance policies assured on the lives of certain partners. They are included in the accounts at cost.

REVALUATION OF LAND AND BUILDINGS Freehold land and buildings, and long leasehold property are revalued every five years at open market value, the increase or decrease being credited to a separate revaluation account by reference to individual profit sharing ratios of partners over the period since the last revaluation or original purchase.

CAPITALISATION OF ASSETS – OPTION 1 All assets with a purchase price in excess of £x are capitalised as fixed assets.

CAPITALISATION OF ASSETS – OPTION 2 With the exception of lease premiums paid, all assets with a purchase price in excess of £x are capitalised as fixed assets. Lease premiums paid are written off on being paid.

LEASE INDUCEMENTS – OPTION 1 Inducements received by the firm to enter into short leasehold agreements in the form of reduced rentals until the first rent review, contribution towards moving and fitting out costs and direct cash payments have been taken as an exceptional profit, and the market value of rents and actual cost of moving and fitting out substituted in the accounts.

Mackenzie, MacDonald and McIntosh

Notes to the accounts for the year ended 30 June 1993

LEASE INDUCEMENTS – OPTION 2 No adjustment has been made to rent payable, moving costs or fitting out costs to take account of inducements received by the firm to enter into short leasehold agreements in the form of reduced rentals, until the first rent review and contribution towards moving and fitting out costs.

DEPRECIATION Depreciation is provided to write off the cost, less estimated residual value, of all tangible fixed assets, other than freehold land and buildings, long leasehold property and the library, over their expected useful lives. It is calculated using the following rates:

- short leasehold property and improvements – equally over the life of the lease;
- furniture and equipment – 12½% per annum;
- computer equipment – 33⅓% per annum;
- motor vehicles – 25% per annum.

LEASES – OPTION 1 Where assets are financed by leasing agreements that give rights that approximate to ownership the assets are treated as if they had been purchased outright. The amount capitalised is the present value of the minimum lease payments payable over the term of the lease. The corresponding leasing commitments are shown as amounts payable to the lessor. Depreciation on the relevant assets is charged to the profit and loss account.

Lease payments are analyzed between capital and interest components so that the interest element of the payment is charged to the income and expenditure account over the period of the lease and represents a constant proportion of the balance of capital repayments outstanding. The capital part of the instalment reduces the amounts payable to the lessor.

All other leases are treated as operating leases. Their annual rentals are charged to the income and expenditure account on a straight line basis over the term of the lease.

LEASES – OPTION 2 All leases are treated as operating leases regardless of their terms. Their annual rentals are charged to the income and expenditure account on a straight line basis over the term of the lease.

WORK IN PROGRESS – OPTION 1 Work in progress is not recognised in the accounts.

WORK IN PROGRESS – OPTION 2 Work in progress comprises the cost of professional staff for the three months to 30 June each year, plus disbursements.

Mackenzie, MacDonald and McIntosh

Notes to the accounts for the year ended 30 June 1993

WORK IN PROGRESS – OPTION 3 The increase in work in progress comprises the increase from one year to the next of professional staff costs charged in the accounts.

WORK IN PROGRESS – OPTION 4 Work in progress comprises non-partner professional time costs, excluding any mark up, plus disbursements, and excluding any non-recoverable work in progress.

WORK IN PROGRESS – OPTION 5 Work in progress comprises non-partner professional time costs, less any progress bills, excluding any mark up, plus disbursements, and excluding any non-recoverable work in progress.

WORK IN PROGRESS – OPTION 6 Work in progress comprises non-partner professional time costs, excluding any mark up, plus disbursements, less any progress bills and excluding any non-recoverable work in progress.

WORK IN PROGRESS – OPTION 7 Work in progress comprises non-partner professionl time costs, excluding any mark up (except in the case of matters completed by the year end), plus disbursements, and excluding any non-recoverable work in progress.

DEBTORS – OPTION 1 Debtors include amounts billed as at 30 June each year.

DEBTORS – OPTION 2 Debtors include amounts billed as at 30 June each year together with any amounts capable of being billed as at that date.

BAD DEBTS Debts, less any recoverable value added tax, in excess of 90/120/240 days old are provided in full.

TAXATION – OPTION 1 Taxation is not provided in the accounts.

TAXATION – OPTION 2 Taxation is provided on the basis of the next instalment due.

TAXATION – OPTION 3 Taxation is provided on the basis of the next two instalments due.

TAXATION – OPTION 4 Taxation is provided on the full provision basis in that account is taken of the liability to taxation in respect of all accounting periods ending on the current balance sheet date.

Mackenzie, MacDonald and McIntosh

Notes to the accounts for the year ended 30 June 1993

TAXATION – OPTION 5 Taxation is provided on the cessation basis in that account is taken of the liability to taxation in respect of all accounting periods ending on the current balance sheet date on the assumption that there is a cessation for tax purposes on the current balance sheet date.

FUNDING OF TAX RESERVES Tax reserves fund specific investments and cash which are shown separately with tax reserves.

DEFERRED TAX-OPTION 1 Deferred tax is not provided in the accounts. The unprovided amount of deferred tax is not disclosed.

DEFERRED TAX-OPTION 2 Deferred tax is not provided in the accounts. The unprovided amount of any deferred tax is disclosed.

DEFERRED TAX-OPTION 3 Provision is made for timing differences between the treatment of certain items for taxation and accounting purposes to the extent that it is probable that a liability or asset will crystallise. Any unprovided deferred tax is separately disclosed.

PENSION COSTS Contributions to the firm's defined benefit scheme are charged to the income and expenditure account so as to spread the cost of pensions over employees' working lives with the firm.

Contributions to the firm's defined contribution scheme are charged to the income and expenditure account in the year in which they become payable.

Mackenzie, MacDonald and McIntosh

Notes to the accounts for the year ended 30 June 1993

	1993	*1992*
	£	£
2. *Interest Receivable*		
Interest receivable on bank accounts	x	x
less paid to clients	(x)	(x)
	x	x
3 *Staff costs*		
Professional salaries	x	x
Professional salaries national insurance	x	x
Professional pension costs	x	x
Administration salaries	x	x
Administration salaries national insurance	x	x
Administration pension costs	x	x
Staff welfare and other costs and benefits	x	x
	x	x
4. *Accommodation costs*		
Rent	x	x
Rates	x	x
Service charges	x	x
Lighting and heating	x	x
Repairs and renewals	x	x
Depreciation and short leasehold property	x	x
Depreciation of fixtures and fittings	x	x
Insurance	x	x
	x	x
5. *Office expenses*		
Telephone	x	x
Postage	x	x
Printing and stationery	x	x
Cost drafting	x	x
Books and publications	x	x
	x	x

Mackenzie, MacDonald and McIntosh

Notes to the accounts for the year ended 30 June 1993

	1993	*1992*
	£	£
6. *Equipment charges*		
Equipment hire and maintenance	x	x
Motor vehicle charges	x	x
Depreciation of equipment and motor vehicles	x	x
	x	x
7. *Professional charges*		
Accountancy	x	x
Public relations	x	x
Counsels' fees	x	x
Professional indemnity insurance	x	x
Practising certificates	x	x
	x	x
8. *Financial charges*		
Amortisation of goodwill	x	x
Bad and doubtful debts	x	x
Bank charges	x	x
Bank loan interest	x	x
Overdraft interest	x	x
	x	x
9. *Goodwill*		
Estimate of value as at 1 July 19X1		x
Amortisation		(x)
Written down value		x

Mackenzie, MacDonald and McIntosh

Notes to the accounts for the year ended 30 June 1993

10. *Fixed assets*

	Freehold Property £	Short Leasehold Property £	Fixtures & Fittings £	Computer Equipment £	Motor Vehicles £	Total £
Cost						
Balance at 1 July 1992	x	x	x	x	x	x
Additions	x	x	x	x	x	x
Disposals	x	x	x	x	x	x
Balance at 30 June 1993	x	x	x	x	x	x
Depreciation						
Balance at 1 July 1992	x	x	x	x	x	x
Provided in year	x	x	x	x	x	x
On disposals	x	x	x	x	x	x
Balance at 30 June 1993	x	x	x	x	x	x
At 30 June 1993	x	x	x	x	x	x
At 30 June 1992	x	x	x	x	x	x

	1993 £	*1992* £
11. *Investments*		
Investment in MMM Limited	x	x
Life assurance policies at cost	x	x
	x	x
Surrender value of life assurance policies at year end	x	x
12. *Work in progress*		
Time costs	x	x
Disbursements	x	x
	x	x

Mackenzie, MacDonald and McIntosh

Notes to the accounts for the year ended 30 June 1993

		1993	*1992*
		£	£
13.	*Debtors and prepayments*		
	Fees rendered at year end	x	x
	Fees rendered after year end in respect	x	x
	of matters completed at year end	x	x
	Insurance	x	x
	Rent and rates	x	x
	Interest receivable	x	x
	Subscriptions	x	x
	Season ticket loans	x	x
	Amounts owed by former partners	x	x
	Other debtors	x	x
	Loaned to MMM Brussels	x	x
		—	—
	Loaned to MMM Brussels	x	x
		—	—
14.	*Creditors and accrued expenses*		
	Purchase ledger	x	x
	Pension liability	x	x
	VAT	x	x
	PAYE control	x	x
	Salary control	x	x
	Amounts owed to former partners	x	x
	Motor, travel and entertaining	x	x
	Rent and rates and service charges	x	x
	Current instalments of medium term loan	x	x
		—	—
		x	x
		═	═
15.	*Provision for taxation*		
	Second instalment 1992/93 due 1 July 1993	x	x
		═	═

Mackenzie, MacDonald and McIntosh

Notes to the accounts for the year ended 30 June 1993

		1993	*1992*
		£	£
16.	*Future tax reserve*		
	1992/93	x	x
	1993/94	x	x
	1994/95	x	x
		—	—
		x	x
	Less investments to fund future tax liabilities	(x)	(x)
		—	—
		x	x
		═	═
17.	*Medium term loan*		
	Ten year loan, repayable in ten annual instalments, first instalment due 1 July 90	x	x
	Less current instalments	(x)	(x)
		—	—
		x	x
		═	═
18.	*Deferred tax*		
	Deferred tax provided on capital gain deferred by way of rollover relief	x	x
		═	═
	Deferred tax not provided on accelerated capital allowances	x	x
		═	═
19.	*Commitments under operating leases*		
	As at 30 June 1993, the firm had annual rental commitments under non-cancellable operating leases as follows:		
	On equipment	x	x
		═	═
	On short leasehold property at (lease expires xx.xx.xx; next rent review xx.xx.xx)	x	x
	On short leasehold property at (lease expires xx.xx.xx; next rent review xx.xx.xx)	x	x
	On short leasehold property at (lease expires xx.xx.xx; next rent review xx.xx.xx)	x	x
	On short leasehold property at (lease expires xx.xx.xx; next rent review xx.xx.xx)	x	x
		—	—
		x	x
		═	═

Mackenzie, MacDonald and McIntosh

Notes to the accounts for the year ended 30 June 1993

20. *Pension schemes*

The firm operates two pension schemes, a defined benefit scheme and a defined contribution scheme.

The pension cost of the defined benefit scheme is assessed every three years in accordance with the advice of a qualified actuary. The most recent valuation, at 30 June 1992, indicated that the scheme's assets were sufficient to meet its liabilities, based on an assumed investment return of eight per cent per annum, salary increases of six per cent per annum, and an increase in pensions of four per cent per annum. Contributions to the scheme by the firm and eligible employees have been maintained in accordance with the recommendations of the actuary.

The pension cost of the defined contribution scheme represents contributions payable by the firm to the fund.

21. *Contingent liabilities*
At 30 June 1993 the firm had guaranteed the borrowings of certain entities which amounted to the following:

	1993	*1992*
MMM Limited	x	x
MMM Brussels	x	x

Appendix 10 – Suggested Accountants Report for solicitors accounts

Preparation of accounts

To the partners of Mackenzie, MacDonald and McIntosh

We have prepared the acccounts on pages xx to xx, without carrying out an audit, from the books and records of the partnership, and from information and explanations supplied to us by the partners.

Additional paragraphs of the Accountant's Report

Confirmation of profit share

We have also prepared the allocation of profits for the year ended 30 June 1993 by partner based on the memorandum of the partnership's compensation committee dated 1 August 1989, such committee being duly empowered under Clause xx of the partnership agreement dated 1 July 1989.

Disclaimer on commentary

We have not reviewed or verified in any way the commentary on the accounts on page xx prepared by Mr xx.

Certification that accounts are in accordance with accounting policies

To the partners of Mackenzie, MacDonald and McIntosh

We have prepared the accounts on pages xx to xx, without carrying out an audit, from the books and records of the partnership, from information and explanations supplied to us by the partners, and in accordance with the accounting policies of the partnership set out on page xx of the accounts.

Certification that accounting policies are appropriate

To the partners of Mackenzie, MacDonald and McIntosh

We have prepared the accounts on pages xx to xx, without carrying out an audit, from the books and records of the partnership, from information and explanations supplied to us by the partners, and in accordance with appropriate accounting policies set out on page xx of the accounts.

Certificate that accounting policies are appropriate to firms of solicitors

To the partners of Mackenzie, MacDonald and McIntosh

We have prepared the accounts on pages xx to xx, without carrying out an audit, from the books and records of the partnership, from information and explanations supplied to us by the partners, and in accordance with accounting policies which are appropriate for a firm of solicitors and which are set out on page xx of the accounts.

Certificate that accounting policies are generally acceptable

To the partners of Mackenzie, MacDonald and McIntosh

We have prepared the accounts on pages xx to xx, without carrying out an audit, from the books and records of the partnership, from information and explanations supplied to us by the partners, and in accordance with the stated accounting policies as set out on page xx of the accounts which are in accordance with generally acceptable accounting principles.

'Audit' certificate

To the partners of Mackenzie, MacDonald and McIntosh

We have audited the accounts on pages xx to xx, in accordance with Auditing Standards. In our opinion the accounts show a true and fair view of the state of affairs of the partnership as at 30 June 1993 and of the profit for the year then ended.

Appendix 11 – Suggested format for partners information pack

MACKENZIE, MACDONALD AND MCINTOSH

ACCOUNTS

Year Ended
30 June 1993

PARTNERS' INFORMATION PACK

Mackenzie, MacDonald and McIntosh

Accounts for the year ended 30 June 1993

Contents

Mackenzie, MacDonald and McIntosh

Summary of capital and current accounts and tax reserves as at 30 June 1993

	Capital Account	*Current Account*	*Tax Reserves*	*Total*
	£	£	£	£
D Mackenzie	x	x	x	x
A MacDonald	x	x	x	x
I McIntosh	x	x	x	x
J McMurdo	x	x	x	x
J McAndrew	x	x	x	x
S McCallister	x	x	x	x
F MacBean	x	x	x	x
G MacAskill	x	x	x	x
J Campbell	x	x	x	x
R Campbell	x	x	x	x
	x	x	x	x

Appendix 11

Mackenzie, MacDonald and McIntosh

Movement on capital account for the year ended 30 June 1993

	As at 1 July 1992	*Introduced*	*Withdrawn*	*As at 30 June 1993*	*Equity Points*
	£	£	£	£	
D Mackenzie	x	x	x	x	x
A MacDonald	x	x	x	x	x
I McIntosh	x	x	x	x	x
J McMurdo	x	x	x	x	x
J McAndrew	x	x	x	x	x
S McCallister	x	x	x	x	x
F MacBean	x	x	x	x	x
G MacAskill	x	x	x	x	x
J Campbell	x	x	x	x	x
R Campbell	x	x	x	x	x
	—	—	—	—	—
	x	x	x	x	x
	═	═	═	═	═

Mackenzie, MacDonald and McIntosh

Movement on current account for the year ended 30 June 1993

	As at 1 July 1992	*Drawings*	*RAPs/PPPs Paid*	*Profit*	*Tax Charge*	*As at 30 June 1993*
	£	£	£	£	£	£
D Mackenzie	x	x	x	x	x	x
A MacDonald	x	x	x	x	x	x
I McIntosh	x	x	x	x	x	x
J McMurdo	x	x	x	x	x	x
J McAndrew	x	x	x	x	x	x
S McCallister	x	x	x	x	x	x
F MacBean	x	x	x	x	x	x
G MacAskill	x	x	x	x	x	x
J Campbell	x	x	x	x	x	x
R Campbell	x	x	x	x	x	x
	x	x	x	x	x	x

Mackenzie, MacDonald and McIntosh

Allocation of profit by partner for the year ended 30 June 1993

	£
Excess of income over expenditure	x
Salaried partners' salaries	
J Campbell	x
R Campbell	x
	x
Add back motor expenses	x
Add back notional interest on capital account	x
Available for distribution	x
Distribution as follows:	
Notional interest	x
Salary	x
Second tranche	x
Motor expenses	x
	x

Mackenzie, MacDonald and McIntosh

Allocation of profit by partner for the year ended 30 June 1993 (Continued)

	Notional Interest	*Salary*	*Second Tranche*	*Less Motor Expenses*	*Total*
	£	£	£	£	£
D Mackenzie	x	x	x	x	x
A MacDonald	x	x	x	x	x
I McIntosh	x	x	x	x	x
J McMurdo	x	x	x	x	x
J McAndrew	x	x	x	x	x
S McCallister	x	x	x	x	x
F MacBean	x	x	x	x	x
G MacAskill	x	x	x	x	x
	x	x	x	x	x

Appendix 11

Mackenzie, MacDonald and McIntosh

Calculation of notional interest by partner for the year ended 30 June 1993

	Capital Account 30 June 1992	*Capital Account 30 June 1993*	*Average Balance*	*Notional Interest @ x%*
	£	£	£	£
D Mackenzie	x	x	x	x
A MacDonald	x	x	x	x
I McIntosh	x	x	x	x
J McMurdo	x	x	x	x
J McAndrew	x	x	x	x
S McCallister	x	x	x	x
F MacBean	x	x	x	x
G MacAskill	x	x	x	x
J Campbell	x	x	x	x
R Campbell	x	x	x	x
	x	x	x	x

Mackenzie, MacDonald and McIntosh

Movement on tax reserve for the year ended 30 June 1993

	As at 1 July 1992	*Paid in year re 1991/92*	*Other adjustments*	*Charge for Year*	*As at 30 June 1993*
	£	£	£	£	£
D Mackenzie	x	x	x	x	x
A MacDonald	x	x	x	x	x
I McIntosh	x	x	x	x	x
J McMurdo	x	x	x	x	x
J McAndrew	x	x	x	x	x
S McCallister	x	x	x	x	x
F MacBean	x	x	x	x	x
G MacAskill	x	x	x	x	x
J Campbell	x	x	x	x	x
R Campbell	x	x	x	x	x
	x	x	x	x	x

Appendix 11

Mackenzie, MacDonald and McIntosh

Composition of tax reserve at 30 June 1993 by open year

	90/91	*91/92*	*92/93*	*93/94*	*94/95*
	£	£	£	£	£
D Mackenzie	x	x	x	x	x
A MacDonald	x	x	x	x	x
I McIntosh	x	x	x	x	x
J McMurdo	x	x	x	x	x
J McAndrew	x	x	x	x	x
S McCallister	x	x	x	x	x
F MacBean	x	x	x	x	x
G MacAskill	x	x	x	x	x
J Campbell	x	x	x	x	x
R Campbell	x	x	x	x	x
	—	—	—	—	—
	x	x	x	x	x
	═	═	═	═	═

Mackenzie, MacDonald and McIntosh

Segmental analysis of fee rendered and profits by department for the year ended 30 June 1993

	Bills	*Profit on Bills*	*Movement on W.I.P Reserves*	*Movement on Bad Debt Reserves*	*Adjusted Profit for the Year*	*1992 Adjusted Profit*
	£	£	£	£	£	£
Commercial	x	x	x	x	x	x
Commercial property	x	x	x	x	x	x
Conveyancing	x	x	x	x	x	x
Criminal	x	x	x	x	x	x
Family	x	x	x	x	x	x
Planning	x	x	x	x	x	x
	—	—	—	—	—	—
	x	x	x	x	x	x
	═	═	═	═	═	═

Mackenzie, MacDonald and McIntosh

Segmental analysis of fee rendered and profits by partner for the year ended 30 June 1993

	Bills	*Profit on Bills*	*Movement on W.I.P Reserve*	*Movement on Bad Debt Reserve*	*Adjusted Profit for Year*	*1992 Adjusted Profit*
	£	£	£	£	£	£
D Mackenzie	x	x	x	x	x	x
A MacDonald	x	x	x	x	x	x
I McIntosh	x	x	x	x	x	x
J McMurdo	x	x	x	x	x	x
J McAndrew	x	x	x	x	x	x
S McCallister	x	x	x	x	x	x
F MacBean	x	x	x	x	x	x
G MacAskill	x	x	x	x	x	x
J Campbell	x	x	x	x	x	x
R Campbell	x	x	x	x	x	x
	x	x	x	x	x	x

Index

*References in **bold** type are to chapters or Appendices that contain an extended treatment of the subject matter concerned. Other references are to section numbers.*